AUG 2007

KOREA

PEOPLE'S REPUBLIC OF CHINA

RUSSIA

Hamyong
Book-Do

Chongjin

Pyong An
Book-Do

Hamyong
Nam-Do

Shinuiju

Hamhung

Pyong An
Nam-Do

DEMOCRATIC PEOPLE'S REPUBLIC OF KOREA
(DPRK, NORTH KOREA)

Pyongyang

Demilitarized Zone
(DMZ)

Hwanghae-Do

EAST SEA
(SEA OF JAPAN)

Haeju

Gangwon-Do

Seoul

Chunchon

Ullung-Do

Inchon

Gyonggi-Do

Tok-Do

YELLOW
SEA

Suwon

Choong Chong
Book-Do

Choong Chong
Nam-Do

Chongju

Gyongsang
Book-Do

Daejon

REPUBLIC OF KOREA
(ROK, SOUTH KOREA)

Jonju

Daegu

Julla
Book-Do

Gyongsang
Nam-Do

Ulsan

Gwangju

Changwon

Busan

Julla
Nam-Do

Korea Strait

JAPAN

Jeju-Do

Jeju

eating
korean

from barbecue to kimchi, recipes from my home

Cecilia Hae-Jin Lee

WILEY

John Wiley & Sons, Inc.

For my family

Published by John Wiley & Sons, Inc., Hoboken, New Jersey

Published simultaneously in Canada

For general information on our other products and services or for technical support, please contact our
Customer Care Department within the United States at (800) 762-2974, outside the United States at (317)
572-3993 or fax (317) 572-4002.

Wiley also publishes its books in a variety of electronic formats. Some content that appears in print may
not be available in electronic books. For more information about Wiley products, visit our web site at
www.wiley.com.

Library of Congress Cataloging-in-Publication Data:
Lee, Cecilia Hae-Jin.
  Eating Korean / By Cecilia Hae-Jin Lee.—1st ed.
    p. cm.
  Includes index.
  ISBN 0-7645-4078-5
  1. Cookery, Korean. 2. Korea—Social life and customs. I. Title.
  TX724.5.K65L44 2005
  641.59519—dc22   2004024092

Cover photographs: All courtesy of Cecilia Hae-Jin Lee, except "Korean Bulgoki," © Fran Geuler/
    FoodPix/Getty Images
Photographs: Courtesy of Cecilia Hae-Jin Lee

Printed in the United States of America

10 9 8 7 6 5 4 3 2 1

Contents

Many of my earliest memories have to do with food and eating. Locked up in the haziness of nostalgia on a peninsula in the Pacific Ocean are family gatherings, mountain picnics, beach roasts, and fishing trips. Even when we moved to the United States, events revolved around food. Everything from weekend trips to weddings involved gathering friends and family together and eating.

When my little brother was born, we were having lunch. The midwife had taken my mom away to another room and there was an anticipatory energy that hung in the air. At some point my dad left, too. I don't know if we were worried or excited, but for once in our lives, my sister and I were eating quietly at the table. Only the occasional sound of chopsticks clinking on metal bowls disturbed the odd silence.

Then we heard a baby crying. We both looked at each other in surprise and bolted down the long corridor to a closed door. We didn't dare go in, but stood outside with our ears pressed against the secret coolness of the wood, listening for clues. When we heard the doorknob being turned, we ran like mad down the hall to our lunches again. Sitting like harried angels, we tried to stifle our giggles and rough breathing as we folded our sweaty hands on our laps. In a moment, a head appeared in the doorway.

"You have a little brother," the head said, and my dad disappeared again.

That was one of the few meals I remember eating as a child without the entire family. Although my parents worked seven days a week, they insisted on eating dinner together. After we immigrated to the states in the late 1970s, it was even more important that we shared a meal as a family every day. My folks wanted to make sure we retained our Korean culture, even insisting that we speak only Korean at the dining table. Whenever my dad enforced this rule, my siblings and I would fall silent, waiting for our stern father to leave the table and begin nodding off in front of the TV before resuming our conversations in English.

In a traditional Korean family, no one is allowed so much as to pick up their chopsticks until the patriarch of the family has taken his first bite. At dinnertime, it was torture. All the side dishes or *banchan* would be set out in front of us, steaming, bubbling, giving off their various tempting aromas. And we would have to wait at the table for my dad to be done with his predinner, after-work shower. I would wait for the water to turn off and would imagine my dad taking his time. First, he would towel off, put on his underwear and socks, then the rest of his clothing. Meanwhile, we kids would be sitting at the table, salivating in anticipation. I thanked my lucky stars for being born into a family of bald men, knowing the lack of hair combing meant the speedier arrival of the food into my mouth. As soon as I heard the sound of the bathroom door opening, I would place my hand closer to my chopsticks, ready to jolt like a racehorse seconds before the gate was released.

Many years and many businesses later, my parents bought a grocery store, which forced them to work longer hours. We were older then, and in our naive adolescence we believed we were more mature. So, the family dinners eventually dissipated into disjointed meals and hurried snacks between work, study, after-school meetings, and athletic events.

Still, our house was always brimming with people. The heart of the house was the kitchen. My mom took pride in the fact that there was always a hot pot of rice steaming in the cooker on the counter, several jars of *kimchi,* and tons of food in the fridge. Amidst the revolving door of family and friends, I learned how to cook.

When I wrote this book, I wanted the experience of reading it to be like cooking and eating with my family. The best way to learn how to cook is by watching, doing, and tasting. Unfortunately, there's not enough room in my kitchen, so you'll just have to make do on your own. But I hope this book helps.

That is not to say that our family members are experts in Korean cuisine. In fact, it had been nearly a decade after we stepped off the plane onto American soil that our family took a trip back to the homeland. Everything had changed. Like our teenage bodies, the city we had remembered as Seoul had grown, too, beyond recognition. The playground where my brother had buried his first pair of glasses was now a motel for lovers. The sub-

CELEBRATING MY ELEVENTH BIRTHDAY WITH MY FAMILY

way where we held tightly onto my mother's hands was an intricate web of trains that extended to the far reaches of the metropolis. Traditions that my parents insisted on maintaining had been discarded long ago by Koreans back home.

Somehow, our customs were frozen in time, while the country we left behind became more progressive. Western habits my folks resisted so staunchly were imported with ease into the Korean culture. Labor-intensive ways of food preparation were discarded for convenient meals that fit better into modern lifestyles. My Korean friends marveled at how I could have lived in America so long, yet still be so old-fashioned. They called it outdated, but I insisted it was good manners.

After college, I went back to Korea alone to relearn my language and culture. For months, I was able to discover my native land with adult eyes, taking in the country's gifts and difficulties in my own time. As I taught English and learned Korean again, I grew to appreciate each language's own characteristics and cultural overtones. I realized then that I was never going to be completely Korean or feel completely American. Somewhere in the middle, I could turn a critical outsider's eye to both cultures, yet be privy to intimate secrets that each country would offer.

The subsequent recipes come from that point of view. Some dishes are super-traditional with preparation methods that haven't changed in centuries. Others are more modern, simplified for convenience and ease, but never sacrificing flavor. They are just guidelines for you to follow. Feel free to experiment and make each dish your own. Add a little salt or a pinch of chili powder here and there, or put in less soy sauce if you want. If you can't find a certain ingredient, try the recipe with something else. You may be surprised to find that you've accidentally improved it. As with all cooking, I encourage you to taste everything as you make it. Then, nothing that makes it to the table will be a mystery. You'll be able to serve your food with pride, already knowing that everything tastes great.

My sister laughs at my mom and me because we take it to the extreme. We both get so excited about tasting the food as we cook that we're full by the time the guests arrive. My mom isn't the typical apologizing Asian woman. With a beaming smile, she brings the platter to the table announcing that this is the best thing we've ever had in our lives. I agree with her style of playing hostess. What kind of dinner guest wants to eat an apology anyway?

So, if you find yourself in Los Angeles wanting a home-cooked Korean meal, there are two homes you can choose from, my folks' or mine. Just let yourself in, take your shoes off at the door, and help yourself. There's always hot rice in the cooker, lively conversations to join, and plenty of food on the table.

Acknowledgments

Like a good celebration, a book comes together best when many people are involved. Although I am grateful for everyone who has supported me, there are some I would like to acknowledge specifically.

This project would have never happened if I hadn't shared a lifetime of meals with such a quirky but wonderful family. My mom, Julia Mi-Ja, taught me to open my doors and my heart to even the strangest of strangers. My dad, Daniel Pal-Woo, gave me the palate for good food and showed me the importance of having good friends to share it with.

Thanks to my sister, Catherine Hae-Ran, and my brother Sang for allowing me to share our stories with the rest of the world. To my nephew Christopher for believing that his Imo is a better cook than his grandma and mom. And to Benjamin who eats with such relish that his enjoyment of a simple meal is a joy to watch.

I would have never had the courage to embark on this journey without the encouragement of former *L.A. Times* food editor, Russ Parsons, and the rest of the food staff. Through Russ, I've had the fortune of meeting my agent, Judith Weber, whose pragmatism and support kept me focused on my creative work.

Of course, a book cannot be produced without the people who worked so diligently to make the words make sense and look good on the page. Thanks to everyone at Wiley, especially my editor Pamela Adler, who has been so patient and encouraging throughout the entire process.

A special thanks to my family in Korea, especially my great-aunt, my aunts Jumi and Young-Gyu, and my Uncle Man-Gyu and his wife for opening up their home to their crazy American niece.

My friend Laura Witsenhausen was thoughtful enough to think of me and my book in the midst of her wedding commotion. Thank you. To my friend Yunju Yeom for driving me all over the Korean countryside as we searched for rice and chile peppers to photograph. Thanks to my friend Sunny Ye, who makes me laugh and makes me food.

Thank you to Bob Davis for emotional support and taking me out when I would tire of my own cooking. To Karen Achenbach for reminding me that a book gets written one word at a time.

Thanks to everyone who allowed me to share their stories and photos in the book.

And my husband, Tim Maloney, who has not only been my food taster, therapist, and editor throughout the process, but who was also a super friend.

Anatomy of a Korean Meal

A Korean meal consists of a balance of flavors and colors. Bits of hot and cold, spicy and mild are thrown together to make a meal. At the core of every meal is rice (*bap*)—unless, that is, the meal is noodle- or porridge-based. Since Koreans don't distinguish between breakfast, lunch, or dinner, rice is eaten all times of the day. Each person gets his or her own serving. • Soups are also served in individual bowls. Hot pots (*Jjigae*), which are a thicker, saltier broth-based dish, are set in the middle of the table for communal enjoyment. Because beverages are rarely served during a traditional Korean meal, there should always be a soup or water *kimchi* to help wash the food down. • Speaking of *kimchi*, there should be at least one type on the table. Usually there are two or three, depending on the season. Served in small dishes, *kimchi* serves as a small side dish (*banchan*) to add an extra kick to whatever else is on the menu. Like the rest of the food, *kimchi* is laid out in the middle of the table for everyone to share. • A variety of smaller side dishes (*mit banchan*), anything

from pickled seafood to seasonal vegetables, rounded out the regular meal. In traditional culture, the table settings varied depending on the occasion (whether the meal was for everyday eating, for special occasions, or for guests) as

 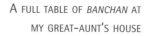

A FULL TABLE OF *BANCHAN* AT
MY GREAT-AUNT'S HOUSE

well as the number of *banchan* on the table. The settings were determined by the number of side dishes, which could vary in number—three, five, seven, nine, or twelve. As with all Korean food, the royal table was different from the commoner's.

There are no real "courses" per se in Korean meals. Generally, all the food is laid out on the table at the same time and eaten in whatever order you wish. Also there is no such thing as "dessert" in Korean tradition; however, an after-dinner drink of hot tea or coffee is generally served with whatever fruit is in season.

Also, Korean meals were traditionally served on low tables with family members sitting on floor cushions. Some households and certain restaurants still adhere to this older custom, but most Koreans I know sit at a regular Western-style dining table. Although certain traditions have gone by the wayside, mealtime etiquette still applies, especially for formal meals.

For starters, you should always wait for the eldest to eat their first bite, unless you are the guest of honor—if you are, then everyone will wait for you to take your first bite before digging in. Koreans always eat their rice with a spoon, never with chopsticks. (*See* Tools and Implements on page 238.) Unlike other Asian countries, rice bowls and soup bowls are not picked up from the table. And completely taboo at the dining table is blowing your nose, chewing with your mouth open, and talking with your mouth full. Leaving chopsticks sticking straight out of a bowl, mixing rice and soup, and overeating are also considered inappropriate. During informal meals, however, these rules are often broken.

A Quick Guide to the Types of Korean Food

Battered Foods (*Jun, Buchingae*)

Any pan-fried foods from flatcakes to simple vegetables cooked in egg batter are called *jun*. *Jun* is cooked over a griddled surface with a little bit of vegetable oil. *Buchingae*, a type of *jun*, are flatcakes and pancakes that contain meat or seafood and a variety of vegetables.

Grilled or Broiled Foods (*Gui*)

Any food cooked over high flames is called *gui*. Usually meats and seafood are prepared this way after being marinated or, in the case of whole fish, sometimes just slightly salted.

Hot Pots (*Jjigae, Jungol*)

Although liquid-based, hot pots are considered main courses for everyone to share. Saltier and chunkier than regular soup, *jjigae* are quite often spicy and contain vegetables, seafood, or meat. *Jungol* is usually set on the table on a small fire or electrical heat source so that the dish can continue cooking and stay warm throughout the meal.

Noodles (*Gooksu*)

Except for mixed noodles and Sweet Potato Noodles (*Japchae*, page 123), most Korean noodle dishes are broth based, whether served hot or cold. Certain noodles are also added to hot pots cooked on the table (*jungol*).

Pickled Foods (*Kimchi, Jjang Achi, Jutgal*)

Any vegetables that are seasoned and pickled in salt-based seasonings are called *kimchi*. Those that are pickled in soy-based sauces are called *jjang achi*. *Jutgal* is a name given to any sort of seafood that is pickled in salt. Very salty and sometimes served as a side dish, *jutgal* is also used as a seasoning for other dishes as well as for *kimchi*.

Porridge (*Jook*)

Jook has been served to people recovering from illnesses in Korea for centuries. Known for its restorative qualities, it has also been considered a delicacy, a breakfast food, as well as a nice afternoon snack to share with friends.

Raw Foods (*Hwae*)

Not only is raw fish popular in Korea, but a wide variety of seafood, such as squid and abalone, are eaten raw as well. Some restaurants even serve raw, seasoned beef. Unlike Japanese sushi, Korean *hwae* is eaten dipped in Vinegar Chili Paste (*Cho Gochujang*, page 9), sometimes wrapped in perilla or lettuce leaves (*sangchu*).

Rice (*Bap*)

Steamed white rice is a staple of Korean food. The word for cooked rice, *bap*, is synonymous with food.

Sauces (*Jang*)

There are three sauces used in Korean cooking—soy sauce (*ganjang*), chili paste (*gochujang*), and fermented soybean paste (*dwenjang*). Traditionally, each household made their own each year.

Simmered or Stewed Foods (*Jjim, Jolim*)

Meat or fish simmered in a soy-sauce-based seasoning is given the name *jjim* or *jolim*. This way of cooking over low heat not only seasons the meat, but also helps tougher cuts become tender. The word *jjim* also refers to steamed food.

Soups (*Gook, Tahng*)

A Korean meal isn't complete without soup. Not considered a separate course, soup is served with the rice and other dishes. Everything from bones to seaweed is used to make soup.

Vegetables (*Namool*)

A huge variety of harvested vegetables and wild greens are part of the Korean diet. Different regions have their own specialties depending on what grows there. *Namool* is a generic word that encompasses all the plants eaten as well as the seasoned side dishes (*ban-chan*) made from those plants. They are usually parboiled or stir-fried and seasoned with garlic, sesame oil, salt/soy sauce, and sesame seeds.

A Few Words About Cutting Food

Quite often in Korean cooking, things are made a certain way not because it necessarily tastes better that way, but rather because it looks better. My dad used to always say, "If it doesn't look good; it doesn't taste good." I remember being sent back into the kitchen to rearrange cut fruit in order to achieve the best presentation. Cutting foods operated under the same rules. Green onions are often cut into lengths on the diagonal because they look better than when they are cut straight. Also, there is a type of cut called "che" in Korean, which is similar to the julienne cut, but smaller. With such vegetables as Korean zucchinis, the "che" cut can be easily done on a mandoline by using the largest holes. Foods are often cut not only to look good, but because bite-size pieces are easily eaten with chopsticks. Of course, there is no absolute way of doing anything. No matter what you're cooking, just make it look good.

CHOPPING GREEN ONIONS

SEED BEARERS

Basics

My family has grown Korean vegetables on American soil
ever since we bought our first small house back in the early eighties. A visitor
would bring mysterious seeds from the homeland; during spring, the seeds
would be planted into the fertile soil. By the time summer rolled around, the
backyard would be teeming with squash vines coiling everywhere, lush
green pepper plants or garlic stalks whose tall stems would burst forth with
beautiful, garlic-smelling flowers. • Any houseplant or cactus given to my
mom as a gift from her offspring would eventually be killed, yet for some
crazy reason, the vegetables in our backyard thrived under her care. I guess
my dad did most of the complicated stuff—the planting, the weeding. My mom
was there to enjoy the fruits of the harvest, when the plants were ready for
the dinner table. • My folks redefined the idea of an "open door" policy.
People came in and out of our house any time of year. Invariably, the visitors would have to sleep in either my brother's room or the room my sister

and I shared. All of us spent half
of our growing-up years sleeping
on the living room floor. • It
didn't help that we had family
trees that extended beyond mere
branches on both sides. My dad
was the eighth son of sixteen

MY SISTER, HAE-RAN, AND
I WITH ONE OF OUR MANY
VISITORS, MR. NOH

children (fourteen boys). In fact, his name, Pal-Woo, means "eight" and "plentiful rain," a symbol of good fortune in the rural community where he grew up. My mom was the eldest of a mere five children, but relatives expanded several generations both up and down her side of the family.

Summers were the most hectic. Vacationing cousins sprawled out comfortably on our beds, while we and our younger friends would sleep on blankets in the living room. Whispered conversations and quiet giggles would reverberate throughout the dark house as we waited for the sound of snoring to emanate from behind my folks' bedroom door. Too hot and excited to sleep, we would turn on the TV with the volume just barely audible over the sound of warm weather insects. Surreptitiously, we'd catch the latest music videos or some late-night B-movie as we snuck food my dad was saving for *anju* (drinking snacks). Sometimes there would be some static on TV screwing up our late-night revelry and my sister and I would try to coax our little brother into walking the two feet required to adjust the antenna, too lazy to move our own sleepy-time selves. When we got tired of whatever was on the tube, we'd play silly games or tell ghost stories well into the wee hours, until we fell asleep accidentally only to wake up with an imprint of a Monopoly game piece on one of our cheeks.

During waking hours, the house would be bustling with activity. Someone was always banging on the bathroom door to tell someone else to hurry, while people ran back and forth chasing each other. It seemed as if someone else was always cooking something, doing the dishes, or eating. It was nonstop action in the kitchen.

This past year, my parents had visitors from several states. They've housed half a dozen priests from all over the world, nieces from three continents, and even an amateur Russian dance troupe—young Korean girls whose grandparents were forced to immigrate to Siberia during Stalin's Reign of Terror.

While their house was abuzz with activity, the garden quietly produced lettuce, peppers, Asian radishes, perilla leaves, and cucumbers. One of their well-meaning friends picked the last cucumbers they were saving for seed. With her usual good nature, my mom just laughed and sent someone else out for more peppers and lettuce to eat with the last cucumbers of the season, while I made Seasoned Fermented Soybean Paste (*yangnyum dwenjang*) for dipping. Soon enough, we were all sitting around the dining table, chatting and snacking away on fresh vegetables from the garden.

Next year will bring more visitors. The seeds they bring will be planted. The people will come and go. The vegetables will grow and die. And the cycle will continue like the revolving door of our lives.

Toasted Sesame Seeds

Ggae

Sesame seeds are one of the major staples of Korean cooking. Although you can buy seeds already toasted, the flavor is much better when you toast the seeds yourself. It's easy to do, and toasting them brings out the wonderful nutty flavor. They will keep for months in an airtight container in the fridge, but keep even longer in the freezer. MAKES 1 CUP

1 cup sesame seeds

1   Place the seeds in a heavy skillet over a very low flame. With a wooden spoon or spatula, stir the sesame seeds until they turn a dark golden brown. Take care since the seeds will occasionally pop in the pan during toasting.

2   Remove from heat and allow the seeds to cool to room temperature. Store in an airtight container in the refrigerator or freezer.

VARIATION: You may wish to crush the seeds before storing for use in certain recipes. Use a mortar and pestle, a blender, or a food processor to crush the seeds. Sesame seeds stored in the refrigerator or freezer will have a longer shelf life.

Seasoned Soy Sauce

Yangnyum Ganjang

A popular dipping sauce, it can also be used for seasoning vegetables, fish, and meat. It also makes a nice accompaniment to some noodle dishes.

MAKES $^1\!/_2$ CUP

4 tablespoons soy sauce

1 green onion, finely chopped

2 garlic cloves, minced

1 tablespoon toasted sesame seeds (page 3)

1 tablespoon sesame oil

$^1\!/_2$ tablespoon chili powder

$^1\!/_2$ teaspoon black pepper (optional)

1   Combine all ingredients in a small bowl.

2   If serving as a dipping sauce, serve in small individual bowls. Leftovers can be stored in the refrigerator in a tightly sealed container for about a week.

Vinegar Soy Sauce

Cho Ganjang

Another popular dipping sauce, it is usually served with dumplings and other dishes. MAKES $^1\!/_2$ CUP

2 tablespoons soy sauce

2 tablespoons rice vinegar or white vinegar

1 tablespoon sesame oil

1 tablespoon toasted sesame seeds (page 3)

1 teaspoon black pepper (optional)

1   Combine all ingredients in a small bowl.

2   For dipping, serve in individual small dishes. Store leftovers in a tightly sealed container for about a week.

Seasoned Fermented Soybean Paste

Yangnyum Dwenjang

This sauce can be served as a dipping sauce for fresh vegetables such as cucumbers, Korean green peppers, and carrots. It's also served on the side to eat with rice and grilled meats wrapped in lettuce or perilla leaves.

MAKES $^1/_2$ CUP

4 tablespoons fermented soybean paste (*dwenjang*)

2 garlic cloves, minced

1 green onion, chopped

2 tablespoons sesame oil

1　Combine all ingredients until they are well mixed.

2　Serve in small individual-sized bowls. When stored in a covered container, this paste will keep in the refrigerator for about a week.

Fresh Red Chili Sauce

Put Gochujang

Made with fresh peppers or chili powder, this is a chili paste that doesn't require fermentation. It's used as a seasoning for certain soups and noodles.

MAKES ABOUT 1 CUP

5 garlic cloves

10 red Korean chile peppers, coarsely chopped or 1 cup chili powder

$^1/_4$ cup sesame oil

$^1/_4$ cup vegetable oil

1　With a mortar and pestle, mash the garlic well. If you don't have a mortar and pestle, use a blender or food processor. Add the chile peppers or chili powder and pound (or grind) into a paste.

2　Transfer into a bowl and add the oils, mixing until it becomes a coarse paste. Transfer into a glass jar with a tight lid and store in the fridge indefinitely.

Red Chili Paste

Gochujang

Hardly anyone makes their own red chili paste at home, since such delicious varieties are readily available in grocery stores. However, if you want the wonderful taste of homemade, it's not that hard to make. It just takes a little bit of time to get it to ferment properly. This spicy chili paste is a staple in Korean cooking and there is really no substitute for it. You will need a well-cleaned, medium-sized glass or clay jar (*hang ali*) with a tightly fitting lid.

MAKES 4 CUPS

1^1/$_2$ cups fine barley malt powder (*yut gilum*)

Water

2 cups sweet rice flour

2 cups red chili powder

1 cup fine soybean malt powder (*meju galu*)

1 cup coarse sea salt

^{1}/$_2$ cup soy sauce

1   In a bowl, combine barley malt powder and 5 cups water (preferably filtered) and stir until powder is completely dissolved. Let stand overnight in a warm place or in an electric rice cooker. Strain into a heavy stockpot. Add sweet rice flour and stir until dissolved. Bring to a boil and simmer uncovered over low heat for about 20 minutes, until its volume is reduced by a third or a half. Cool and set aside.

2   In a large bowl, combine chili powder, soybean malt powder, rice flour and malt mixture, ^{1}/$_4$ cup of the salt, and the soy sauce. Mix thoroughly with a wooden spoon. Let stand overnight.

3   Transfer the chili paste to the jar and sprinkle the remaining ^{3}/$_4$ cup of salt on top. Leave some space on top of the jar, because the mixture will rise as it ferments. Cover with cheesecloth or some other breathable fabric. Sun-dry every day and cover at night. It may be used right away but for best results, let the chili paste mature for at least a month. Afterward, store in a tightly sealed container in the fridge and it will keep indefinitely.

Not Only Skin Deep

My American husband, Tim, has been made an honorary Korean, first by my mom, then confirmed by countless relatives and friends. His status was not bestowed upon him just because he enjoys spicy foods and stinky hot pots of fermented soybean paste. That doesn't hurt, but Koreanness goes way beyond the superficial *kimchi* eating.

I would venture to say, that in some ways, he is more Korean than I am. He loves the scratchy feel of the Korean washcloths on his skin, while I shy away from their

cat tongue texture. He gets up and bows whenever any elder family member enters a room; I usually wave from my seated position. When I'm too lazy to make dipping sauce for some flatcakes we've just thrown together, Tim's already in the kitchen mincing garlic and pouring soy sauce and other ingredients into a small bowl.

So, when my uncle visited from Korea, none of us was surprised when Tim took a huge dip of the

MY HUSBAND, TIM, EATING WHILE OUR FRIEND, YUNJU, WATCHES

spicy chili paste (*gochujang*) to eat with his dried anchovies (*myulchi*). He almost succeeded in getting the dipped fish into his mouth, but my uncle, his eyes as wide as saucers, stopped him short of his first bite.

In his broken English, he kept saying, "No ketchup! No ketchup!" Puzzled, I asked him what he was going on about. He thought Tim had mistaken the chile paste for ketchup and was going to make the mistake of putting the whole spicy mess into his unaware mouth. He was probably fooled by the light hair and hazel eyes. What my uncle didn't realize was that if you sliced Tim in half, you'd have a lot of Korean in the middle of all that Polish, Irish, German, and Luxembourg blood. After some translations and much laughing, Tim popped the chili-covered anchovy into his mouth, while my uncle shook his head in amazement.

Seasoned Chili Paste

Yangnyum Gochujang

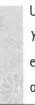 Used to season such dishes as Mixed Rice Bowl (*Bibim Bap*, recipe page 23), *Yangnyum Gochujang* can also be served as a dipping sauce for fresh vegetables such as cucumbers, Korean green peppers, and carrots. The spiciness of the sauce will depend on how hot the *gochujang* is. MAKES ¹/₂ CUP

4 tablespoons chili paste (*gochujang*)

2 garlic cloves, minced

2 tablespoons sesame oil

1 tablespoon soy sauce

2 teaspoons sugar or Korean malt syrup (*mool yut*)

2 teaspoons toasted sesame seeds (page 3), optional

1 green onion, chopped (optional)

1   Combine all ingredients until they are well mixed.

2   When stored in a covered container, this paste will keep in the fridge for over a week.

Vinegar Chili Paste

Cho Gochujang

 This vinegar dipping sauce can be served with just sliced vegetables or used as a dipping sauce for many dishes. MAKES ¹/₂ CUP

2 tablespoons chili paste
(*gochujang*)

1 tablespoon soy sauce

2 tablespoons vinegar
(white or cider)

1 tablespoon sugar

1 tablespoon toasted sesame
seeds (page 3), optional

Black pepper (optional)

1   Combine chili paste, soy sauce, vinegar, and sugar. Sprinkle with optional seeds and black pepper just before serving.

2   Store leftovers in a tightly sealed container in the fridge for about a week.

Seasoned Green Onions

Pa Muchim

 Usually served on the side with Sliced Roast Beef (*Roseh Gui*, page 168), this green onion "salad" also makes a nice flavor addition to any grilled meats. Serve with some red-leaf lettuce on the side. MAKES 4 TO 5 SERVINGS

1 bundle of green onions

3 tablespoons sesame oil

1 teaspoon chili powder

Salt

1   After washing and cleaning the green onions, cut them into about 2-inch lengths. Using a sharp knife, continue cutting the green onions, lengthwise, into strips as thin as possible.

2   Combine green onions in a medium bowl with the sesame oil, chili powder, and salt. Serve immediately as a side dish for grilled meats or *gui*.

Anchovy Stock

Myulchi Gookmul

Dried anchovies are a staple in any Korean kitchen. Although soup stock is made from beef, chicken, and a variety of seafood, dried anchovies are most commonly used. Purists like to devein the little fish and remove their heads before cooking with them. If you don't have the time or don't want to bother, you can use the fish whole or buy them beheaded and deveined in the dried goods section of any Korean grocery. Dried anchovies range in size from tiny little creatures, whose eyes are barely distinguishable from the rest of their bodies, to the larger silvery fish. The medium- to larger-sized ones are best for making soup stock. MAKES 5 CUPS

About 15 dried medium-sized anchovies (use fewer if they are extra large)

Water

1 Place the anchovies in a large stockpot.

2 Add 6 cups water and bring to a boil. Reduce heat to medium and simmer for about 8 to 10 minutes. Pour through a wire strainer or use a small strainer to fish the anchovies out of the stock. Discard the fish. Although it is best to use the stock immediately, it will keep in the refrigerator for a few days.

Beef Stock

Gogi Gookmul

Beef stock is used in beef-based Korean soups. Although some of the beef used to make the stock is often used in the soup itself, there is leftover beef in some cases. I recommend using the beef in such recipes as Soy Stewed Beef (*Jang Jolim*, page 175). MAKES ABOUT 12 CUPS

1 pound beef brisket

Water

In a large pot, boil the beef brisket in about 16 cups of water for approximately 2 to 3 hours over low heat, until stock has reduced about a fourth. Occasionally skim the foam and fat that rises to the top.

NOTE To skim fat, wait until the stock cools a bit. Then take a piece of cling wrap and place over the surface of the liquid. Discard and repeat until the fat is removed. Alternatively, refrigerate the stock until the fat congeals. Then remove and discard the fat.

Rice and Porridges

In Korea, the word for cooked rice (*bap*) is synonymous with the word meal. A standard greeting, left over from when the country was seeing hard times, is "Have you eaten?/Have you had your rice?" Basically, if you were able to eat, then things were good. Cooking rice, in and of itself, is an art form. Even with the widespread use of automatic rice cookers, getting the rice just perfect—not too dry, not too mushy—is considered an admirable skill. • I learned how to make rice when I was about five. I would carry a chair into the kitchen so that I could climb up to reach the sink. My mom taught me how to get just the right level of rice and water with my hands and fingers. To this day, I still use only my hands as measuring implements to make rice. On winter days, it was torturous to dunk my sensitive flesh in the icy cold water, swishing the white grains around to rinse them clean. I would never think to wash rice in warm water and ruin the rice. Instead, I would let my hands turn rosy with cold. • Like all Korean families, rice was as important to us as money. So, the year our apartment flooded—it was around the annual monsoon season, which generally happened in July or August—none of us questioned our mom when she began yelling at us to grab the sacks of

MY DAD IN THE RICE FIELDS
JUST BEFORE HARVEST

rice and hurry upstairs to Third-Floor Grandma's place. Third-Floor Grandma was my mom's godmother who lived on—where else but—the third floor. All of her kids were much older than we were, so there was nothing much to do at her place but to read. Luckily, we brought our books with us after lugging the rice upstairs.

My sister and I used to each have a set of books of fairy tales and other stories. Her books were beige with pink spines, while mine were a golden yellow with deep red spines. With these stories, I was able to enter the world of naked kings, frog princes, and dancing princesses. I don't remember actually learning how to read them. Magically, one day I was able to make sense out of the lines and circles on the page. The only thing that emerges from my memory's swamp is how I would never tire of the incredible stories, losing myself in the words and running my fingers over the pictures until the spines grew weak and torn.

My favorite story was one of two young lovers, well known by schoolchildren throughout Korea and Japan. The couple was so starry-eyed in love with each other that they would not do their work, preferring, instead, to while the days away basking in each other's company. This made the gods very angry. When the lovers refused to heed their warnings, the gods banished them to opposite sides of the earth.

Luckily for them, the young woman had a magpie, her solitary companion and confidant. She would send love letters back and forth to her faraway man by tying them to the bird's leg. The magpie felt deeply sorry for these separated young ones, so she devised a plan. She got together with all her feathered friends and created a bridge with their bodies. The lovers were able to step on the bird bridge and be reunited, if only for a brief moment. Eventually, the birds would get tired and would have to break up the bridge. It is said the torrential rains were caused by the bittersweet tears of the lovers.

The day of the flood, I read the story again. I stared out at the flooded

RICE FIELDS JUST AFTER HARVEST IN MY FAMILY'S OLD VILLAGE IN KOREA

streets, my nose pressed against the cold glass, wondering what true love would really be like. Since I had no illusions that my mom would ever buy me a bird, I decided that I wouldn't upset the gods, no matter how much in love I was. Outside the window, there was a man sitting on a wall holding what seemed to be a fishing pole. The wall, usually quite high, just kept him above the floodwaters, as the bottoms of his rubber boots touched the temporary river. The rain continued to fall and I was lost, deep in my own thoughts when my little brother began pulling my hair.

"It's time for lunch!" he tugged at my pigtails.

"Stupid!" I yelled, laughing as I chased him around the room.

"Come eat your rice!" my mom called from the kitchen. When I sat down at the table, I forgot all about those silly lovers as I stuffed my mouth with the hot goodness of freshly cooked white grains.

Rice

Bap

With automatic rice cookers these days, we no longer have any excuses for making a bad (too wet or too dry) batch of rice. Whether you're using a rice cooker or making rice on the stovetop, use slightly more water than you do rice. MAKES 6 TO 8 SERVINGS

3 cups uncooked rice

Water

1   Rinse the rice in cold water. Drain and place in a rice cooker. Add $3^1/_4$ cups water. Push the button and let the rice cooker do its job. After the button pops up, let the rice sit and steam about 5 to 10 minutes longer before serving.

2   If cooking on a stovetop, bring rice and $3^1/_4$ cups water to a boil, keeping the pot covered. Then, lower the heat, cover, and simmer for about 20 minutes until done. The grains should stick together but be fluffy. Remove from heat and let sit, covered, for about 10 minutes, so the steam can continue cooking the rice. Each cup of uncooked rice makes about $1^1/_2$ to $1^3/_4$ cups of cooked rice.

NOTE If the rice seems too dry, add a couple of tablespoons of water, stir, cover, and let cook a bit longer. If it's too wet, remove the lid, stir, and cook uncovered for a bit longer.

OUR FAMILY FRIEND, MR. LEE, ENJOYING A HUGE SPOON OF RICE

Red Bean Rice

Pot Bap

When you cook rice with red beans, the rice turns a lovely purplish color. This dish can be eaten in place of regular white rice on special occasions or for a more nutritious everyday meal. MAKES 4 TO 5 SERVINGS

---

¹/₂ cup red beans

2 cups rice

Water

1   Soak the red beans in cold water for about a day. Alternatively, you can simmer the red beans for about 20 minutes in about a cup of water. In either case, reserve the water.

2   Rinse the rice in cold water.

3   In a rice cooker, place together the red beans, rice, and the reserved water. Add more water to bring the amount to 2¹/₄ cups. Follow the directions of your rice cooker. Serve hot and steaming.

NOTE If you don't have a rice cooker, cook in a heavy pot. First, bring to a boil. Reduce heat to medium and simmer for about 15 minutes. Decrease the heat to low and cook for another 10 minutes. Turn off the heat and leave covered for about 10 minutes, allowing the rice and beans to steam a bit longer.

Five Grain Rice

Ogok Bap

 This special rice is eaten during the first full moon of the lunar year (*Dae Borum, see* page 222). Made from five different dried grains, hence the name, I consider it the rice equivalent to the really multigrained, whole wheat bread you'd find in health stores. MAKES 8 TO 10 SERVINGS

$^1/_2$ cup black soybeans

$^1/_2$ cup red beans

4 cups rice

1 cup sorghum

1 cup millet

Pinch of salt

1   Soak the black soybeans in cold water for at least 1 hour and drain.

2   Rinse the red beans. Simmer them in a pot with about a cup of water for about 20 minutes and drain, retaining the water for use later.

3   Wash the rice and drain. Clean the sorghum by putting it in a bowl of water and rubbing it with your hands until the water no longer turns red. Wash the millet and drain.

4   Combine black soybeans, red beans, rice, and sorghum in a large pot. Add the reserved red bean water and additional water to equal 7 cups. Add the salt and bring to a boil. Reduce heat and let simmer for about 20 minutes. Add the millet evenly over the top. Cover and cook for another 10 minutes longer, cooking until all the grains are well done.

Serve immediately with a simple soup, *kimchi*, and various vegetable *banchan* (*namool*).

Chestnut Rice

Bahm Bap

During autumn, you can see the glistening piles of dark brown chestnuts all over Korea's markets. Now with the availability of chestnuts year-round, *bahm bap* can be enjoyed any time of year. For this dish, dried chestnuts are easier to peel than fresh ones. In order to dry them, simply keep them at room temperature a couple of days. Then, use a small, sharp knife to peel them. If you can't find chestnuts in the produce section, Korean grocers sell chestnuts, peeled and ready in their freezers. The nuts add a slightly sweet flavor and nice texture to this simple rice dish. MAKES 6 TO 8 SERVINGS

3 cups uncooked rice

About a dozen chestnuts

Water

1   Rinse the rice in cold water. Drain. If using fresh chestnuts, peel them. If the chestnuts are large, cut them in half. Otherwise, leave them whole.

2   Combine the rice, chestnuts, and 4 cups water in a rice cooker and let cook. If cooking on a stovetop, add them to a medium pot with a well-fitting lid. Bring to a boil, then reduce heat to low and let cook until chestnuts are cooked through, about 15 minutes. Stir once or twice within the last 5 minutes of cooking to avoid having burnt rice sticking to the bottom of your pot. Remove from heat and let sit, covered, for about 10 minutes (allowing the rice to steam a bit longer).

Serve with various vegetable *banchan* (*namool*).

NOTE If you're having trouble peeling your chestnuts, cut off about half of the outer shell and drop the chestnuts in boiling water. Cover and let simmer for about 5 minutes. Drain and let cool. You'll find the inner skins are much easier to remove after parboiling them.

Soybean Sprout Rice

Kohng Namool Bap

This is an especially easy and nutritious way to eat rice and soybean sprouts. Did I mention it tastes good, too? Preparing this dish can be made into a labor-intensive affair by removing all the "tails" from the soybean sprouts.

I never bother and have never regretted the time spent doing something else. MAKES 5 TO 6 SERVINGS

3 cups rice

$^1/_2$ pound soybean sprouts

Water

1   Rinse the rice and place in a rice cooker. Rinse the sprouts, removing and discarding any bean skins. Add the sprouts to the rice cooker.

2   Cover with 3 cups water and follow directions for your particular cooker. Do not open the lid during cooking, because a raw taste will infuse into the rice and your kitchen will smell fishy.

Serve hot with a side of Seasoned Soy Sauce (*Yangnyum Ganjang*, page 4), *kimchi*, and various side dishes.

———

NOTE If you don't have a rice cooker, cook in a heavy pot. First, bring to a boil. Reduce heat to medium and simmer for about 15 minutes. Decrease the heat to low and cook for another 10 minutes. Turn off the heat and leave covered for about 10 minutes, allowing the rice to steam a bit longer.

Mountain Rice

The bus continued up the winding mountain road for what seemed like hours. The parents up front were singing some old-time Korean songs at the top of their lungs. Our photo albums are full of scenes like these: my dad in one of his U-neck undershirts with some silly visor on his head, my mom in a sillier visor with her huge sunglasses on, their friends singing a song from the Onions or some other sixties Korean pop group. Meanwhile, their teenage kids were sprawled out in the back of the bus sleeping or listening to their Walkmen. I turned up the volume on mine, hoping the Ramones could drown out their voices.

Occasionally, we could see through the thick growth of trees down to the rocky landscape below as our crazy bus driver sped through the precarious turns without even thinking about locating the brake pedal. This was the first time my family had

MY DAD IN THAILAND DURING THE SEVENTIES

been back to Korea since we immigrated to America in the late seventies. If we were going to die in some flaming bus crash, at least we would be together on home soil, I thought.

We finally arrived at our destination after what seemed like days. Getting out to stretch our legs, we looked presentable except when we turned around, showing wrinkles on our clothes and thighs. All the kids were cranky and hot, which wasn't helping the mood of the parents either. My dad somehow remembered a place that made really good country-style food; he hoped it was still there after a decade.

Knowing my dad, it couldn't be some easy walk to the place. We had to trek another mile or so up a steep overgrown mountain. Maybe there was a trail there ten years prior, but now there was none to be seen. Once we reached a clearing, we were relieved to find some signs of human life. Some women were washing vegetables from a hand pump as little orange-bellied green frogs splashed in the puddles that gathered nearby. Young children in bare feet and dirty faces chased after them as hundreds of iridescent dragonflies flew around. I was too hungry, tired, and cranky to care.

Some of us spotted a few benches and tables underneath an awning and sat down. My dad was thrilled! Apparently, this was the restaurant he remembered. Since there was no kitchen or waitress in sight, the kids were immediately skeptical. Even my siblings and I began to worry.

First, let me tell you a little something about my dad. This is the man who took us to eat live squid in Jeju Do (the southernmost island in Korea). In our family photo album, there is a picture of him in Thailand or Laos or some unidentifiable Southeastern Asian country—he is wearing a suit and tie with a fat boa constrictor around his neck. When we asked him if he was scared of the snake, he just replied, "Do you know what I did right after taking that photo?" He grinned and paused for effect, "I ate that snake for dinner!" Then he threw his head back and laughed, pausing only to take another swig of his beer before laughing again.

This is the same guy who would put something on your plate and tell you to eat it and he'd tell you what it was after you'd finished.

"What was it?" my siblings and I would ask innocently.

Sometimes, the answer would be "cow brain" or "pig feet." Other times, it would be a more palatable answer, such as "sparrow" or "deer." He was a tough dad to have growing up, but I am grateful to him now for my iron stomach.

A short *ajumma* (slang for an older married woman) suddenly appeared out of nowhere. She surprised us when she smiled, revealing the shiniest gold tooth behind her thin lips. Abruptly, she disappeared again after some gruff and brief instructions from my dad. Since her tooth distracted me during the ordering process, I began to worry that he had requested some regional "delicacies," like fish intestine or black goat soup. When she started bringing the large bowls of *bibim bap* (Korean mixed rice bowl), however, my fears were allayed.

My brother gingerly picked out a green stem and waved it in the air some distance from his bowl, "What is *this*?" he quipped, still cautious after the live squid incident.

"That's *soot*, stupid," I replied while I grabbed the stem from his chopsticks to mine, greedily adding it to my already brimming bowl.

"What's it called in English?"

"I don't know," I mumbled between bites. "It's some kind of weed."

"We have that in America, too," my sister piped in. "It's that stuff grandma used to pick from the neighbor's yard."

Actually, I discovered later that it was the leaves of the crown daisy. There were some other vegetables in my bowl that I didn't recognize and I hoped no one would ask me about those. Luckily for me, everyone was too busy shoveling food into their mouths for any more questions.

That was the best *bibim bap* I had ever eaten before or since. Maybe it was the mountain air. Maybe it was the unidentifiable vegetables. Whatever the case, I will never doubt my father again. Well . . . at least in matters of food, anyway.

Mixed Rice Bowl

Bibim Bap

Every cook has a different way of making his or her own *bibim bap*. This recipe may seem complicated at first glance, but it really isn't. Most of the ingredients are prepared by stir-frying in a little bit of oil and garlic with a touch of salt for seasoning. I have found it easiest to do all the preparations beforehand (slicing, chopping, etc.) and do the stir-frying in succession in the same skillet, setting each ingredient aside as they are done. The rice should be served hot, but the toppings can be at room temperature.

MAKES 5 SERVINGS

BOOLGOGI

1 pound sliced rib eye
(or *boolgogi* beef)

1 teaspoon soy sauce

1 teaspoon sesame oil

1 teaspoon sugar

3 garlic cloves, minced

About $^1/_2$ teaspoon black pepper (optional)

Marinate the sliced rib eye in soy sauce, sesame oil, sugar, and garlic for at least 30 minutes. Stir-fry the meat until thoroughly cooked, about 5 to 7 minutes. Add the black pepper, if you like. Set aside.

SPINACH
Shigumchi Namool

2 bundles of spinach, trimmed and thoroughly washed

1 tablespoon vegetable oil

1 garlic clove, minced

$^1/_2$ teaspoon salt

1 Blanch the spinach by quickly dunking the leaves in boiling water. Rinse immediately in cold water to stop cooking.

2 In a skillet, heat the vegetable oil. Add the garlic and stir-fry for about 1 to 2 minutes. Add spinach. Remove from heat, add salt, and toss. Set aside.

MUSHROOMS
Buhsut Namool

10 shiitake mushrooms, sliced

1 tablespoon vegetable oil

1 garlic clove, minced

$^1/_2$ teaspoon salt

1   If using dried mushrooms, soak them in water for about 1 hour before slicing.

2   In a skillet, heat the vegetable oil. Add the garlic and mushrooms and stir-fry for about 2 to 3 minutes. Add salt and toss. Set aside.

SOYBEAN SPROUTS
Kohng Namool

Water

1 pound soybean sprouts, washed and trimmed, if desired

1 tablespoon vegetable oil

1 garlic clove, minced

$^1/_2$ teaspoon salt

In a medium-sized pot, bring about $^1/_2$ cup of water to a boil. Add the soybean sprouts and cover. Only some of the spouts will be covered in water. The steam will cook the rest. Reduce the heat and simmer for about 10 minutes. Remove from heat and set aside.

In a skillet, heat the vegetable oil. Add the garlic and stir-fry for about 1 to 2 minutes. Add sprouts. Remove from heat, add salt, and toss. Set aside.

N O T E   Soybean sprouts can be found in the produce section of Korean supermarkets. They are white with large yellow bean heads. Do *not* lift the lid to see if the sprouts are cooked. Don't worry. They will cook. If you lift the lid before the sprouts are completely done, a fishy smell will fill your kitchen and boy, will you be sorry!

KOREAN ZUCCHINIS
Hobak Namool

1 tablespoon vegetable oil

1 garlic clove, minced

2 medium Korean zucchinis, Korean julienned or *che* cut

$^1/_2$ teaspoon salt

In a skillet, heat the vegetable oil. Add the garlic and stir-fry for about 1 to 2 minutes. Add Korean zucchinis and stir-fry for another 2 to 3 minutes until the zucchinis are slightly limp. Remove from heat, add salt, and toss. Set aside.

FERN BRACKEN
Gosali Namool

2 tablespoons vegetable oil

1 garlic clove, minced

$^1/_2$ pound fern bracken

1 teaspoon salt

In a skillet, heat the vegetable oil. Add the garlic and stir-fry for about 1 to 2 minutes. Add the fern bracken and stir-fry for another 2 to 3 minutes. Remove from heat, add salt. and toss. Set aside.

———

NOTE Fern bracken, which can be found prepared in the deli section of Korean supermarkets, looks brown and stringy.

CARROTS

1 tablespoon vegetable oil

2 medium carrots, Korean julienned or *che* cut

$^1/_2$ teaspoon salt

In a skillet, heat the vegetable oil. Add carrots and stir-fry for about 2 to 3 minutes (until carrots soften but do not lose their color). Add salt and toss. Set aside.

5 cups of short grain rice, cooked

5 eggs, fried sunny side up

5 sprigs crown daisy leaves (*soot*)

Seasoned Chili Paste (optional) or sesame oil and soy sauce, to taste

ASSEMBLY AND PRESENTATION

Place 1 cup of rice in each of five separate bowls. Arrange the vegetables and meat on top of the rice in a circle by color. Make sure there are no similar-colored vegetables next to each other. Place a fried egg in each bowl. Garnish each bowl with a sprig of crown daisy. Serve immediately with Seasoned Chili Paste (*Yangnyum Gochujang*, page 8), if you like it spicy, or with sesame oil and soy sauce.

Stone Pot Mixed Rice Bowl

Dolsot Bibim Bap

You can get stone pots at Korean houseware stores. Before you use your stone pot for the first time, you must treat it to keep it from cracking. Place your stone pot in another pot large enough to hold the stone pot fully immersed in water. Bring to a boil and let it simmer for about 1 hour. Remove from heat and let cool before removing the stone pot. Let the pot dry completely, then coat the inside of the pot completely with any vegetable oil. Let sit for three to four days. Wash completely and your pot is now ready to use.

1   Prepare the vegetables and meat as you would for the Mixed Rice Bowl (*Bibim Bap*, page 23).

2   Grease the inside of the stone pot. Cover and place over medium heat for about 3 to 4 minutes.

3   Add a cup of rice in each stone pot and top with remaining ingredients, arranged in a circle. Serve immediately with optional raw egg (the egg will cook from the stone pot's heat) and seasonings.

A CHEAT You can find all the toppings for *bibim bap* in the deli section of some Korean markets. Just add freshly cooked rice and a fried egg, if you want, and voilà! You can have *bibim bap* instantly. Of course, it doesn't taste as good as homemade, but what really does?

Field Trips

Field trips (*so-poong*) were the best things in the world for my kindergarten soul. Getting ready was always a ritual. First, I would have to put on my white tights, my white blouse, my yellow skirt and suspenders, and my yellow blazer. The last things I put on were my shiny black shoes. They kept my feet inside with little black straps that would snap on with a click. I would tap around in them in front of the house waiting impatiently for my mom to walk me to school.

She would be busy packing my lunch into my lunchbox (*doshilak*). When she knew I would be going on a field trip, she would make me *gim bap*—rice, vegetables, and meat wrapped in a seaweed roll. It was like a sushi roll, but with other things in the middle. (*See* Seaweed Rolled Rice, page 29.)

More often than not, I would forget my hat in the house and would have to unsnap my shoes, run back inside, and hastily snap them back on before running to school, my backpack flapping on my back. A bus would be waiting in front of the building, while other kids in their yellow uniforms filed in. The trip always seemed to last forever, while we sang songs, played games, or dozed off drooling on our friend sleeping next to us.

FIELD TRIP IN KINDERGARTEN

We would eventually arrive at our destination—the zoo, a park, a factory. Whatever it was, it was always new and exciting.

One of my favorite trips was to some hillside in the country. We all carried our sketch pads and oil pastels up this grassy slope and spent hours sketching the landscape around us. My best friend, Yunju, and I would roll down that hill, laughing and panting to catch our breath just long enough to run back up to roll down all over again. Eventually, we'd tire ourselves and sit in the grass making clover flower wreaths to crown each other with. Or we'd lay down to watch the cloud shapes turn into animals, while the blades of grass tickled us through our cotton tights.

We would work up such an appetite that my *gim bap* tasted like the best food in the whole wide world. You never saw a group of kids sit so quietly as you would during the first bites of lunch, each of us eating seaweed rolls made with a mother's care and love. Who had time to talk when you were gobbling up the best food in the world?

Even at that young age, I realized how important little things like scenery, weather, and good company made a seemingly simple meal taste so wonderful. The *gim bap* shared on a grassy hillside with your best friend did not taste at all the same as when you were trying to eat it right after having a fight with your little brother. A simple bowl of rice tasted different when eaten in sunshine than when you were trapped inside a house because of a violent storm.

As we got older, the same *gim bap* had different connotations. I would be embarrassed when my mom pulled out the sliced and wrapped rolls in front of Disneyland or some other public place. While other parents were buying fresh pizza and hamburgers for their brats, we had to swallow cold rice rolls before we could have any fun.

Years later, while supporting myself through art school, I lived the reality of the "starving artist," opting to buy prohibitively expensive red sable brushes over having warm meals during any given week. Yet, even as I was wolfing down a day-old bagel I'd bought for a dime, the life lessons I learned as a young child helped me enjoy it a little more with the company of good friends, or in the warm glow of a sunny beach. No matter how simple the food, the meals I remember the most are those in good company, in beautiful scenery, or especially those made with love.

Seaweed Rolled Rice

Gim Bap

Rice rolled in seaweed makes a healthy snack or portable lunch. Don't be afraid to experiment with different ingredients, colors, and combinations. You can really put anything you want inside and roll it up. The rolling itself takes a little bit of practice, but with a bamboo roller, it's actually quite easy to make nice tight rolls. MAKES 10 TO 12 ROLLS

4 cups cooked rice

$^1/_2$ teaspoon salt plus additional for seasoning

1 teaspoon rice vinegar

1 carrot

1 bunch of spinach

$1^1/_2$ teaspoons sesame oil

2 eggs

Vegetable oil for cooking

About $^1/_4$ pound *boolgogi* beef or ground beef

Black pepper

About 8 ounces of yellow pickled Asian radish (*mu*)

10 to 12 sheets seaweed/laver (*gim*)

1 tablespoon toasted sesame seeds (page 3), optional

1   If the rice is hot, let it cool until it stops steaming. Dissolve $^1/_2$ teaspoon salt in the vinegar and add to the rice. Mix well. Set aside.

2   Cut the carrot into long thin strips and blanch in a bit of salt water. Set aside.

3   Thoroughly wash the spinach and blanch in boiling water. Remove and run through cold water, then squeeze out as much water as you can. Mix the spinach with $^1/_2$ teaspoon sesame oil and salt as needed. Set aside.

4   Beat the eggs in a small bowl. In a heated frying pan, add a bit of vegetable oil and pour in the eggs, moving the frying pan to cover the surface. Cook over low heat until one side is slightly browned, then flip and finish cooking the other side. Remove from heat and let cool. Slice into long thin strips. Set aside.

5   Cook the beef in a frying pan, adding a bit of salt and pepper. Set aside.

6   Slice the pickled radish into thin long strips. Set aside.

ASSEMBLING

1   Have all the ingredients laid out in front of you, as well as a bowl of cold water to dip your fingers. Using a cutting board or other flat surface, lay down a bamboo roller and a sheet of seaweed, placed right to the edge closest to you.

2   Dip a spoon in the cold water, then spoon the rice, spreading it out into a rectangle over $2/3$ of the seaweed closest to you. If you want to shape the rice with your fingers, dip them in cold water first to keep the grains from sticking. Lay a bit of each ingredient in lines on top of the rice, starting right near the edge of the rice closest to you and working away from you until a bit of each ingredient fills the length of the seaweed. Roll away from you, curling your fingers around and pulling the bamboo roller out from under as you roll. Do not be afraid to squeeze as you roll. When the roll is done, dip your finger in the cold water and run it across the loose end of the seaweed to help seal it closed. Repeat rolling until you've run out of rice.

3   Once all the rolls are done, brush each roll with a bit of sesame oil and sprinkle with sesame seeds, if you like. To slice the rolls, dip a large knife in cold water and cut each piece about $1/2$ inch thick. Slice just before serving. Serve at room temperature with a bit of barley or corn tea, or a small bowl of soup and some slices of pickled Asian radish, if you like.

NOTE   Prepare all the ingredients, then assemble the rolls. Make these rolls the morning you intend to eat them because they won't keep well in the refrigerator.

VARIATION   Instead of beef, you can add sliced sausages, crabmeat, or keep it vegetarian. You can also add cucumber, drained *kimchi*, blanched bean sprouts, or anything you like. For a different look and flavor, you can also wrap the rolls in sheets of egg instead of seaweed.

To make thin sheets of egg, beat a dozen eggs in a medium bowl with $1/2$ teaspoon of salt. Add a bit of oil into a frying pan. Pour a thin layer of egg, enough to cover the bottom of the pan thinly, but completely. Let the egg cook, browning slightly. Flip and cook on the other side. Repeat until all the eggs are used. Then use the egg sheets instead of the seaweed to roll the rice.

Kimchi Fried Rice

Kimchi Bokkum Bap

I think of fried rice as the meat loaf of Asian cuisine—a dish you make when you have leftover food. That's why you'll hardly ever see any Koreans order fried rice in a restaurant or serve it to special guests. Any fried rice dish works best with chilled rice. If you don't have any leftover rice, use undercooked, drier rice, otherwise the dish will be mushy. This recipe is quick and easy to make with overripe *kimchi* and a few simple ingredients. MAKES 2 SERVINGS

1 garlic clove, minced

$1/2$ medium onion, chopped

$1/4$ pound pork, sliced into bite-size pieces

2 tablespoons vegetable oil

3 cups leftover rice

1 cup *kimchi*, loosely chopped

2 green onions, chopped

1 tablespoon sesame oil

Sesame seeds for garnish (optional)

1   In a large frying pan (with deep sides) or wok, sauté garlic, onion, and pork in vegetable oil until pork is browned. Add rice and cook over medium heat until grains are no longer hard, about 7 to 10 minutes.

2   Add *kimchi*, green onions, and sesame oil and cook, mixing the ingredients together, for another 2 or 3 minutes, until green onions are limp but have not lost their color and the *kimchi* is limp.

Serve immediately sprinkled with sesame seeds, if you wish. Serve with Roasted Seaweed Sheets (*Gim*, page 61), Fire Meat (*Boolgogi*, page 166) and other leftover *banchan*.

VARIATION To make a vegetarian version, simply omit the pork.

Comfort Food

My dad trained as an acupuncturist when I was a young child. Growing up, there was hardly even a bottle of aspirin in the house. If you had a stomachache, dad would poke some needles in the right pressure points and you'd feel better in moments. Depending on the nature of your headache, a few more needles would be inserted into the skull, the nasal passages, or other points and the headache would miraculously disappear in a matter of minutes.

With his metal box of needles on hand, my father was the terror of neighborhood children. If we were misbehaving or making too much noise, all he had to do was pull out that tin from his pocket and shake it menacingly at us and all the kids would run away screaming. I even had a friend who refused to step into the house while my dad was around. My non-Asian friends would watch in both horror and fascination as my dad put needles into various points of our bodies, while my siblings and I would calmly watch TV.

During the acupuncture treatment, my mom would be making rice porridge (*jook*) for us. Proper *jook* takes a certain amount of patience, requiring long moments of stirring while the white grains turn soft and mushy. Plain rice porridge bears just the subtle flavor of rice. Yet, with a side of soy sauce and toasted sesame seeds, it's about the only thing you want to eat when you're feeling sick with no appetite.

Whoever was sick would sit in bed, milking the sickness for all it was worth with a bowlful of *jook* and a pile of books by the bedside. My mom would make us get things for the sick one, as we did our chores grumblingly while casting dirty glances their way. The one in bed would gloat between coughs, sticking their tongue out in defiance at the healthy ones.

Rice porridge is not just food for sick people, though. With the addition of certain seafood, vegetables, or beans, *jook* can make a wonderfully warm winter breakfast or a nice snack to share with a visiting friend. Certain *jook* are eaten for health benefits or special occasions. But nothing comforts a cold like a nice bowl of steaming *jook.*

Pine Nut Porridge

Jat Jook

 A mild, but nutty porridge, *Jat Jook* makes a nice autumn or winter breakfast or special snack to share with friends. *Jat Jook* is also served to sick
people to rehydrate them and restore their strength. MAKES 6 TO 8 SERVINGS

2 cups rice

1 cup pine nuts plus
additional for garnish

Water

Salt

Honey

1   Place the rice in a medium-sized bowl. Cover with water
and let sit overnight.

2   Place the pine nuts and 1 cup of water in a blender or food
processor. Blend until smooth. Strain through a sieve and discard the tips. Set aside.

3   Drain the rice and add it to a blender or food processor
with 2 cups water. In a medium pot, add the ground rice and
3 cups of water. Bring to a boil. Then reduce heat and let simmer for about 15 minutes, stirring frequently until the mixture thickens. Add the pine nut liquid slowly, stirring as you
pour. Bring the mixture to a boil again, reduce heat, and let simmer for about 10 more minutes, stirring frequently until the mixture is a thick porridge.

Serve warm or at room temperature, sprinkling a few pine nuts into each bowl.
Serve with salt and honey on the side for each person to add according to his or
her particular taste.

NOTE If the porridge takes a long time to thicken, add some rice flour as a thickener.

VARIATION Instead of pine nuts, you can use sliced red dates/jujubes for garnish.

Abalone Porridge

The chewy meatiness of the abalone is a nice texture surprise in this mushy porridge. Freshly made, it can serve as a warm snack or light winter meal.

MAKES 8 TO 10 SERVINGS

1¹/₂ cups rice

¹/₂ pound fresh abalone

Water

Salt

Sesame oil

1   Soak the rice in water for at least 2 hours. Drain and set aside.

2   Shuck the shells from the abalone. Clean abalone meat thoroughly in cold water. Cut into slices.

3   In a large frying pan, stir-fry the abalone slices for about 2 to 3 minutes over high heat. Add the drained rice and pan-fry for several more minutes. Add 8 cups water and bring to a boil. Reduce heat and let simmer for about 20 minutes, stirring occasionally at first and more frequently as the rice becomes mushier. Add salt to taste.

Serve immediately sprinkled with sesame oil and with a side of *kimchi*.

Red Bean Porridge

Pot Jook

According to old customs, red bean porridge is eaten on the shortest day of the year, the Winter Solstice (*Dongji*). Bowls of red bean porridge were presented to the household shrine, placed in rooms and in the shed. The red bean (red being the color of Yang, the sun, the positive, the masculine) was supposed to chase away evil spirits, who had the greatest strength when the days were short. The porridge was also applied to the main gate or the walls to the main gate of the house. When the porridge cooled, the family shared a meal to celebrate the solstice, the day the sun comes to life again. MAKES 5 TO 6 SERVINGS

2 cups red beans

Water

1/2 cup rice

About 2 dozen Sweet Rice Balls (page 199)

1   Place the red beans and 16 cups (1 gallon) water in a large pot. Simmer for about 2 hours until soft, stirring occasionally, then more frequently as the liquid thickens. Remove from heat and let cool. Drain the beans, but retain the water. Then push the beans through a mesh strainer, adding some of the reserved water to help strain. Discard the peels and residue. Pour the strained bean soup back into the pot.

2   Wash and soak the rice in cold water for about 20 minutes. Add the rice to the soup and simmer for about 30 minutes, stirring constantly. Add the rice balls and cook for a few minutes longer.

Serve either hot or at room temperature with either a side of salt or honey, depending if you like your porridge savory or sweet.

———

NOTE After you've added the rice, adjust the thickness of the porridge to your liking. If the mixture is too thick, add a little bit of water at a time, stirring and adding until you have the right consistency. If the mixture is too thin, simmer a bit longer until some of the water evaporates.

Sweet Pumpkin Porridge

Hobak Jook

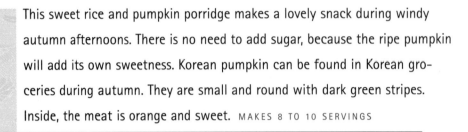

This sweet rice and pumpkin porridge makes a lovely snack during windy autumn afternoons. There is no need to add sugar, because the ripe pumpkin will add its own sweetness. Korean pumpkin can be found in Korean groceries during autumn. They are small and round with dark green stripes. Inside, the meat is orange and sweet. MAKES 8 TO 10 SERVINGS

1 pound sweet Korean pumpkin

4 cups glutinous rice flour

Salt

Water

1   Wash the pumpkin and cut it into 4 pieces. Remove the seeds and place into a large pot, skins facing up. Add water to cover and bring to a boil. Boil for about 25 to 30 minutes, until pumpkin is soft. Remove the pumpkin and let cool. Scrape out the insides of the pumpkin with a wooden spoon or spatula.

2   Place the pumpkin back into the pot, add the rice flour and about 10 cups water. Continue to cook over medium heat. Add salt as needed and continue cooking, stirring continuously to keep the porridge from sticking to the bottom of the pot. Cook for about 30 minutes, then turn off heat and cover, letting it steam for another 10 minutes or so.

3   Serve warm or at room temperature.

VARIATION For a fun texture, add rice balls before removing from heat. (See Sweet Rice Balls, page 199.)

A BIT OF HISTORY AND TRADITION

Kimchi

While shopping at a Korean grocery one day, I saw two young girls in the produce section. They were both hanging onto the shopping cart like little rag dolls as their mom meticulously picked out Napa cabbages for their *kimchi.* Seeing their bored faces took me back to my younger days, when my sister and I had to help my mom. • The monthly *kimchi* making was how the neighborhood women saved money and found out the latest gossip. I remember how my sister and I hated squatting on the kitchen floor with the rest of them, peeling garlic as the pungent scent of chili powder made our noses itch. • Listening to their mindless chatter about people I vaguely knew and peeling clove after clove of the endless

pile of garlic, it was all I could do to stay awake. The only thing that would cure me of my drowsiness was the morsel of fresh *kimchi* that my mom would put into my mouth. Even after the drudgery, seeing the jars full of *kimchi* at the end of the day filled me with a sense of accomplishment, as my mouth watered with anticipation. But it really wasn't until I became an adult that I grew to appreciate this cultural tradition. • *Kimchi* is a source of national pride for Koreans. When hungry, any Korean would swear that a bowl of rice and some *kimchi* are all

MY MOM AND MRS. SUH MAKING *KIMCHI*

that's needed to complete a meal. According to a national nutrition survey in South Korea, an average adult consumes two to four ounces a day in the summer and five to seven ounces a day in the winter. That translates to about 12.5 percent of the average South Korean's daily food intake.

Not only is *kimchi* eaten as part of a meal, it is also used as an ingredient in other dishes. For instance, there is *kimchi* fried rice, *kimchi jjigae* (a hot pot of *kimchi,* meat, tofu, and vegetables), *kimchi mandu* (like wontons), *kimchi buchingae* (flatcakes), *kimchi* ramen—the list is endless.

My father is such a *kimchi* eater that our family has found creative ways of preparing it. We have had *kimchi* pizza, *kimchi* hamburgers, and even *kimchi* stuffing in our Thanksgiving turkey.

In Korean culture, a woman's value as a wife is tested by her cooking abilities, especially by how well she makes her *kimchi.* When my sister was newly married, she made her first batch by herself. She followed all the procedures and ingredients except for one crucial step, the last bit of salt in the seasoning. A couple of days later, we sat down to dinner to enjoy my sister's first *kimchi.* My younger brother exclaimed in horror, "What is this tasteless thing?" It was as raw as if she had just taken some chili powder and poured it over the naked cabbage. Laughing, my mom pulled her famous *kimchi* from the fridge and saved the day.

Although it is considered such an important dish, no written record of it is found in Korea until the seventh century. It is believed that *kimchi* originated from Chinese pickles (*ju,* pronounced "*cho*" in Korean) imported during the Shilla and Koryo dynasties—roughly beginning in 57 B.C.

When most Koreans hear the word *kimchi,* the image commonly conjured up is that of the traditional type made with Napa cabbage. Although this kind is the best known, *kimchi* can be made with a variety of vegetables, spices, and other ingredients. It is also prepared in different ways and to different degrees of fermentation. In areas near the ocean, people tend to add seafood. Some people may even add fruit or nuts. Although any Korean on the street would say there are hundreds of types, an independent study conducted by the Korean Food Research Institute counted only 187 varieties.

As when pickling, *kimchi* vegetables are soaked in a salt solution. Sea salt is best because of its high magnesium chloride content, which helps the vegetables stay crisp. Ordinary table salt can be used, but it will not yield the best results. The earliest salt used to preserve vegetables was found in sea water, rock-salt deposits, or salt flats. A peninsula, Korea has a ready supply of rock salt. *Kimchi* from northern regions generally contains less salt because of the colder winters. Those from southern regions require more salt because more is needed for preservation during the milder winters.

Historically, winter *kimchi* was prepared in late fall to preserve the harvest until the springtime. The tradition of burying the *kimchi* in large clay pots in the snow was developed to slow fermentation during storage. In the summer, the large clay jars were stored in near-by streams or in wells.

The major *kimchi* making (*gimjang*) usually started in late October or early November, after the fall harvest. *Gimjang* was a major task that lasted two to three days and involved several people. Close relatives and neighboring housewives got together at one house and pickled anywhere from 100 to 200 Napa cabbages, depending on the size of the family. It was the hostess's responsibility to make a big lunch for all her helpers during the days of *gimjang*. When one of the other women was ready to make her own winter *kimchi,* everyone else helped out again, taking turns until everyone had several large clay jars of *kimchi* laying in wait for the winter months.

Kimchi was an important source of nutrition during the frost when fresh vegetables were not available. There is an inscription from the Shilla dynasty: "A family of ten needs eight jars to make it through the winter." With the advancement of agricultural techniques and the availability of vegetables year-round, there is no longer a need to prepare such large stocks. And, of course, no one digs a hole in the backyard anymore when it is so much easier to put it in the refrigerator.

Until the Koryo Dynasty (roughly A.D. 918 to 1392), the main vegetable used was the radish. Diversity grew as Buddhists preserved many other vegetables to maintain their vegetarian diet during the harsh winters. What we know as *kimchi* today did not come into existence until the fifteenth century, when the first chile peppers were imported to Korea from the New World. Along with chile peppers, salted seafood became an important *kimchi* ingredient. Small shrimps, anchovies, hairtail, squid, or pollack are among the many fish that can be added. Also around that time, Napa cabbage and Asian radish became increasingly popular in making *kimchi.* Even before chile peppers were introduced, Koreans used various ingredients, like violet-colored mustard leaf, cockscomb, and safflower, to give *kimchi* a reddish color.

Factory production of *kimchi* started in the 1960s so that it could be exported to the South Korean army stationed in Vietnam. Since the 1970s, with technological advances and increased consumption, commercial production has increased significantly.

Kimchi is such a staple in Korea that there is even a museum dedicated to it. The P'ulmuwon Kimchi Museum in Seoul covers its history, the tools used to make it, and the regional varieties, among many other related displays. In Gwangju, *kimchi* is celebrated in an annual festival (around mid-October), with traditional folk music, cultural events, and, of course, *kimchi*-making contests.

Like any good Korean American, I would swear that my mother's *kimchi* is the best, although every household has a different way of preparing it. My mom's secret is to add ample amounts of fish sauce; she just likes the taste of it. My aunt, who grew up in a seaside town, likes to put raw oysters in hers. One of our friends makes hers too salty for my taste; she's from Busan, in the southern part of the country.

Kimchi is a tradition passed down from generation to generation. It's a purely female tradition: My mom learned from her mom, who learned from her mom, and so on. Like Korean folktales, the recipes aren't really written down, but are passed along orally and by experience, adding a different twist to each family's recipe. Because Korea is a Confucian society, the cycle of life and ancestral lineage are very important. The passing down of stories and cooking to the next generation is like passing the torch. Out in the country, it was easier for the family to gather to make *kimchi* because the extended family lived in the same village, sometimes in the same house. When aunts, nieces, and cousins would gather to cook for special occasions, it was also an excuse to share the latest gossip.

Even when the older women get together today, there is always a lot of bickering and boasting about which is the correct way to make *kimchi,* how to cut things, how much of what to put in and whatnot. Now that I'm older, I sometimes put in my two cents' worth, but I generally like to listen and learn from the other women. Unfortunately, younger women like me don't get together to make *kimchi*. Because of our modern lives, most of us make it alone or buy it at the store. I get worried knowing that even my mom and the women of her generation in America rarely make their own *kimchi* anymore. But as long as there are enough weary little girls peeling garlic in the kitchen with their mothers, *kimchi* making is a tradition that will continue for generations to come.

Traditional Napa Cabbage Kimchi

Baechu Kimchi

This is the mother of all *kimchi*. When Koreans say "kimchi," this is the kind that comes to everyone's minds. Good either fresh or fermented, it goes with everything from meats to noodles. You will need a one-gallon glass jar or four 1-quart jars. MAKES ENOUGH *KIMCHI* TO FILL 1-GALLON JAR

1 cup plus 1 tablespoon coarse sea salt or kosher salt

Water

2 heads Napa cabbage, cut in quarters or 2-inch wedges, depending on size of cabbage

1 bulb garlic, cloves separated and peeled

1 (2-inch) piece of ginger root

$^1/_4$ cup fish sauce or Korean salted shrimp

1 Asian radish, peeled and grated

1 bunch of green onions, cut into 1-inch lengths

1 bunch of mustard greens, chopped into 1-inch pieces

$^1/_2$ cup Korean chili powder

1 teaspoon sugar (optional)

Sesame oil (optional)

Sesame seeds (optional)

1   Dissolve 1 cup salt in $^1/_2$ gallon water. Soak cabbage in the salt water for 3 to 4 hours.

2   Combine garlic, ginger, and fish sauce or shrimp in food processor or blender until finely minced.

3   In large bowl, combine radish, green onions, mustard greens, garlic mixture, chili powder, 1 tablespoon salt and optional sugar. Toss gently but thoroughly. (If mixing with your hands, be sure to wear rubber gloves to avoid chili burn.)

4   Remove cabbage from water and rinse thoroughly. Drain cabbage in colander, squeezing as much water from the leaves as possible. Take cabbage and stuff radish mixture between leaves, working from outside in, starting with largest leaf to smallest. Do not overstuff, but make sure radish mixture adequately fills leaves. When entire cabbage is stuffed, take one of the larger leaves and wrap tightly around the rest of the cabbage. Divide cabbage among 4 (1-quart) jars or one 1-gallon jar, pressing down firmly to remove any air bubbles.

5   Let sit 2 to 3 days in a cool place before serving. Remove *kimchi* from jar and slice into 1-inch-length pieces. If serving before *kimchi* is fermented, sprinkle with a little bit of sesame oil and sesame seeds. Refrigerate after opening.

NOTE   *Kimchi* will be good enough to eat straight for up to about 3 weeks. After about 4 weeks, once the *kimchi* gets too fermented to eat by itself, use it to make hot pots, flatcakes, dumplings, or just plain fried rice.

Quick Kimchi

Mak Kimchi

This recipe is easy to make with readily available ingredients and without a lot of prep work. Because all the vegetables are sliced into bite-size pieces before pickling, it's convenient to eat as well. For a more complex flavor, you can substitute the salt with salted shrimp or fish sauce. MAKES 1 GALLON

2 Napa cabbages

1 medium Asian radish

$^1/_4$ cup coarse sea salt or kosher salt

Water

4 green onions, sliced into pieces about 1-inch long

5 garlic cloves, minced

2 tablespoons fresh ginger, minced

2 tablespoons chili powder

1   Thoroughly wash the leaves of the Napa cabbages and cut them into about 2-inch lengths. Peel the Asian radish and halve it lengthwise down the center, cut lengthwise again, and then slice into $^1/_2$-inch thin squares.

2   Dissolve the salt in 1 cup water. Place the vegetables in a large bowl and pour the salt water over them. Let soak at least 6 hours or preferably overnight.

3   The next day, drain the vegetables and retain the salty water. Add the green onions, garlic, ginger, and chili powder. Mix the vegetables by hand (use gloves because the chili may sting and stain your hands). Pack into a 1-gallon jar. Pour the salted water over the mixture. Leave about an inch of space on top of the jar.

4   Let sit about 2 or 3 days, depending on how warm the weather is and how fermented you like your *kimchi*. Refrigerate after opening.

TRADITIONAL *KIMCHI* INGREDIENTS

Wrapped Kimchi

Bossam Kimchi

This traditional *kimchi* is beautiful to look at but rather labor intensive. Except for special occasions and for extra special guests, hardly anyone makes this *kimchi* anymore. The seafood and the Asian pear add a nice balance of crunchy and chewy textures with sweet and salty tastes. FILLS 3 1-GALLON JARS

5 Napa cabbages

1 medium Asian radish

3 cups plus $^{1}/_{4}$ cup coarse sea salt or kosher salt

Water

2 Asian pears

1 small octopus

3 cups red chili powder

$^{1}/_{4}$ cup sugar

$^{1}/_{2}$ cup salted shrimp, chopped

5 garlic cloves, minced

2 tablespoons fresh ginger, minced

1 bunch of Korean watercress (*minari*), cut into about 2-inch lengths

1 bunch of mustard greens, cut into about 2-inch lengths

3 green onions, cut into about 2-inch lengths

1 cup raw oysters

5 raw chestnuts, sliced

1   Thoroughly wash the leaves of the Napa cabbages and cut the cabbages in half, lengthwise. Peel the Asian radish and halve it lengthwise down the center.

2   Dissolve 3 cups of salt in about 1 gallon of water. Place the cabbages and radish in a large bowl and pour the salt water over them. Let soak at least 6 hours or preferably overnight.

3   The next day, drain the vegetables, but retain the salty water. Remove the leafy parts of the cabbages and set aside for wrapping later. Cut the cabbage stems into pieces about 1 $^{1}/_{2}$ inches long. Slice the radish halves into semicircles about $^{1}/_{2}$ inch thick. Then cut the slices into about 2 or 3 pieces, depending on how big they are. Peel and cut the pears into pieces similar in size to the radish pieces. Cut the octopus into narrow strips about 1$^{1}/_{2}$ inches long.

4   Add enough water to the chili powder to make a paste. Add $^{1}/_{4}$ cup salt, sugar, salted shrimp, garlic, and ginger and mix.

5   In a large bowl, add the Korean watercress, mustard greens, green onions, radishes, the cabbage stems, pears, chestnuts, octopus, and oysters. Add the seasoning and mix, being careful not to break the oysters.

6   In a medium bowl, lay out about 2 or 3 cabbage leaves. Add enough stuffing to fill. Sprinkle a few pieces of the raw chestnuts on top. Securely wrap with the leaves and place in

FOR GARNISH

Pine nuts

Chile pepper threads

5 raw chestnuts, cut into slivers

5 dried dates, cut into slivers

5 shiitake mushrooms, cut into slivers

a 1-gallon glass jar. Repeat until all the leaves are used, stacking each wrapped bundle into the jar. Cover the tops of the glass jars with any remaining stuffing. Pour in the reserved salty water, making sure there are no air bubbles.

7   Let sit about 2 or 3 days, depending on how warm the weather is and how fermented you like your *kimchi*. Refrigerate after opening. Serve each bundle by slicing or lifting the leaf to expose the filling inside.

Regional Kimchi

When you look at a map of Korea, you can see that it is a small peninsula, surrounded by the Yellow Sea on one side and the East Sea on the other. It would make sense that products of the sea would affect the cuisine. What is more difficult to realize from looking at a map is that Korea is one of the most mountainous regions in the world. About 70 percent of its landmass is mountain, so imagine the variety of subclimates that would be created, as well as the difficulty of farming such land. It is considered to be in the subarctic climate zone, which means that its climate exhibits characteristics of both arctic and tropical zones. The winters are dry with temperatures well below freezing. Summers are incredibly humid with temperatures above 100 degrees Fahrenheit.

Due to historical, natural, topographical, and social factors, different regions have developed their own distinctive foods. As would stand to reason, each region

TRADITIONAL CLAY JARS IN SEOUL

has its own way of making *kimchi*. Each family in turn, also has its own recipe, which is handed down through generations.

The flavor of the *kimchi* depends on the ingredients available, the amount of salt used, and the degree of spiciness. In the southern part of the peninsula, where the winters are milder than the northern provinces, more salt is used to help preserve the vegetables. Thus, the *kimchi* from the south tends to contain more seafood and be sweeter with a stronger flavor. Northern *kimchi* tastes less salty and milder with fewer fiery peppers.

Gyonggi Province

Gyonggi Do is in the heart of the Korean peninsula. It's no wonder that the capital city, Seoul, has been located here since the Josun Dynasty. The Charyong Mountain range ends on the eastern and southern parts of this province, leaving the wonderfully fertile plains of Gyonggi, Kimpo, and Pyongtek. Crops like rice and barley are plentiful here, as well as herbs from the mountains and fruits such as grapes and pears. Like all the provinces of Korea, there is plenty of access to seafood from the western coast.

Seoul food retains many traces of royal culinary traditions. Typical Gyonggi Do food tends to be extravagant and aristocratic, since the area has been the center of trade for hundreds of years. *Kimchi* from this region include ones made from baby ginseng (*misam kimchi*), Wrapped *Kimchi* (*Bossam Kimchi*) and Asian Radish *Kimchi* (*Mu Kimchi*).

North and South Choongchong Provinces

Located in the middle of the peninsula, just below Gyonggi Do, the Choongchong Provinces have a relatively mild climate and fertile land, which is great for farming. The provinces encompass the Nonsan Plains, one of Korea's largest rice-growing areas. South Choongchong Do borders the Yellow Sea. Local seafood specialties include salted oysters with chili powder (*oligool jut*) from Ganwol Island (*Ganwol Do*) and salted tiny shrimps (*saewu jut*).

In the central part of North Chungchong Do are wonderful mountain herbs and mushrooms. Although there is no access to the ocean, there are well-known freshwater fish available for local cuisines. People use mainly salted and fermented baby freshwater shrimp. Oyster Asian radish kimchi (*gul ggakdoogi*), eggplant *kimchi* (*gaji kimchi*), pumpkin *kimchi* (*hobak kimchi*) and spinach *kimchi* (*shigumchi kimchi*) are local specialties.

Gangwon Province

On the East side of the peninsula, Gangwon Do borders the Hamgyong and Hwanghae provinces. The western part of the province grows crops, such as potatoes, corn, beans and buckwheat. The eastern part, whose coast meets the East Sea, boasts such ocean foods as pollack, squid, sea mustard, and Alaskan pollack. Seafoods such as clams and anchovies are preferred to meat. Cuttlefish and Alaskan pollack from the East Sea are widely used in *kimchi* from this region. Particularly well known is a *Shikhae* made with dried pollack mixed with grains and vegetables.

Kimchi made from dried squid and sliced radishes (*mu malleng-i*) are also regional specialties. Although seafood is a main ingredient, acorn, arrowroot, and other medicinal and mountain herbs give the *kimchi* of this region a distinctive taste.

North and South Julla Provinces

Julla Do is in the southwestern part of the peninsula. One of the most fertile areas, the northern part of this region produces most of the grains of Korea. On the plateau between the Noryong and Sobaek Mountains, crops like gingseng, chile peppers, herbs, bracken, and mushrooms are grown. High-quality ginger, persimmons and citron are also grown in this region. From the sea, oysters, sea laver, and sea mustard are cultivated.

Being a wealthy region, foods from this area are refined from generations of aristocratic living. Due to the warmer weather, the regional *kimchi*'s spices are stronger and hotter. Chili powder and pickled seafoods are used in large quantities to preserve the *kimchi*. Regional specialties include *Gat kimchi* (mustard leaf *kimchi*). Citron (*Yuja*), abundant in this region, is added to White Radish Water Kimchi (*Dong Chimi*, page 51). People from this region like their *kimchi* with intense and complex flavors.

North and South Gyongsang Provinces

Located in the southeastern part of the peninsula, Gyongsang Do is well known for its seafood. The people from this region like their *kimchi* to have simpler tastes, preferring that to a wide variety of flavors. Pickled seafood, such as anchovy, hairtail, or mackerel pike, give *kimchi* from this region a distinctive flavor. Regional specialties include sesame leaf *kimchi*, soybean leaf *kimchi*, leek *kimchi*, sliced green onion *kimchi*, persimmon *kimchi* (*gam kimchi*), garlic stalk *kimchi* (*manul julgi kimchi*), crown daisy *kimchi*, and burdock *kimchi* (*uong kimchi*).

Jeju Island

The country's largest island, Jeju Do, is located off the southwest coast of the peninsula. As sea resources are abundant, a variety of seafood *kimchi* is produced. Abalone *kimchi* (*junbok kimchi*), mixed seafood kimchi (*haemul kimchi*) and square-cut radish *kimchi* (*nabak kimchi*) are well known.

Hwanghae Province (North Korea)

Famous for their hospitality, Hwanghae Do is in the west side of the central part of the peninsula. The food is plentiful and so it follows that people from this region are known for their generosity. The *kimchi* from this region is neither salty nor flat, but has a clear taste and uses spices called *gosu* and *bundi*. Water *kimchi* (*dong chimi*) from this region is made with pickled shrimp or salted croakers or fermented crushed fish. Squash *kimchi* is another specialty from this region.

Pyongyang Province (North Korea)

Pyong An Do is located in the northwestern part of the Korean peninsula. With its characteristic cold winters, fermentation of *kimchi* is slow. Thus, the *kimchi* from this region is flat and not very pungent. Spices and large amounts of salt are not needed to preserve the *kimchi*, so the taste is light, but refreshing. *Dong chimi* from this region is made with beef broth (made from boiling beef ribs).

Hamgyong Province (North Korea)

Located in the northeastern part of the peninsula, Hamyong Do is the coldest and most remote region. Like its neighbor, *kimchi* from this province is not very salty or spicy; less salt and chili powder are used here than in other regions. Indigenous fish products, like flatfish, are widely used. For instance, flatfish punch is made by fermenting a mix of vegetables, grain rice and fish. Other regional specialties also include bean sprout *kimchi* and cod fish (*daegu*) *ggakdoogi*.

Asian Radish Kimchi

Ggakdoogi

Another easy one to make, the radishes make this *kimchi* crispy and refreshing. This is one of my favorite *kimchi* to make in the summer, but it can really be enjoyed all year long. You will need a 1-gallon glass jar or four 1-quart jars. MAKES 1 GALLON

1 bulb garlic, cloves separated and peeled

1 (2-inch) piece of ginger root

2 tablespoons Korean chili powder

2 tablespoons salt

2 large Asian radishes, peeled and cut into 1-inch cubes

1 bunch of mustard greens, chopped into 1-inch pieces

2 tablespoons sugar

1   Combine garlic, ginger, chili powder, and salt in food processor or blender until finely minced.

2   In large bowl, combine garlic mixture with radishes, making sure to rub seasoning into radishes. (If mixing with your hands, wear rubber gloves to avoid chili burn.)

3   Place 4 (1-quart) jars on work surface. Fill jar about one-quarter full with seasoned radishes. Top with thin layer of mustard greens and sprinkle with about $1/2$ tablespoon sugar. Add more seasoned radishes to jar until half full, top with mustard greens and sugar again. Repeat two more times until first jar is filled. Fill remaining jars following the same steps.

4   Place jars in a cool place and do not move until *kimchi* has fully fermented, about 3 to 4 days, before serving. You will know it is ready when water rises from radishes. Refrigerate after opening.

"Bachelor" Kimchi

Chong Gak Kimchi

Some *kimchis* may be eaten fresh, but this *kimchi* is not one of them. One of the easiest to make, *Chong Gak Kimchi* is best when fermented. Ponytail radishes can be found in Korean supermarkets. They look like miniature radishes with long green stems and leaves (the ponytail) attached to them. You can serve the radishes whole, but I recommend slicing them for easier eating. You will need two 1-quart jars. MAKES 2 QUARTS

3 bunches of Korean ponytail radishes

1 cup plus 1 tablespoon salt

1 bulb garlic, cloves separated and peeled

2 (1-inch) pieces of ginger root, peeled

1 bunch of green onions, sliced into 1-inch lengths

1/2 cup chili powder

1 tablespoon salted shrimp

1   Peel radishes, taking care to leave green stalks attached. Wash radishes thoroughly. Drain in colander. Place on baking sheet or in large bowl and sprinkle with 1 cup salt. Mix and let sit 30 minutes.

2   Place garlic and ginger in food processor or blender and mince. Combine garlic mixture with green onions, chili powder, salted shrimp, and 1 tablespoon salt. (If mixing with your hands, be sure to wear gloves to avoid chili burn.)

3   Rinse salt from radishes. Drain in colander. Rub seasoning mix onto radishes. Set two 1-quart jars on work surface. Divide radishes among jars. Let sit 2 to 3 days before serving. Refrigerate after opening.

White Radish Water Kimchi

Dong Chimi

Dong Chimi is a light and refreshingly chilled *kimchi*, perfect for those who enjoy pickled foods that aren't spicy. Although it originated as a winter *kimchi*, it makes a great accompaniment for any summer meal. To get the best tasting *dong chimi*, ferment it slowly by storing it in lower temperatures. Various regional ingredients add special flavors to this *kimchi*. In the south, some people like to add a bit of citron (*yuja*) for an extra refreshing zest. People in the north sometimes add broth from beef or bone. The *kimchi* made with beef broth is sometimes used as a noodle base, quite possibly an origin of the Cold Noodle Soup (*Naengmyun*, page 118). MAKES ABOUT 1 QUART

1 pound Asian radishes

Coarse salt or kosher salt

3 green onions

3 stalks mustard greens

3 or 4 small green peppers

1 (2-inch) piece fresh ginger, sliced

2 garlic cloves, sliced

2 tablespoons salt

Water

1 teaspoon sugar

1   Cut the stems off the radishes and wash well. Roll them over coarse salt, coating them evenly. Place them in a jar, adding just enough water to cover them. Let sit for about 2 days in a cool place. Drain, reserving the salted water.

2   Slice the radishes into thin pieces about $1^1/_2$ inches long by $1/_2$ inch wide. Cut the green onions and mustard greens into $1^1/_2$-inch lengths. Place the radishes, green onions, mustard greens, green peppers, ginger, and garlic in a glass jar and sprinkle with 1 tablespoon salt. Mix well and let sit covered, overnight.

3   Mix 2 cups water with 1 tablespoon of the salt and the sugar until completely dissolved. Pour over the vegetables. Let sit for about 2 or 3 days in a cool place. Store in the refrigerator after opening. Serve chilled.

Why I Used to Hate Making Kimchi

When my parents bought a grocery store, my dad was thrilled. He bought this rickety white truck that was so old, the markings showing what brand of car it was had worn down or fallen off years before my dad acquired it. The back had a wooden cagelike structure to allow him to load it up high with boxes. It looked something like a white, picket fence around the back. My sister and I found it embarrassing to ride around with him in that thing. For my dad, it was his pride and joy.

Twice a week, my dad would get up around four or five in the morning to go downtown for fresh produce. I could hear him trying to get that white beast to start in the cold dawn, the sound of the engine revving and revving in the driveway just below my bedroom window. Even with my eyes still closed, I'd roll them back in teenage girl fashion as I burrowed deeper under the covers. After stalling a couple of times, he would eventually get that clunker moving and somehow make it to the produce market and back in time to open the store at 8 A.M.

GREEN ONIONS AND KOREAN LEEKS

My dad loved going to the Central Market, a large industrial warehouse-type place where local farmers sold their products wholesale to grocery stores, for fresh fruits and vegetables. One summer morning, he thought it would be good for me to go with him. Even after screams of protest and an impromptu bout of tug-of-war with blankets, I got my sleepy self out of bed and climbed into his white monster. Neither the truck's lack of shocks nor its defective heating system could keep me awake during the ride there. From the moment we got on that wide expanse of empty freeway, I was snoozing again. What seemed like a second later, the engine was quiet and my dad was jostling me awake in the middle of some crazy industrial place. Large semis were loaded full with the fruits of the season hauled down from the Central Valley. Smaller local growers were selling their wares straight from the backs of their trucks. The bustling market was indeed a sight to behold.

I followed my dad around as he made his regular rounds. Fifty boxes of tomatoes from this guy, ten boxes of avocados from that guy, and so on. It seemed my dad knew everyone and everyone knew him by name.

"Hey Pal! (My dad's Korean name is Pal-Woo.) Is that your daughter with you there?"

"Good morning, Pal. What can I get for you today?"

You could see my dad's pride in his grin as he showed off his daughter to the produce sellers. I tried to make a good impression, admiring their stuff and smiling a lot. I also shook a lot of rough hands, callused from countless years of honest labor. The men in turn would pick out their best things and hand them to me, sometimes winking at me as if the fruit in their hand was some shared secret between us. I was happy to accept the beautiful leafy green or a handful of handsome plump peaches. One guy even gave me a whole watermelon, so big that it took all my effort to pretend not to strain as I accepted the prize with both of my teenage arms.

By the time we got the truck completely loaded up, the morning sky was already light. My dad and I wolfed down a couple breakfast burritos from a nearby taco truck before we headed back to open the store.

I never went with him to the early morning market again. But whenever he brought home a particularly colorful box of mangoes or crispy green celery, I would always remember the produce sellers' generous smiles and the feel of their weathered skin on my young girl's hand.

Remembering that morning, I always appreciated the produce my dad brought back. Except for the one day he bought the huge box of green onions. When my sister and I got to the market that afternoon, we thought we would be stocking or doing inventory for a few hours, like any other after-school day. But that day, my dad hauled out the green onion box from the walk-in refrigerator and told us that we had to make green onion *kimchi* (*pa kimchi*), saying something about this being the right season and all that. We stood aghast as we peered into that seemingly bottomless box. There must have been at least a hundred bundles of green onions in there! Trimming and cleaning those little things would be no easy task.

Any other afternoon, he would've only heard the usual grumblings and whinings of teenage girls. But that evening, we were supposed to go to some dance. How were we supposed to get the stench of garlic and onions off our hands after making that much *kimchi*? Our complaints fell on deaf ears as my sister and I succumbed to our menial task.

What seemed like days later, we had the green onions all trimmed and cleaned. My mom came over and seasoned the whole lot as we helped her pack the jars. Amongst the three of us, we somehow managed to fill several gallon jars. I knew this was my dad's favorite *kimchi*, but there was no way even he could finish that much *pa kimchi* before it became too fermented to enjoy.

Nevertheless, we were so thrilled to be done with the *kimchi* making that we ran off in a mad rush to get ready for the dance that night. It was the first dance of the year and even hours of *kimchi* making couldn't dampen our excitement. Although it wasn't as important as a homecoming or prom, there were still plenty of cute guys we wanted to impress.

Once we got home, my sister and I must have washed our hands a dozen times before we bathed them in lotion and doused them with perfume, trying to conceal the fact that we had been handling green onions and garlic all afternoon. After squeezing ourselves into our dresses and dabbing ourselves all over with even more perfume, we were ready to go.

During the dance, we probably looked pretty hilarious as we tried to dance without bringing our hands too close to anyone's faces. Eventually, we were having such a good time that we forgot all about our afternoon task and enjoyed ourselves with our friends.

Afterward, as we were enjoying drinks and fries at some late-night establishment, the faint smell of garlic and green onions wafted into my nostrils.

"Oh man!" I exclaimed quietly to my sister.

"What?" my sister gave me her usual oblivious look.

"Smell," I commanded as I thrust my hand under her nose.

"Aw man!" she exclaimed in return, as she pushed my hand away she smelled her own hands. "Aw man!" she said again, as she put her hand under my nose.

I pushed her hand away and I reached for my milkshake.

"All I can say is that the *kimchi* better be good," I shrugged and slurped the thick beverage through my straw.

"Tell me about it," my sister agreed as she grabbed my milkshake and took a drink.

"What are you two going on about?" one of our friends asked.

"Nothing," we both replied in unison. I caught my sister putting her hands in her pockets while nonchalantly slurping my milkshake, as I was slipping my hands between my thighs and the vinyl seat underneath.

Green Onion Kimchi

Although green onions can be spicy when raw, their flavor mellows when pickled in *kimchi*. One of my dad's favorite, *pa kimchi* is actually very easy to make. MAKES ABOUT 1 QUART

40 green onions

1 tablespoon coarse sea salt or kosher salt

1 tablespoon chili powder

2 garlic cloves, minced

1 teaspoon fresh ginger, grated

2 tablespoons water

1 Remove any withered or browned leaves from the green onions. Trim the roots and dry ends off and wash in cold water. Place the green onions in a bowl and sprinkle with salt. Let stand about 30 minutes until the onions become limp. Rinse with cold water and drain.

2 In a large bowl, mix together the chili powder, garlic, and ginger. Add the green onions and mix well. Bunch 5 green onion stems together and wrap the green parts around the bundle, tying a knot, if possible, and leaving the white bulbs exposed. Repeat with the rest of the green onions. Pack the bundles into a 1-quart jar, pressing down with each addition.

3 Add the water to the bowl and swish it around to gather any spices collected in the bowl. Pour over the onions and seal jar tightly. Let sit in a cool place for about 2 to 3 days. Refrigerate after opening.

Mustard Green Kimchi

Got Kimchi

 Mustard greens make a nice flavorful and fragrant *kimchi* that goes well with beef and other meats. MAKES 1 QUART

1 bunch of mustard greens

1 tablespoon coarse sea salt or kosher salt

Water

1 cup salted shrimp

1 onion, grated

2 garlic cloves, minced

1 tablespoon red chile powder

1 teaspoon fresh ginger, grated

1   Thoroughly wash the mustard greens, discarding any yellowed leaves. In a large bowl, add the salt and cover the greens with about 4 cups water. Let sit for about 1 hour or longer, until the leaves have gone limp. Rinse.

2   In a large bowl, combine the shrimp, onion, garlic, chili powder, and ginger. Add the mustard greens and mix until all the greens are covered with the seasoning.

3   Place the greens in a glass jar at least a quart in size, folding them to fit. Pour any remaining seasoning on top and press down. Store in a cool place for at least 2 or 3 days. Refrigerate after opening.

cherish was now an embarrassment. Other kids would crowd around my desk to watch me eat as if I were some sort of zoo animal to be scrutinized during feeding time.

"What's *that?*" they would point as I detected a tone of disgust in their voice.

"That smells funny," someone else would say.

I would barely be able to swallow, let alone answer, as I washed my food down with the hot tea in the only thermos that our family owned. It was a Buck Rogers thermos. I had hastily covered it with paper and tape that morning in a vain effort to hide the fact that it was a Buck Rogers thermos.

That was about the time I decided I would learn how to cook. I had eaten one too many Hungryman dinners when my folks had to work late. I was tired of having to eat my lunch under the scrutiny of my classmates. I just wanted a peanut butter and jelly sandwich like everyone else.

I wish I could have been like my nephew is now. When his mom packs him a *doshilak,* he loves it. He doesn't care about other kids pointing at his food. When they ask, "What's that?" he gives them the only answer anyone should give:

"That's *gim,* stupid." As if to say, "How can you not know what it is? We eat it all the time."

It wouldn't be until I was much older that I would appreciate the food of my heritage. Nowadays I love introducing Korean food to new friends by making it for them or taking them out to eat. When I take friends to a Korean restaurant, I always feel like I spend more time explaining than actually eating. Whenever a dish is placed on the table, everyone points and asks "What's that?" as they wave their chopsticks cautiously about the food. Depending on which restaurant we're in, that could be repeated anywhere from five to twenty times.

If I'm in a particularly nice mood, I will carefully explain the dish, list all the ingredients, and describe how it's prepared, how spicy it is, and how it should be eaten. On days that I'm feeling lazy, annoyed, or just plain mischievous, I give some noncommittal answer: "It's just some stuff thrown together" or "Just try it and see if you like it."

Anything that's eaten with rice is given the all-purpose name, *banchan*. It can be anything from an elaborate fish dish to *kimchi* to some sautéed vegetables. All the little dishes that come with a meal are called *mit banchan*, which loosely translates to something like bottom or base *banchan*. They are the foundation and support for the main *banchan*. A Korean meal isn't complete without a couple of main dishes (or *banchan*), at least half a dozen small dishes (*mit banchan*), and some sort of soup or water *kimchi* to help wash it all down.

When I'm entertaining at home, not only do I have to make a couple of main dishes, I also have to make sure there are plenty of *mit banchan*, too. Once when I was rushing around trying to put a meal together, I realized that I'd forgotten to make a soup. My husband didn't know what the big deal was. "Can't we just skip the soup?" he asked innocently.

No, we can't just skip the soup. My mom raised me right; there was going to be a liquid with that meal.

When you look out on a Korean table filled with little dishes, you may think it took a tremendous amount of time and effort, but that's not necessarily the case. I've been able to

BANCHAN IN A RESTAURANT

put together a last-minute feast in little more than an hour. It's easier for me because I have most of the ingredients at hand, but take one trip to the Korean grocer and you, too, can whip together a great dinner in no time.

When putting a meal together, just make sure you have the following: rice, at least one type of *kim-chi,* a liquid (soup or water *kimchi*), at least a couple of main *banchan* (usually with meat, chicken, or fish), and a handful of *mit banchan*.

Let's take it in steps. First, the rice: This part is easy, especially if you have an electric rice cooker. Even if you don't, you can prepare the rice first and do something else while it's cooking.

Next, the *kimchi*: You should always have some *kimchi* in the house anyway, but if you don't, you can buy it ready-made, packaged in glass jars, plastic containers, or even bags. Some of the less common *kimchi* may be harder to find, but the traditional Napa cabbage kind can be found in the refrigerated sections of even non-Asian supermarkets.

Next, there's the main *banchan*: A main *banchan* can be something easy like *Boolgogi* (Fire Meat, page 166) or something complicated like *Japchae* (Sweet Potato Noodles, page 123). It's up to you.

Now, the fun part—the *mit banchan*: In the deli section of larger Korean supermarkets, you may see a variety of these *mit banchan* laid out for your convenience. The little dishes can be anything from pickled lotus roots to sautéed spinach. It can be salty, sour, sweet, spicy, or any combination.

Some of the dishes need to be prepared weeks ahead (especially if you're pickling any-thing). Other dishes can be made in a matter of minutes. Once you get the hang of making certain dishes, you can mix and match the ingredients. Just as long as there is a balance of hot and cold, spicy and sweet, crispy and soft, the meal will be great.

Oh yeah, and don't forget the soup.

Roasted Seaweed Sheets

Gim

Although you can now find sheets of *gim* (laver) preseasoned and toasted, it always tastes best to make it fresh. It's a very quick and simple dish to prepare. The only thing to remember is that sesame oil burns easily in high heat, so cook it over low heat. MAKES 40 SMALL SHEETS

10 sheets seaweed (*gim*)

Sesame oil

Salt

1   On a cutting board or other flat surface, place the 10 sheets in a stack. Pour about 1 tablespoon of sesame oil into a small bowl. Using a pastry brush, brush a thin layer of oil onto the seaweed. Sprinkle with a little bit of salt over the entire sheet. Turn over and repeat on the other side. Repeat with the remaining sheets, pouring more sesame oil as needed.

2   Heat a large griddle surface with low heat. Carefully toast each sheet, one at a time, flipping and cooking both sides until the sheets turn lighter green and become crispy, but do not brown. Repeat with the remaining sheets.

3   Cut each sheet into 4 pieces and serve with rice and other dishes. Store any leftovers in a tightly sealed container or bag in the refrigerator.

Sautéed Dried Anchovies

Myulchi Bokkum

Use smaller or medium-sized dried anchovies for this dish. Although larger ones can be used, they are best for making soup stock. MAKES ABOUT 6 SERVINGS, DEPENDING ON WHAT OTHER *BANCHAN* ARE BEING SERVED

2 tablespoons vegetable oil

5 garlic cloves, minced

$^1/_2$ medium onion, chopped

1 cup small dried anchovies

3 tablespoons Korean malt syrup (*mool yut*) or 2 tablespoons honey

1 tablespoon sugar

1 tablespoon sesame oil

2 tablespoons soy sauce or chili paste (*gochujang*)

Sesame seeds, for garnish

1   Put 1 tablespoon of vegetable oil in a skillet until heated. Add garlic and onion and stir-fry until onion is soft. Add the remaining vegetable oil and the dried anchovies and stir-fry over low heat for about 10 to 15 minutes until the anchovies get slightly crispy on the outside.

2   Add the malt syrup or honey, sugar, sesame oil, and soy sauce or chili paste, and mix until combined. Remove from heat and serve warm or cold sprinkled with sesame seeds.

Simmered Tofu

Dubu Jolim

Jolim is any dish that has been simmered in a soy-based sauce until the liquid has reduced, allowing the seasoning to soak in. A *jolim* can be made from beef, chicken, fish, tofu, or any number of meaty vegetables. The intensity of the fire must be carefully adjusted in making a *jolim* to make sure that the liquid continues to simmer, but doesn't burn on the bottom. MAKES ABOUT 4 SERVINGS, DEPENDING ON WHAT OTHER *BANCHAN* ARE BEING SERVED

1 (18-ounce) package of firm tofu

2 tablespoons soy sauce

1 garlic clove, minced

2 green onions, thinly chopped

$^1/_4$ red bell pepper, chopped, or 1 teaspoon Korean red chili powder (optional)

1 tablespoon vegetable oil

1   Rinse tofu in cold water. Cut the cube of tofu in half, then into approximately $^1/_2$-inch pieces. Set aside on some paper towels or in a wire-mesh colander to drain.

2   To prepare the seasoning, combine soy sauce, garlic, green onions, and optional red pepper or chili powder. Set aside.

3   In a large skillet, heat the vegetable oil. Then place the tofu carefully into the skillet, making sure each rectangle is flat on the bottom of the skillet. (Be careful because the water in the tofu will make the oil splash!) Cover with a wire-mesh splash-guard, if you wish. Cook on medium to high heat until the tofu is lightly browned on both sides (about 4 to 5 minutes). But be careful not to overcook or the tofu will lose its moisture and texture.

4   Lower the heat and spoon the soy mixture over each tofu slice. Cover and cook for another 2 to 3 minutes until the tofu is slightly steamed and infused with the seasoning.

Soy-Seasoned Potatoes

Gamja Jolim

Although potatoes are a New World crop, Koreans have found creative ways of introducing them into the cuisine. This dish is quick and easy to make when you have a couple of potatoes on hand. MAKES ABOUT 4 SERVINGS, DEPENDING ON WHAT OTHER *BANCHAN* ARE BEING SERVED

2 medium potatoes

2 tablespoons soy sauce

1 garlic clove, minced

1 tablespoon sugar

1 tablespoon sesame oil

1 teaspoon toasted sesame seeds (page 3)

$^1/_2$ teaspoon chili powder (optional)

1   Peel potatoes and cut into 1-inch cubes. Boil in a small pot or saucepan for about 5 or 6 minutes, until the potatoes are cooked through but not soft. Drain.

2   Add soy sauce, garlic, sugar, and sesame oil and toss, cooking the potatoes over low heat for another 2 or 3 minutes, until the soy sauce thickens slightly.

Serve warm or cold, sprinkled with sesame seeds and optional chili powder.

Seasoned Black Beans

Kohng Jang

A simple side dish to prepare. *Kohng Jang* will keep in the refrigerator for a long time. MAKES 1 POUND, ENOUGH FOR SEVERAL MEALS

1 pound dried black beans

Water

4 tablespoons sugar

$^1/_2$ cup soy sauce

1 tablespoon Korean malt syrup (*mool yut*), optional

Toasted Sesame seeds, for garnish (page 3)

1   Thoroughly rinse the black beans in cold water, taking care to remove any small stones. Place the beans in a pot and cover with 3 cups of water. Bring to a boil and simmer for about 30 minutes until the beans have softened slightly and the water is reduced drastically. If there is too much water, cook the beans uncovered a little longer.

2   Add the sugar, stirring until the sugar has dissolved. Then add the soy sauce, continuing to simmer an additional 10 minutes. Add the optional malt syrup and combine.

Serve chilled sprinkled with sesame seeds.

Seasoned Fern Bracken

Gosali Namool

Fern bracken can be found prepared in the deli section of Korean markets. They look brown and stringy and are an essential ingredient for Mixed Rice Bowl (*Bibim Bap,* page 23) and Spicy Beef Soup (*Yookgaejang,* page 101).

MAKES $^1/_2$ POUND, ENOUGH FOR A COUPLE OF MEALS

1 tablespoon sesame oil

1 tablespoon vegetable oil

1 garlic clove, minced

$^1/_2$ pound fern bracken

Salt

1   In a skillet, heat the sesame oil and vegetable oil.

2   Add the garlic and stir-fry for about 1 to 2 minutes. Add the fern bracken and cook another 2 to 3 minutes. Remove from heat, add salt as needed, and toss.

Serve either warm or cold.

Marinated Perilla Leaves

Ggaetnip

 Use large perilla leaves for this recipe. YIELDS 24 LEAVES, SERVING ABOUT 6 PEOPLE, DEPENDING ON WHAT OTHER *BANCHAN* ARE BEING SERVED

About 24 perilla leaves

5 tablespoons soy sauce

2 green onions, chopped

2 garlic cloves, minced

2 tablespoons sesame oil

1 tablespoon toasted sesame seeds, crushed (page 3)

1 tablespoon chili powder

1 teaspoon sugar

1   Wash and dry the perilla leaves.

2   In a small bowl, combine the soy sauce, green onions, garlic, sesame oil, toasted sesame seeds, chili powder, and sugar. In a deep bowl or container, spoon a little bit of the marinade on the bottom. Place a perilla leaf on top. Add a little bit of the marinade on the leaf and continue until all the leaves have been stacked. Pour any remaining marinade over the whole pile. Refrigerate for at least 2 or 3 days before serving. Serve either at room temperature or chilled.

Pickled Garlic

Manul Jang-ajji

Use young garlic for this recipe, if you can. Otherwise, remove the garlic skin. MAKES 10 BULBS OF GARLIC, ENOUGH FOR SEVERAL MEALS

10 garlic bulbs

1 cup plus $^1/_2$ cup white vinegar

Water

$^1/_2$ cup soy sauce

1 tablespoon sugar

1   You can either peel all the garlic, or just cut the tops off of each clove, making sure that each clove is exposed.

2   Place the garlic in a glass jar, cover tightly with 1 cup vinegar and enough water to cover bulbs completely, then set aside in a cool, dry place for 2 weeks. After 2 weeks, drain the vinegar water from the garlic. Combine the soy sauce, sugar, and $^1/_2$ cup of vinegar until the sugar is completely dissolved. Pour over the garlic, adding just enough water to completely cover the bulbs. Cover and let sit another 2 weeks.

Serve at either room temperature or chilled. Refrigerate after opening.

Pickled Green Chile Peppers

Gochu Jang-ajji

Jang-ajji is the word used to describe any number of vegetables that are pickled in a soy sauce and vinegar base. It can be anything from cucumbers to garlic that is preserved in this way. Generally, most of the dishes have a salty, yet tangy, and slightly sweet taste. Although it takes a long time for *jang-ajji* to be ready, like any other pickling process, you can enjoy the dishes for a long time. To ensure that the vegetables will be pickled properly, they should be fully immersed in the pickling liquid and free of any air bubbles.

MAKES 1 POUND, ENOUGH FOR SEVERAL MEALS

1 pound Korean green chile peppers

$^3/_4$ cup soy sauce

Water

$^3/_4$ cup white vinegar

2 tablespoons sugar

1   Wash and rinse the peppers and place them in a medium-sized glass jar. Combine the soy sauce, $^3/_4$ cup water, vinegar, and sugar until the sugar is dissolved completely. Slowly pour the soy mixture over the peppers making sure that no air bubbles form. If they do, shake the jar slightly or stir with a chopstick until the air bubbles disappear.

2   Take a pair of wooden chopsticks and cut them so that they will fit just under the lip of the jar. Jam the chopsticks in a cross pattern over the peppers to make sure that they are immersed in the pickling seasoning. Cover tightly and store in a cool, dry place for about 2 weeks.

Serve peppers whole either at room temperature or chilled. Refrigerate after opening.

When my father decided that he was going to "Americanize" our names, as in most decisions regarding his children, he neglected to garner our consent. My dad came home at his usual time after closing the store that night. He went to take a shower while my sister, my mom, and I set the table with some *banchan* and put the chopsticks out. When I heard the water turn off in the bathroom, I began doling out the rice onto five plates.

My father sat at his usual spot—the head of the table—while the rest of us filed into our respective seats. I poured him a beer and the rest of the family waited for him to take the first bite of *banchan* before we could dig in. As teenagers, we gossiped about someone at school, my mom talked about something or other, and my father sat quietly chewing his food, probably not listening to any of us, as usual. It was a regular weeknight.

Then he took a swig of his beer and put the glass down on the table with a loud clink. He put his chopsticks down beside it and cleared his throat. No one paid attention.

He commanded attention, "Listen." The table went quiet save for the sound of chewing and chopsticks clinking on ceramic bowls.

"I've changed your names," he announced with a hint of pride in his tone.

"What?!" his three children cried out in unison.

"I've changed all our names to our baptismal names on our naturalization forms, our social security records, everything." He pointed to each of us. "You're Catherine. You're Cecilia. You're Anthony. You'll start school with your new names next year." He went back to eating his dinner.

"What do you mean you changed our names? You can't just change our names without asking us!" my sister shouted at him. He continued chewing with a blank expression on his face. I glared at him as only a teenage girl could. Then I slammed my chopsticks on the table.

"I'm not hungry anymore," I declared, crossing my arms across my chest. I continued to glare at my unsuspecting father, who just kept eating dinner as if nothing had happened.

To a fifteen-year-old, your name was sacred. It was a huge part of your identity. You practiced handwriting your name in your notebook, trying to perfect the most floral signatures. You imagined your name with a new last name, the last name of your one true crush, at least for that month. I felt like my dad had taken a part of me away, that he had taken away a part of each of us.

Although I'd been teased because of my name, it was still special to me. It looked beautiful written in Korean and in Chinese characters. Even my very common last name looked good written in Chinese characters—the pictograph of a boy relaxing under a tree. My first name, Hae-Jin, had a meaning, "graced truth," which could never be equaled by the name of some Italian saint, even if she was the patron saint of music.

If I had known how difficult the transition would be, I would have been angrier with him that night. I wouldn't know until later how many drunk men I had to endure at parties singing that stupid Simon and Garfunkel song to me. I didn't know then how many times I would have to spell my name for strangers, repeating again and again "with two i's" anytime someone had to fill out a form for me.

That night, I was so upset, it was the first time in my life I couldn't eat dinner. My mom tried to coax me to eat, but I stubbornly refused, pushing the plates and bowls farther away from me. Later, after the whole house had fallen asleep, I snuck down to the refrigerator to eat my dinner. Cold *banchan* at midnight never tasted so good as it did then. With each swallow, the fires of anger inside of me subsided to a simmering glow. Maybe someday I could learn to live with my name, but no one was going to take away my identity. I washed my determination down with barley tea and went to bed that night to dream of warm rice fields in the middle of a shimmering ocean.

Seasoned Soybean Sprouts

Kohng Namool

"Namool" is a word used to describe a certain group of greens, herbs, sprouts, and vegetables. It is also used to describe *banchan* made from these plants. Usually the vegetables are sautéed or steamed and mixed with a sesame oil and garlic-based seasoning. Salt is often used in place of soy sauce to preserve the natural color of the vegetable. MAKES A POUND OF SPROUTS, ENOUGH FOR SEVERAL MEALS

1 pound soybean sprouts

Water

2 green onions, thinly chopped

3 garlic cloves, minced

1 tablespoon toasted sesame seeds, crushed (page 3)

1 tablespoon sesame oil

$1^1/_2$ to 2 teaspoons salt

1 to 2 teaspoons chili powder

1   Wash the bean sprouts in cold water, removing any bean husks. Place them in a pot and add about 1 cup water. Do not fill the pot. Bring to a boil and cook for about 5 minutes. (Do not lift the lid to check if the pot is boiling because an unpleasant, fishy odor will fill your kitchen.) Remove from heat, rinse in cold water, and drain.

2   Add green onions, garlic, toasted sesame seeds, sesame oil, salt, and chili powder and combine thoroughly, adjusting the salt and chili powder to your taste. Serve warm or chilled.

Seasoned Spinach

Shigumchi Namool

As a child, I never quite got that the Popeye cartoons were a ploy to get young children to eat their spinach because the way it is prepared in Korea, it has always been a joy to eat it. The most popular way to enjoy spinach is to make this simple side dish for everyday meals. MAKES ABOUT 1 1/2 CUPS OF SPINACH, ENOUGH FOR A COUPLE OF MEALS

2 bundles of spinach

1 tablespoon sesame oil

1 garlic clove, minced

Salt

1 teaspoon toasted sesame seeds, crushed (page 3)

Toasted sesame seeds for garnish

1   Thoroughly wash and trim the spinach, cutting off the roots and removing any withered leaves. Blanch the spinach by quickly dunking in boiling water. Rinse immediately in cold water to stop cooking. Squeeze the water from the spinach.

2   In a skillet, heat the sesame oil. Add the garlic and stir-fry for about 1 to 2 minutes. Add spinach. Remove from heat, add salt as needed and crushed sesame seeds, and toss. Let sit for about 10 minutes to let the flavors seep into the spinach. Add a little more salt, if necessary.

Serve either warm or cold, sprinkled with some toasted sesame seeds.

Seasoned Mushrooms

Buhsut Namool

In Korea, we used any sort of wild mushrooms in season. Since the variety of mushrooms is not as available in the states, I recommend using *pyongo*, also known as shiitake, for this dish. Use fresh mushrooms if you can, but dried ones will work as well if fresh ones aren't available. MAKES ABOUT 4 TO 5 SERVINGS, DEPENDING ON WHAT OTHER *BANCHAN* ARE BEING SERVED

10 *pyongo* or shiitake mushrooms

1 tablespoon sesame oil

1 garlic clove, minced

1 teaspoon soy sauce

1 teaspoon toasted sesame seeds (page 3)

1   If using dried mushrooms, soak them in water for about 1 hour, stem sides down. Squeeze any excess water and slice mushrooms into $^1/_4$-inch pieces.

2   In a skillet, heat the sesame oil. Add the garlic and mushrooms and stir-fry for about 2 minutes. Add soy sauce, toss, and remove from heat. Let sit for about 10 minutes to let the flavors seep into the mushrooms.

Serve either warm or cold, sprinkled with toasted sesame seeds.

Seasoned Korean Zucchini

Hobak Namool

Korean zucchinis are fatter and lighter in color than their Italian cousins.
If you can't find the Korean versions, the Italian ones work just fine in this
recipe. MAKES ABOUT 5 SERVINGS, DEPENDING ON WHAT OTHER *BANCHAN* ARE
SERVED

2 Korean zucchinis

1 tablespoon sesame oil

1 garlic clove, minced

1 green onion, chopped

Salt

1 teaspoon toasted sesame
seeds, crushed (page 3)

1   Cut the Korean zucchinis in half lengthwise, then slice
the lengths into $^1/_4$-inch thin semicircles.

2   In a skillet, heat the sesame oil. Add the garlic and Korean
zucchinis and stir-fry for about 2 to 3 minutes, until the zucchinis start going limp. Add the green onions and salt and
cook another minute or so. Remove from heat and let sit for
about 10 minutes to let the flavors seep into the Korean zucchinis. Add a little more salt if necessary.

Serve either warm or cold, sprinkled with toasted sesame seeds.

Seasoned Eggplant

Gaji Namool

Korean eggplants are similar to Chinese and Japanese ones. If you can't find the Korean variety, use any type of small eggplant. Unfortunately, the large Italian ones won't do. MAKES ABOUT 5 SERVINGS, DEPENDING ON WHAT OTHER *BANCHAN* ARE SERVED

2 medium eggplants

1 tablespoon sesame oil

1 garlic clove, minced

1 green onion, chopped

Salt

1 teaspoon toasted sesame seeds, crushed (page 3)

1   Trim the ends off the eggplants and place them in boiling water until just barely tender, about 5 minutes. Drain and let cool. Cut or tear the eggplants into thin strips about 3 inches long.

2   In a skillet, heat the sesame oil. Add the garlic and stir-fry for about 1 to 2 minutes. Add eggplants and green onion, stir-frying for another minute or so. Remove from heat, add a little salt and toss. Let sit for about 10 minutes to let the flavors seep into the eggplant. Add more salt, if necessary.

Serve either warm or cold, sprinkled with toasted sesame seeds.

Seasoned Bellflower Root

Doraji Namool

Fresh bellflower root can be found in the produce section of Korean groceries. Preshredded ones can be found in the deli section. If using dried roots, reconstitute them by soaking them in water for at least an hour.

MAKES $^1/_2$ POUND, ENOUGH FOR A COUPLE OF MEALS

1 tablespoon sesame oil

1 tablespoon vegetable oil

1 garlic clove, minced

$^1/_2$ pound bellflower root, shredded

Salt

1 teaspoon toasted sesame seeds, crushed (page 3)

1   In a skillet, heat the sesame oil and vegetable oil.

2   Add the garlic and bellflower root and stir-fry for about 2 to 3 minutes. Remove from heat, add salt as needed, and toss.

Serve either warm or cold, sprinkled with toasted sesame seeds.

Spicy Radish Salad

Mu Sangchae

This salad has a wonderful combination of sweet and sour with the light crispness of Asian radish. Although it adds a bit of spiciness, the chili powder also adds a wonderful color to the dish. MAKES ENOUGH FOR A COUPLE OF MEALS

1 medium Asian radish

1 teaspoon fine chili powder

2 tablespoons vinegar

1 tablespoon sugar

1 tablespoon salt

1   Peel the radish and cut or grate into thin strips. Add the chili powder to the radish and mix.

2   In a medium bowl, add the vinegar, sugar, and salt, stirring until completely dissolved. Pour over the radish and mix well. Let marinate in the refrigerator for at least a couple of hours before serving. Serve chilled.

Chilled Cucumber Soup

Oi Naengook

During hot summer months, this cold soup is a nice addition to any meal.

MAKES ABOUT 3 TO 4 SERVINGS, DEPENDING ON WHAT OTHER *BANCHAN* ARE

BEING SERVED

2 cucumbers

Water

$^1/_4$ cup vinegar

1 tablespoon sugar

Salt

1 teaspoon sesame oil

1 green onion, chopped

2 tablespoons toasted sesame seeds (page 3)

Ice cubes

1   Wash and shred the cucumbers.

2   In a medium bowl, add 2 cups cold water, vinegar, sugar and salt, stirring until the sugar and salt are dissolved. Add the cucumbers, sesame oil and green onions and stir.

3   Serve in individual-sized bowls sprinkled with toasted sesame seeds and with a few ice cubes in each serving to keep chilled.

VARIATION Add about 2 ounces of dried kelp (*miyuk*) that has been reconstituted by being soaked in water for about 5 to 10 minutes. The seaweed will swell up to about 1 cup and turn dark green. Cut the kelp into pieces about 2 inches long and add to the dish.

Deep-Fried Kelp

Dashima Twigim

Large sheets of kelp are sold in the dried goods section of Korean, Japanese, and Chinese groceries. Kelp sheets used for deep frying are different from the softer kelp (*miyuk*) used in soups. MAKES ABOUT 5 SERVINGS, DEPENDING ON WHAT OTHER *BANCHAN* ARE BEING SERVED

1 large sheet of sea kelp (*dashima*)

Vegetable oil for frying

Sugar

1   With a pair of kitchen scissors, cut each piece of kelp into about 2- or 3-inch lengths.

2   Heat enough vegetable oil in a small saucepan or skillet deep enough to immerse the kelp. Carefully add the kelp into the oil, one piece at a time, until the surface is full. Using a pair of long chopsticks, flip each piece if necessary, making sure all parts of the kelp become cooked. The kelp will become crispy and change to a lighter dark green and bubble up on the surface as it cooks.

3   Remove from heat and place on a plate lined with paper towels or napkins. Immediately sprinkle each piece with sugar on both sides while the oil is still hot. Repeat with the rest of the kelp until finished.

Serve warm or at room temperature.

Flatcakes and Jun

PARTY GIRL

My parents were party fanatics. Whenever there was a holiday, the celebration was at our house. A birthday? A promotion? A new car? Any excuse to throw a party, and our doors were wide open. • I always thought my mom was the instigator, but in retrospect, my dad was happiest with a drink in his hand, sitting at the head of a table full of his friends and family. I remember when I was about eleven or twelve we had an impromptu New Year's Eve bash. At six o'clock, my dad called from work with this crazy idea to have a party (or "*janchi*") that night. By ten o'clock, our house was brimming with dozens of people. • You can imagine what it was like feeding those frenzied guests. Many weekends of my childhood were filled with smiling faces, loud chatter, days in the kitchen, and piles and piles of food. Cooking for forty, fifty, or even sixty people wasn't so much a chore as it was a habit. • And don't even tell me about the dishes. We were crying with joy the day we moved

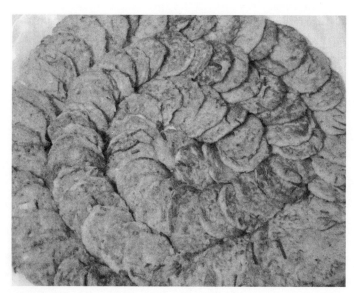

into a house with a built-in dishwasher, especially my brother. He had never forgiven me for convincing my parents that he should help with the household

A WHOLE LOT OF FLATCAKES
(*NOKDU BUCHINGAE*)

chores, even if he was a boy. In fact, my siblings and I used to say that my parents only had us because they needed caterers for their parties.

I remember when I was leaving home to go away for college and my folks were seeing me off. When my mom noticed the tears welling up in my dad's eyes, she asked him if he was sad because he was losing his little girl. My dad, however, was lamenting the fact that he was losing his cook.

Weekend after weekend, it was work, work, work for my siblings and me.

The excitement would start early. By the time I rolled out of bed and made it down to the kitchen, my mom and her friends would already be cooking. All day long, the troops would arrive, one by one. Grabbing another apron off the wall hook, they would tie it around their waist, wash their hands, and start working, not breaking the flow of the conversation they started when they took their shoes off at the door.

I loved to hear about how things were in Korea when they were growing up——funny anecdotes about some dumb relative or even exaggerated tales of their adventures. Still, the best ones were those about my mom and dad, prechildren, premarriage. It was like hearing about someone I didn't know, because as a girl or even as a teenager, I couldn't imagine that my parents had a life before the family.

More often than not, there would be several conversations going on at once. Every once in a while, I'd catch some juicy bit of information about my parents twenty or thirty years ago and look over at my sister, who would exchange a surprised look with me.

We'd slice, dice, fry, boil, mince, crush, chop, and mix for hours until the tables were overflowing with a fabulous feast.

Jun was my major responsibility. "Jun" is a generic word loosely used to describe such foods as flatcakes, battered fish, vegetables stuffed with meat, and basically foods cooked in a little bit of oil over a flat frying pan surface.

I would stake out my territory in a corner by laying out a bunch of newspapers in anticipation of splattering grease, plugging in my electric frying pan and getting a seat cushion for my tender bum. Armed with a pair of chopsticks in one hand and a spatula in the other, I would be prepared for many hours of uninterrupted labor—it would take quite some force to dislodge me from my station.

I would be bombarded with a constant stream of food that needed to be prepared. Sometimes it would be some fish that needed to be dipped in flour, then in egg batter, and prepared with just the right green garnish on top. Sometimes it would be a bottomless bowl of mix for *nokdu buchingae* (a type of flatcake made from mung beans, page 82).

I was the champion *buchingae*-maker. My sister may argue with me. She may even say that *she's* the champion *buchingae*-maker. Sure, she may have spent her share of hours in the trenches with me, making one after another of those endless flatcakes. She might even be better at the flipping, skillfully turning them with one flick of the wrist. I would chase those pesky things around the whole surface of the frying pan, trying in vain to get that unwieldy plastic spatula under their elusive bottoms.

No one can argue that I made the best-looking ones. I could pour those flatcakes exactly the same size, as if I were a machine stamping them out. Then I'd cook them to just the right golden brown, perfect for eating hot off the griddle.

Everyone would grab a hot *buchingae* right off the frying pan, slapping it back and forth to keep it from burning their hands. Everyone, that is, but my brother. He didn't eat them right off the frying pan. No, that would have been uncharacteristically nice. He waited for just the right moment, when I had them laid out on the large platters, arranged beautifully fanning out from the center. He learned to wait until I had the last *buchingae* in just the perfect place before he snuck out of nowhere and grabbed the one that would throw off the balance of the whole presentation. He must have learned that kind of patience in little brother school. Then, as quickly as he materialized, he would disappear, while I shook my fist, waving my spatula in the air with fury.

Despite my little brother's efforts, I still enjoyed cooking for a party. I especially liked looking over at the women swarming in the kitchen, laughing and gabbing and chopping and stirring.

I must have inherited this love for throwing parties from my folks. I'm usually the one calling up ten or so friends for an impromptu dinner. People call to invite themselves over for celebrations I never even intended to throw, and I'm always ready for them. Although some of my friends balk at the idea of cooking for thirty or forty people, I welcome the challenge. Besides, that's nothing. Try making dinner for a hundred people. Now, that's a party!

Some Tips on Making *Jun*

Korean party food is easy to make. But because some of us grew up watching our moms and aunts cook all day for a party or special holiday, there is the mistaken belief that *jun* and *buchingae* take a long time to make. Any food prepared for a hundred people is going to take forever to cook. Yet, making *jun* doesn't have to be an all day event. Smaller portions and a little planning are all you need to have a feast laid out in no time. From many years of experience, I've compiled a list to help you along.

MY COUSIN, JAE-HAK, HELPING

Things to remember when making *jun* or *buchingae*:

- Use very cold water to make your batter and your flat-cakes will be nice and crispy around the edges.

- Just like when making pancakes or waffles, don't overmix your batter. Just mix enough to moisten the ingredients.

- Get all the stuff you need—your ingredients, oil , spatula, etc.—ready in one place before you turn on the heat.

- Use a large, nonstick pan for cooking. When I make *jun* for a large party, I use an electric frying pan so I can sit comfortably on the floor and work.

- *Jun* tastes best served right off the griddle (my brother can attest to that). Plan your cooking so that the *jun* is the last thing you cook before eating.

- Use all the batter the day you make it. Batter won't keep but cooked *jun* will.

- If you have to save the *jun*, refrigerate or freeze for a couple of days, tightly wrapped in plastic or in a tightly sealed container. Reheat in the pan, not the microwave. Better yet, use leftover *jun* in a hot pot.

Mung Bean Flatcakes

Nokdu Buchingae

Be careful when selecting the mung beans. Check to see that the beans are yellow in color and that the package is not too dated. I discovered that some companies dye their beans, so you may wish to choose a more expensive brand for the quality. This recipe is proportioned for large parties; feel free to reduce for smaller meals. MAKES 50 TO 60 FLATCAKES

4 cups dried mung beans (*nokdu*)

10 to 12 dried *pyongo* or shiitake mushrooms

2 pounds green bean sprouts (*sookju* or *nokdu namool*)

1 pound sliced pork loin

1 garlic bulb, minced

3 teaspoons toasted sesame seeds, crushed (page 3)

3 teaspoons sesame oil

1 head of Napa cabbage kimchi (*baechu kimchi*), sliced into 1¹/₂-inch pieces

1 tablespoon salt

Vegetable oil for cooking

1   Soak the dried mung beans in cold water for at least 2 hours or overnight. Soak the mushrooms in cold water for about 1 hour. Squeeze the liquid from the mushrooms and slice. Set aside in a bowl.

2   Slightly blanch the bean sprouts in boiling water. Rinse in cold water immediately. Drain and squeeze the water from the sprouts. Set aside in a second bowl.

3   Place the pork in a third bowl.

4   Divide the minced garlic evenly amongst the bowls of mushrooms, sprouts, and pork. Then, add 1 teaspoon toasted sesame seeds and 1 teaspoon sesame oil into each of the 3 bowls. Mix.

5   Drain the mung beans. Put about ¹/₃ of them into a food processor or blender, add ³/₄ cup of water, and puree. Pour the puree into a large bowl. Repeat with the remaining mung beans. Add the *kimchi,* mushrooms, sprouts, and pork mixtures into the bowl of mung bean puree. Add the salt and mix thoroughly.

6   Preheat a large nonstick frying pan. Sprinkle some vegetable oil onto the surface. Spoon the batter into circles about 3 inches in diameter. Cook about 3 to 4 minutes on each side until the *buchingae* are golden brown.

Serve warm arranged on a platter with a side of Seasoned Soy Sauce (*Yangnyum Ganjang*, page 4).

MAKING *NOKDU BUNCHINGAE*

Egg-Battered Pollack

Dong Tae Jun

My dad always says, "If it doesn't look good, it doesn't taste good." In the case of most *jun*, it's true. This *jun* is easy to make and has high presentation value. If you can't find crown daisy, you can substitute Italian parsley (not the curly leaf variety), which has flat leaves, or even a little slice of green onion. Plain, ungarnished fish looks naked to me. I guess my dad's training stuck. MAKES 25 TO 30 PIECES

1 pound frozen pollack, thawed slightly

1 teaspoon salt

Flour for dusting

2 eggs, whisked with a pinch of salt

Vegetable oil for cooking

5 to 6 stalks crown daisies (*soot*), for garnish

1   Slice the fish on the diagonal into 1 to 2 inch pieces, about $1/4$ inch thick. Sprinkle salt on the fish.

2   Put some flour on a plate. Coat the fish evenly on both sides with flour. Then dip the mini fillets in the egg batter.

3   Preheat a large nonstick frying pan. Sprinkle some vegetable oil onto the surface. Place the fish on the frying pan and put one leaf of crown daisy flat on each mini fillet for garnish. Cook for about 3 to 4 minutes on both sides, until the egg is slightly browned on the edges.

Serve warm arranged on a platter with a side of Seasoned Soy Sauce (*Yangnyum Ganjang*, page 4).

Meat Fritters

Jencha

An easy dish to make, *jencha* can be made with ground turkey, as well. These flattened, egg-battered meatballs can also be made from any leftover *mandu* filling (recipe, page 130). MAKES 50 TO 60 FRITTERS

2 pounds beef (preferably sirloin tip)

3 green onions, chopped

1 garlic clove, minced

$^1/_2$ cup soy sauce

2 tablespoons sesame oil

1 tablespoon sesame seeds

Dash of freshly ground black pepper

Flour

4 to 5 eggs

Vegetable oil for cooking

1   Slice beef into pieces about 2 × 3 inches in size and about $^1/_4$ inch thick. Combine green onions, garlic, soy sauce, sesame oil, sesame seeds, and pepper. Add beef and let marinate in the refrigerator for about an hour.

2   Add a layer of flour on a plate or other flat surface. Whisk together the eggs in a bowl. Heat a little bit of vegetable oil in a large skillet over medium heat. Coat the beef on both sides with flour. Then dip the beef in the egg and place immediately on the frying surface. Let cook on both sides, until the meat is browned completely, but the egg is not too brown. Repeat with the rest of the meat, adding more oil as needed. Reduce the heat, if necessary.

Serve warm arranged on a platter or woven plate with Seasoned Soy Sauce (*Yangnyum Ganjang*, page 4), if you wish.

Little Island

When I got home one afternoon, my Aunt Jumi was waiting impatiently by the front door. Even before I had unlaced my shoes, she was pulling out a magazine, showing me some article that had been carefully earmarked on the bottom right corner. It was a map showing a tiny speck of an island off the eastern coast.

"We can take the boat across from where the bus lets us off," she said as she pointed somewhere on the magazine's page, her eyes shining with the excitement of a child anticipating Christmas morning. "We can go for a couple of days and it won't cost very much."

I just laughed and nodded, giving her a deep bow and gesturing to her with my arms in surrender. "Whatever you want," I said. "I'm at your mercy."

The bus to the shore was surprisingly crowded, as I gave up my seat to a very old grandma (*halmuhni*). Warm bodies pressed me against the vinyl seats as I held onto the handrails in resignation. It was a typical Korean bus, full of people carrying mysterious bundles, packed in like human sardines, ready to be peeled open from our metal container.

As we proceeded farther and farther from the city, the crowd began to thin out and so did the miles of paved road. Eventually, my aunt and I were the only ones left on the bus. The driver pulled into a dirt lot, turned off the engine and walked out without a word.

"Is this it?" we wondered out loud to no one else in particular, as we shared a quizzical look between us. After a second of uncertainty, we gathered our bags and uncurled our crinkled selves, walking out into the sunlight. Although we couldn't see the ocean, the moist salt hanging heavily in the air betrayed its proximity as a flock of seagulls circled overhead.

We accidentally, but quickly, found a boat and persuaded the man (*ahjuhshi*) to take us across the water. He gave us the once over twice, then decided to let us on his little motorboat. He was a friendly and talkative fellow, telling us stories of myths and adventures with his funny accent. It was a pleasure to see the wrinkles wake up on his face when he laughed, showing off the gap where his front teeth had left his mouth long ago.

"We're on vacation," my aunt shouted to the wind with the excitement of a child on her way to an amusement park.

The *ahjuhshi* laughed, his head thrown back in delight, as his hair danced wildly in the ocean wind. "Nobody takes a vacation there this time of year," he chuckled.

"That's why we're going," my aunt answered, unflappable by either the wind or the man's coarseness.

It was a wonderful boat ride across the vast stretch of sea.

Right by the boating docks where we landed, we found a friendly woman (*ahjumma*), who ran a small restaurant. My aunt looked around worriedly as she and I were the only women in the place, the rest of the seats occupied by construction workers, fishermen, and random rugged-looking characters shoveling fistfuls of food into their famished faces. I just enjoyed our simple meal of rice and *banchan* sitting by the spray of the sea.

Although there were a couple of taxis waiting by the docks, the restaurant owner insisted on making a special call.

"He's the best one on the island," she shouted over the din of conversing men. "Besides, you'll need his four-by-four to get to where you want to go."

Our "taxi" arrived within a matter of minutes, eager to have a customer. We asked our driver if he could take us to the motel (*yukgwan*) on the other side of the island.

"Sure," he said, not even acknowledging the map in my aunt's hand as he loaded our bags into his jeep. "That's right next to my house."

"You ladies must be from Seoul," he said as we climbed into the back seat.

"She is," I said, putting my arms around my aunt's shoulders. "I'm from L.A."

With the last words tumbling from my mouth, even from the back seat I could feel his excitement as I watched his eyes light up in the rearview mirror.

"I don't think I've ever met anyone from America," he feigned coolness. "I love American music and . . . " his voice trailed off as he bent down and began fumbling through his glove compartment.

"Watch the road, *ahjuhshi*!" my aunt exclaimed, as the vehicle tumbled over some dirt path parading as a road.

"No problem, lady." I could detect a note of condescension in his voice. "I can drive here blindfolded. I was born on this island," he said, popping in a tape as the first guitar licks of "Hotel California" drowned out his last words. I imagined this man's dreams to tour the world as the Korean Don Henley. I turned to look at the passing scenery outside, suppressing an incredible urge to start cracking up.

Once we arrived at our sleeping quarters, he helped with our bags.

"What are you ladies doing tonight?" It sounded suspiciously like a come on, but I decided to suppress my city-girl distrust of men just this once.

My aunt, on the other hand, raised an eyebrow. "We're busy," she said in the flattest tone possible.

"Busy?!" The taxi driver threw his head back and laughed. "There's nothing to do on this island! Listen," he said, looking over at me. "We're having a bonfire on the beach later tonight. Come on by and meet my friends."

"Alright," I answered. "But how will we know how to find you?"

He began walking away, still chuckling to himself. "You won't be able to miss us!" he called back over his shoulder.

He was right. When we got to the beach, there was a single fire glowing on the moonlit shore. There were about a dozen or so young people surrounding the blaze. Everyone was expecting us—the American girl and her aunt from Seoul. They were trying to warm up flatcakes (*buchingae*) over the fire. Cold beer and Korean rice wine (*soju*) were being passed all around and we enjoyed a fine dinner in the openness of an empty beach. A variety of flatcakes were made by expert hands. Some were familiar to me, containing delicious seafood and green onions, while others contained some regional ingredients I'd never tasted before. Even cold, the *buchingae* were delicious.

My aunt decided to turn in early, making me promise to wake her for a five A.M. sunrise. I quickly saw through her unsuccessful attempt to get me to come with her. She didn't know how much I liked to stay up and talk to strangers around a bonfire. I promised to wake her up at dawn, as I gestured good-bye with my bottle in hand toward the darkness into which she had disappeared. With our stomachs full and faces glowing, toasted warm by the fire's relentless heat, I was thoroughly enjoying myself.

When a group of Koreans gather together, something strange happens, especially when you fill their bellies with good vittles and alcohol—they invariably begin breaking out in song. This group on the beach was no different. I began to feel like my parents—gathering around outside, eating, drinking, and making fools of themselves.

The island people sang old standards and new hits, songs that were familiar to me and songs I had never heard before. Everyone else knew all the lyrics to every song. I sat in the circle but didn't join in.

At one point, someone requested that I sing for them—an American song. I felt my cheeks burn red hot with the embarrassment of years of performing for my parents' house guests. As a very young child, I supposedly used to know the entire oeuvre of Korean seventies band, "The Onions," backwards and forwards. I hated those moments, when my parents called us from our play to perform like trained monkeys, holding our hands clasped together in little girl demure fashion. And here I was, stuck on some beach with complete strangers being asked to carry on that stupid Korean tradition.

"I don't know any songs that you may have heard of," I squirmed, attempting very badly to get off the hot seat.

"Sing something by the Beatles!" somebody quipped. I neglected to mention that the Beatles weren't American.

"Which song by the Beatles?" I said softly.

"How about 'Yesterday'?" said my taxi driver.

"Thank God," I thought to myself. I was afraid he would request his favorite "Hotel California." I paused to recollect the lyrics. A respectful but anticipatory silence hung over the group.

"Yesterday," my voice quivered slightly. "All my troubles seemed so far away . . ." I somehow made it through the first verse, then suddenly, like the waves washing away the footprints on the sand, my mind went blank. I tried concentrating, looking up at the stars, trying to remember the lyrics to this standard. Finally, I laughed.

Then, like some practiced chorus, everyone else began singing the words. Relieved, I joined in. And we sang song after song of Beatles favorites well into the night.

The next morning, I sat up from a strange dream and fumbled around for my watch. It was 5:01 A.M. By some miracle I had managed to keep my promise to my aunt, who was still sleeping soundly next to me under the blanket we shared.

"*Imo*," I shook her shapeless form beneath the blanket. "It's time for the sunrise."

We folded up our bedding and hurriedly threw on some clothes to make our way to the ocean. The gray of the morning was as beautiful as cold slate to me. We walked by the remnants of last night's fire and sat on the empty beach, lost in our own thoughts. My aunt began humming a tune. It was as if she had plucked it from the air. It was "Yesterday." She stopped humming for a moment.

"I like that song," she said to no one in particular, a serene smile on her face.

"It's okay," I shrugged and looked out toward the light emanating from the horizon.

Green Onion Pancakes

Pa Jun

Eaten as a snack, appetizer or meal, the secret to making any *jun* crispy is to use very cold water in the batter. Rice flour gives it a slightly chewier, stickier texture. If you can't find rice flour, you can use all-purpose flour instead. This is the recipe for basic green onion pancakes, but you can add sliced mushrooms (oyster or shiitake), carrots, mung bean sprouts, or red peppers.

MAKES 4 SERVINGS

$3/4$ cup all-purpose flour

$1/4$ cup rice flour

Cold water

5 green onions, cut on the diagonal into about $1^1/2$-inch pieces

Dash of black pepper (optional)

Vegetable oil for frying

1   Combine the flours and about $3/4$ cup cold water, adding water a little bit at a time and mixing until the mixture is the consistency of thin pancake batter. Add the green onions and optional black pepper and mix.

2   In a large skillet or on a griddle, add just enough vegetable oil to thinly cover the surface, about 1 tablespoon at a time. Turn the heat to medium high. Add $1/2$ the batter onto the frying pan in a large flat circle. Cook on one side until golden brown. Flip and cook the other side. Lower the heat as necessary to prevent burning, adding more oil as needed. Remove the pancake. Pour the remaining batter and repeat.

3   Cut the pancake into 4 or 8 pieces.

Serve hot with Seasoned Soy Sauce (*Yangnyum Ganjang*, page 4) or Vinegar Soy Sauce (*Cho Ganjang*, page 4).

VARIATION To add a little color and a different flavor, julienne a few sweet red peppers and add to the batter. Make the recipe as usual.

Seafood Pancakes

Haemul Jun

A variation of the basic Green Onion Pancakes recipe (*Pa Jun*, page 90), these flatcakes take advantage of seafood varieties available in the area. Of course, the type of seafood used varies with the region. MAKES 4 SERVINGS

1 cup all-purpose flour

$^1/_4$ cup rice flour

Water

5 green onions, cut on the diagonal, into about $1^1/_2$-inch pieces

$^1/_2$ cup of small raw oysters

$^1/_2$ cup of raw squid, cleaned and sliced

Dash of black pepper (optional)

Vegetable oil for frying

1   Combine the flours and about $^3/_4$ cup cold water, adding water a little bit at a time and mixing until the mixture is the consistency of pancake batter. Add the green onions, seafood and optional black pepper and mix. Add more flour or water as needed to maintain consistency.

2   In a large skillet or on a griddle, add just enough vegetable oil to thinly cover the surface, about a tablespoon at a time. Turn the heat to medium high. Add $^1/_2$ the batter onto the frying pan in a large flat circle. Cook on one side until golden brown. Flip and cook the other side. Lower the heat as necessary to prevent burning, adding more oil as needed. Remove the pancake. Pour the remaining batter and repeat.

3   Cut the pancake into 4 or 8 pieces.

Serve hot with Seasoned Soy Sauce (*Yangnyum Ganjang*, page 4) or Vinegar Soy Sauce (*Cho Ganjang*, page 4).

NOTE You can also add any combination of shrimp, crab, mussels, octopus, etc. Just be sure to add enough flour and/or water to the batter to get the right consistency.

Kimchi Potato Pancakes

Gamja Buchingae

These little pancakes are a cinch to make and yummy, too. Another great recipe to make with leftover *kimchi*, be sure to use traditional cabbage *kimchi* in any stage of fermentation, although the riper the better. MAKES 4 PANCAKES

1 pound potatoes, peeled and shredded

$^1/_2$ cup finely chopped *kimchi*, drained

5 green onions, chopped

1 egg

1 tablespoon flour

1 tablespoon salt

Vegetable oil for frying

2 small red chile peppers, sliced into thin circles for garnish (optional)

A few sprigs of crown daisies (*soot*) for garnish (optional)

1   In a large bowl, add the potatoes, *kimchi,* green onions, egg, flour, and salt. Mix well until the potatoes are well coated.

2   In a large skillet or on a griddle, add just enough vegetable oil to thinly cover the surface, about 1 tablespoon at a time. Turn the heat to medium high. Take about $^1/_4$ of the batter and form into a ball. Flatten into a pancake, about $^1/_2$ inch thick and carefully place into the pan. If you wish, garnish with a few slices of red pepper and/or a sprig of crown daisy in the middle. Cook on one side until it turns golden brown and the potatoes are crispy around the edges (like hash browns). Flip and cook the other side. Adjust the heat as necessary to prevent burning, adding more oil as needed. Remove the pancake. Repeat with the remaining batter

3   Cut the pancakes into 4 or 8 pieces.

Serve hot with Seasoned Soy Sauce (*Yangnyum Ganjang*, page 4).

Dinner Date

The first time I made Korean food for a boyfriend, it was a total disaster. I was attempting to do the nearly impossible, make an elaborate meal with improper implements all cooked with the inadequate facilities of the shared dorm kitchen.

I started early that morning. Shopping list in hand, I boarded the bus imagining the supposed feast I would prepare. After my hunting and gathering mission, I managed to haul all the ingredients back to my dorm room only to realize that there was no way in hell I was going to get the contents of those bulging bags into my pint-sized refrigerator.

Undeterred, I decided to get to work. I knocked on doors, begging and borrowing skillets, plates, and other ridiculous kitchenware from anyone who happened to be around. Eventually, I had managed to assemble quite an impressive array of inadequate supplies. I began to slice and dice and mince and chop ingredients to make *jun* and *buchingae*. Used to cooking for a family of five, I had not yet mastered the fine art of portioning a meal. I soon found myself with piles of food covering every available surface of the dorm's lounge.

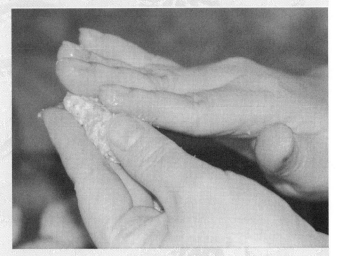

MAKING JUN

Any resident lured by the smell of cooking garlic and green onions was treated to an afternoon snack. Even casual passersby still hung over from the previous night's revelries didn't escape without a flatcake or two in hand. Some time later, I had a teenager's version of a romantic dinner for two set, complete with candles and just the right dash of institutional ambiance thrown in for good measure.

Finally, the boyfriend arrived. He was eager, clean shaven and sheepishly hiding a bouquet of flowers. He sat down at the makeshift table and tried not to appear intimidated by the overflowing amount of food covering all visible surfaces of the room. Nervous and eager to please, I waited for him to begin eating before I started. He sat there, fingering his chopsticks, not eating.

"What's wrong?" I finally asked.

He laughed, still twiddling his two sticks. "How do you use these things?" he said.

I showed him how to use them properly, the way my father showed me how. "Don't learn by watching me," I said. "I learned from watching my mom and I used them wrong. I can use them properly if I wanted to, but I'm lazy. Old habits die hard."

He fumbled around a bit, but managed to get some food into his mouth. I tried not to laugh. He nibbled a bit, but hardly ate a thing.

"I have a secret to tell you," he finally confessed. "I think I have some kind of stomach flu."

My chopsticks and jaws fell with a clank on the floor. Although it wasn't his fault, I felt like flinging flatcakes across the table at him.

"Why didn't you tell me?" I asked in the least accusatory voice I could muster at that moment.

"I was hoping I'd feel better by now," he looked down at his plate.

"It's okay," I mumbled, as I busied myself with clearing the table.

Needless to say, that relationship ended disastrously. For some time afterwards, I wouldn't make Korean food for anyone on whom I had even a little crush. I would prepare elaborate Mexican feasts, complete Middle Eastern mezzas, and large Italian dinners. Yet, if anyone asked me about making Korean food for them, I would make some lame excuse and not-so-smoothly change the subject to something more innocuous.

Since then, I had become a savvier dater. I would test the waters by first taking the guy to a Korean restaurant before letting him into my kitchen and into my heart. My mental scoreboard would go something like this. Bonus points for knowing how to use chopsticks. Minus points for being afraid to eat *kimchi*. More points for trying all the small *banchan* on the table. Super minus points if he committed a faux pas, such as putting soy sauce on his rice or sugar in his tea.

So, the first time I took my last boyfriend to a Korean restaurant, my heart warmed to him immediately as I watched him skillfully navigate the table with his chopsticks. And when he flagged the waitress down for more *kimchi*, I knew he would be a guy even a Korean mother could love. You can even ask my mom. She'd be proud to introduce you to him, her son-in-law.

Fried Oysters

Gool Jun

Get large fresh oysters for this dish. If you love oysters, this is a quick and
tasty way to prepare them. MAKES 35 TO 50 PIECES, DEPENDING ON THE SIZE
OF THE OYSTERS

1 pound oysters

Dash of freshly ground black
pepper

1 tablespoon ginger, grated

3 eggs

$^3/_4$ cup flour

Vegetable oil for frying

Pinch of salt

1   Remove the oysters from their shells, wash them in water
with a pinch of salt, and drain. Sprinkle the oysters with black
pepper and ginger. Set aside.

2   Crack the 3 eggs into a medium bowl and beat until well
mixed. Put the flour in a flat dish. Heat enough vegetable oil
over medium-low heat in a large skillet to cover the surface,
about 1 tablespoon at a time. Dust the oysters in the flour,
then into the beaten egg. Cook them until the egg is golden
brown. Flip and cook other side. Add more oil and adjust
heat as necessary.

Serve immediately with Seasoned Soy Sauce (*Yangnyum Ganjang*, page 4).

———
NOTE Serve as with rice and other *banchan* or as an *anju* to eat with beer and *soju*.

Stuffed Perilla Leaves

Ggaetnip Buchim

Perilla leaves have a fragrant mint-like flavor and texture. They add a wonderful elegance and complexity to this dish. Use larger, broad perilla leaves for this recipe. MAKES 24 STUFFED LEAVES

24 large perilla leaves

$1/4$ pound ground beef

5 ounces tofu ($1/2$ cake from a 10-ounce package)

$1/2$ teaspoon salt

1 green onion, chopped

3 garlic cloves, minced

2 teaspoons sesame oil

Flour for dusting

2 eggs, beaten

Vegetable oil for cooking

1   Wash and dry the perilla leaves, removing any large stems.

2   In a bowl, mix the beef, tofu, salt, green onion, garlic, and sesame oil until thoroughly mixed. Take one leaf in your hand and spoon about 1 tablespoon of the beef mixture onto the bottom half of the leaf, spreading it about $1/4$ inch thick. Fold the leaf in half over the filling. (It's okay if some of the beef is not covered by the leaf.) Repeat with the rest of the leaves.

3   Pour some flour on a plate. In a medium bowl, beat the eggs as if you're making scrambled eggs. In a large skillet, heat enough vegetable oil to thinly cover the surface.

4   Dust the stuffed leaves on both sides with flour. Then dip in the egg. Cook over low-to-medium heat until the meat is cooked thoroughly. The egg batter should become golden brown and the leaves will turn limp and turn dark green. Continue cooking the rest of the peppers, adjusting the heat as necessary and adding vegetable oil as needed, about 1 tablespoon at a time.

Serve immediately with a side of Seasoned Soy Sauce (*Yangnyum Ganjang*, page 4) for dipping.

———

N O T E If you find yourself low in stuffing, squeeze some of the stuffing from the fattest leaves to fill the remaining leaves. On the other hand, if you find yourself with too much stuffing, make small Meat Fritters (*Jencha*, page 85) with the rest of the stuffing.

Stuffed Peppers

Gochu Buchim

Korean chile peppers come in varying degrees of spiciness. Green peppers harvested in early summer are mild and similar to bell peppers. In the late summer, as these peppers hang out longer in the sun, they get hotter and hotter. By the time late autumn rolls around, the peppers will have turned a bright red, fiery in both color and taste. For this dish, I recommend using mild green peppers, but if you can't find them, you may substitute bell peppers.

MAKES 24 STUFFED PEPPER HALVES

12 small green peppers

$^1/_4$ pound ground beef

5 ounces tofu ($^1/_2$ cake of a 10-ounce package)

$^1/_2$ teaspoon salt

1 green onion, chopped

3 garlic cloves, minced

2 teaspoons sesame oil

Flour for dusting

2 eggs

Vegetable oil for cooking

1   Cut the green peppers in half. Remove the seeds and the stem. Set aside.

2   In a bowl, mix the beef, tofu, salt, onion, garlic, and sesame oil until mixed thoroughly. Stuff the pepper halves with the beef mixture.

3   Pour some flour on a plate. In a medium bowl, beat the eggs as if you're making scrambled eggs. In a large skillet, heat enough vegetable oil to thinly cover the surface.

4   Dip the stuffed side of the peppers in flour, then in the egg. Cook over low-to-medium heat until the meat is cooked thoroughly. The egg side should become golden brown and the pepper should be slightly browned and cooked on the skin side. Continue cooking the rest of the peppers, adjusting the heat as necessary and adding vegetable oil as needed, about a tablespoon at a time.

Serve immediately with a side of Seasoned Soy Sauce (*Yangnyum Ganjang*, page 4) for dipping.

VARIATION If using bell peppers (either green or red will work), cut them into rings about $^1/_4$ thick) and stuff with the beef filling. Dip the stuffed peppers on both sides and cook until the meat is cooked through and the egg batter is golden brown on both sides.

Soups and Hot Pots

MORNING HIKES

My family has moved several dozen times in my lifetime. Some homes are inconsequential memories, but others are as tangible as if I had only moved from there yesterday. One such home was a place in Seoul, on the base of a mountain at the edge of the city. It was a tiny little apartment, even by Korean standards. Back in those days, no one slept on Western-style beds. It wasn't because we were poor; it was just tradition. Everyone slept on thick blankets on the floor with several generations sometimes sleeping in the same room. In fact, I never slept in a bed until we moved to Los Angeles in the late seventies. And we were much poorer starting out in America than we ever were in Korea. • In the winter, large, noisy trucks would clunk down our narrow street delivering coal to everyone's homes. I loved to sit and listen to the sound of the coals falling into the basement below. We were never allowed to go under the house, but there was some sort of heating mechanism below that would warm the floor, so that on winter nights, it was an incredible comfort to sleep on fluffy blankets in the cozy room, wiggling under the covers between my siblings. • Cold mornings, however, were a different story entirely. My dad, the notoriously early riser, would rouse us from our sleep at some god-awful hour, long before the welcome light of the sun. Sometimes, that character-building hour was well before the first crows of the rooster. We would tumble around, bumping into each other as we bundled up in thick sweaters, all the while trying not to wake up my mom, who appeared oblivious to the morning ritual. Yawning, stretching, rubbing eyes, we would follow our bushy-tailed dad out into the cold dawn.

The chill of the morning air was so refreshing, it almost hurt to inhale too deeply. It was usually the space between the seasons, that knife's edge between the bare trees of autumn and the first snowfall of winter. My father would lead us in our morning calisthenics, as we bent and stretched as best we could, bundled up in our multiple layers. Then, like a father goose, my dad would proudly march down the street into the fog, followed by his goslings, who had to take extra steps with their toddler legs to keep up with his brisk pace.

The enormous dark shape of the mountain would emerge from the early morning haze like some imposing monster waiting to swallow us up. Once we began our incline, stoic and silent trees would appear slowly from the shadows, listening to our visible breaths as we trudged uphill. We were usually the only ones crazy enough to be up there at that hour. But, every so often, an old man, his clothes as gray as the morning, would materialize from the mist, silently startling us like a ghostly apparition from the forest.

By the time we reached the top, the sun would be just peeking over the horizon, reflecting off the cityscape below. There was a beautiful stream at the lookout point, where someone had left a wooden ladle to scoop up the crystal clarity of the water. We would take turns drinking, always going from oldest to youngest, my dad going first with my brother last. Sometimes, early morning frost would slow the stream down to just a trickle, so that you could crack the thin layer of ice on the edges with your fingers. The water was like pure liquid ice, so clear and cold that I swear my stomach shuddered in amazement and delight.

As we began our descent, I had already forgotten to be envious of our dear mom still slumbering peacefully snug in the coal-heated room. At the base of the mountain, the sane people were beginning to wake up. The sights and sounds of their morning routine signaled the waking rhythms of the city.

At home, my mom had already begun preparing breakfast. The smell of freshly cooked rice was enough to get me to start running toward our front door. On certain days, the smell of chicken soup overpowered the rice and I would run faster.

It may be difficult to imagine eating chicken soup for breakfast, but Koreans eat rice three meals a day (unless you're having noodles instead). Although Korean chicken soup (*samgaetahng*) is believed to cure listlessness in the summer months, it is also eaten as a preventative measure to guard against winter colds and flues. Medicinally beneficial ingredients (like ginseng, garlic, gingko nuts, and dried red dates) are added to make a delicious and healthy soup.

Chicken Ginseng Soup

Samgaetahng

 Usually made from young chickens, this soup is traditionally eaten during the hottest days of summer to help deal with the heat. It also makes a wonderful meal when you're fighting off a cold or flu. MAKES 1 TO 2 SERVINGS

1 (1¹/₂– to 2-pound) chicken (preferably young)

Salt

¹/₂ cup glutinous rice

1 ginseng root, sliced (2 if the roots are small)

5 gingko nuts

3 dried red dates or jujubes

3 garlic cloves, peeled

Water

2 chestnuts, peeled

Salt

Black pepper

1   Clean the chicken, removing any organs and neck. Sprinkle with salt inside and out.

2   Wash the rice, ginseng, gingko nuts, and red dates or jujubes. Stuff the chicken's cavity with rice, ginseng, gingko nuts, and garlic. Cross the legs and bind them to keep the stuffing in.

3   Put the chicken in a large pot and add 8 cups water. Bring to a boil. Lower the heat and add the chestnuts. Let simmer over low heat for about 1 hour. Then add the red dates or jujubes and let simmer another hour or so, until the chicken is thoroughly cooked. (You can check to see if the chicken is cooked by slicing where the leg joins the body. The meat should be opaque throughout and the juices run clear.)

Serve chicken in a large bowl with the broth with a small dish of salt and pepper. The diners can add the salt and pepper as they wish.

Spicy Beef Soup

Yookgaejang

This traditional dish is a wonderfully spicy soup for cold weather. It may seem like a lot of green onions, but once they are cooked, you'll see that it's just the right amount. MAKES 5 TO 6 SERVINGS

1 pound beef brisket

Water

1 garlic bulb, peeled and minced

3 tablespoons chili powder

1 tablespoon soy sauce

2 tablespoons salt

3 eggs

1 tablespoon Korean sesame oil

3 bundles of green onions, cut into about 3-inch lengths

$1/8$ teaspoon black pepper

1   Place beef in a large stockpot and add about 16 cups (1 gallon) of water. Bring to a boil. Reduce heat and simmer for at least 1 hour. Remove the meat from the broth. Skim the fat and foam from the broth.

2   Once the meat has cooled, shred it into thin strips. Set aside.

3   In a large bowl, combine the garlic, chili powder, soy sauce, and salt. Add the beef and mix thoroughly. Cover and let marinate for about 10 minutes.

4   Combine the eggs and sesame oil in a small bowl and beat until well mixed.

5   Bring the broth to a boil again. Add the seasoned meat, green onions, and black pepper. Bring to a boil again, then add the egg mix, drizzling it slowly over the boiling broth.

Serve immediately with rice and *banchan*.

HOT POT COOKING
ON THE TABLE

Spicy Hot Chicken Soup

Dak Yookgaejang

 Yookgaejang is usually made with shredded beef; however, chicken is substituted here. Hot chicken-based soups are thought to prevent illness and fatigue on hot days. MAKES 5 TO 6 SERVINGS

1 whole chicken

Water

1 garlic bulb, peeled and minced

3 tablespoons chili powder

1 tablespoon soy sauce

2 tablespoons salt

3 eggs

1 tablespoon sesame oil

3 bundles of green onions, cut into about 3-inch lengths

1/8 teaspoon black pepper

1   Place chicken in a large pot and add about 1 gallon of water. Bring to a boil. Reduce heat and simmer for at least 1 hour. Remove the chicken from the broth. Skim the fat from the chicken broth.

2   Debone and de-skin the chicken. Then, shred the meat into thin strips. Set aside.

3   In a large bowl, combine the garlic, chili powder, soy sauce, salt, and 2 tablespoons chicken broth. Add the chicken and mix thoroughly. Cover and set aside for about 10 minutes allowing the chicken to season and the chili powder to soften.

4   Combine the eggs and sesame oil in a small bowl and beat until well mixed.

5   Bring the broth to a boil again. Add the seasoned meat, green onions, and black pepper. Bring to a boil again, then add the egg mix, drizzling it slowly over the boiling broth.

Serve immediately with rice and *banchan*.

Seaweed Soup

Miyuk Gook

In addition to cake and candles, seaweed soup was always a part of a birthday celebration. You may think it's hardly a treat, but I looked forward to the soup as much as I did the cake that would follow. After my sister gave birth to her first child, my mom insisted she eat *miyuk gook* for strength. For how much soup my mom fed her, it was a surprise my sister didn't turn green. Seaweed for the soup can be found in the dried goods section of Korean groceries. MAKES 4 TO 5 SERVINGS

About 4 ounces of dried kelp or wakame (*miyuk*)

$^1/_4$ pound beef, sliced or shredded

5 garlic cloves, minced

Black pepper

2 tablespoons sesame oil

2 tablespoons soy sauce

12 cups Beef Stock (page 11)

Salt

2 green onions, thinly sliced into little circles, for garnish

1   To rehydrate the dried kelp, soak in water for about 5 to 10 minutes. The seaweed will swell up to about 2 cups and turn dark green. Cut the kelp into pieces about 2 inches long.

2   Mix the beef, garlic, pepper, 1 tablespoon sesame oil, and soy sauce in a bowl. Let marinate for about 5 to 10 minutes.

3   In a large stockpot, heat 1 tablespoon sesame oil over medium heat until hot. Add beef and sauté until the meat is browned, about 2 to 3 minutes. Add the kelp and stock and bring to a boil. Lower the heat to medium and simmer for about 10 to 15 minutes. Remove from heat and season with salt and pepper.

Serve immediately into individual serving bowls. Garnish with green onions and serve with a bowls of rice and a variety of *kimchi*.

Taro Soup

Torang Gook

Taro roots are said to cure many ailments in Korea. I don't know how many of those old wives' tales are true, but I do know that the roots are very high in nutrients, especially calcium, protein, and phosphorous. Although they can be found year-round, the roots reach their maturity during the fall. If you've never seen one before, look for a small brown tuber, similar to a potato, except it is a bit hairy on the outside like a coconut. Make sure you always cook taro roots before eating, because they can be toxic in their raw state. You may wish to use gloves when handling them raw, as well. This soup makes a hearty autumn dish. MAKES 10 TO 12 SERVINGS

1 small onion, peeled

$^1/_2$ medium Asian radish

1 ounce sea kelp (*dashima*)

12 cups Beef Stock (page 11)

$2^1/_2$ pounds taro roots, peeled

Water

Salt

2 tablespoons soy sauce

2 garlic cloves, minced

1 teaspoon toasted sesame seeds, crushed (page 3)

1 teaspoon black pepper

1 large green onion (*keun pa*) or 3 regular-sized ones, cut on the diagonal into about 2- to 3-inch pieces

1 Add the whole onion, the radish, and kelp to the beef stock. Bring to a boil. Then, reduce heat to simmer for another $^1/_2$ hour. Remove from heat. Remove the ingredients from the broth, being careful not to lose too much liquid. Set aside to cool.

2 If the taro roots are large, cut in half or quarters. In a medium pot, bring about 12 cups of water and a little salt to a boil. Add the taro and cook for about 10 minutes. Rinse in cold water, drain, and set aside.

3 Shred the beef brisket from the stock into small pieces and cut the kelp into approximately 1 × $^1/_2$-inch pieces. Combine the shredded beef, kelp, soy sauce, garlic, sesame seeds, and black pepper. Mix thoroughly and press together. Set aside for about 10 to 15 minutes to marinate.

4 Cut the radish into flat cubes, about $^1/_4$ inch thick. Cube the onion.

5 Bring the broth to a boil again and add the beef, radish, and onion. Remove from heat, add the green onions, and serve immediately.

Soybean Sprout Soup

Kohng Namool Gook

The last time I was really sick, my mom called me to ask me what I wanted to eat. As silly as it may sound, I couldn't shake the idea of this simple soup. The refreshing broth and nutritious sprouts make it an everyday food that's nice to eat anytime. Traditionally, the root tips are supposed to be trimmed, but I've found that it's way too time-consuming and not trimming them doesn't affect the taste one bit! MAKES 5 TO 6 SERVINGS

4 cups soybean sprouts

Water

1 garlic clove, minced

1 teaspoon chile powder

1 teaspoon salt

5 cups Anchovy Stock (page 10)

3 green onions, chopped

1   Wash and clean the bean sprouts, removing any bean skins and blackened parts.

2   In the meantime, in a large pot, bring about 2 cups water to a boil. Add the sprouts, reduce the heat to low and cook for about 8 to 10 minutes. Add the garlic, chili powder, and salt, and mix. Add the anchovy stock and let simmer for about 10 minutes. Add the green onions and cook for 1 to 2 minutes longer. Season with additional salt, if necessary.

Serve immediately with rice, *kimchi*, and other sides.

Oxtail Soup

Ggoli Gomtahng

One of the staple soups of Korean cuisine, this soup is an example of how every part of the animal can be used to produce something delicious, in this case, the tail. The meat on the bone gets very tender after being boiled for a long time. The secret to the flavor is in the seasoning. MAKES 5 TO 6 SERVINGS

3 pounds beef oxtail

Water

1 (1-inch) piece of ginger, sliced

10 garlic cloves

2 garlic cloves, minced

1 Asian radish, peeled and cubed

1 tablespoon salt

$^1/_2$ tablespoon black pepper

1 teaspoon chili powder

3 green onions, chopped, for garnish

1   Soak the oxtail in cold water for about an hour, to drain all the blood and to produce a clear broth. Rinse well.

2   In a large stock pot, add the oxtail, ginger, and about 16 cups (1 gallon) water. Bring to a boil and skim off the foam. Reduce heat, add the 10 garlic cloves, cover, and let simmer for about 2 hours. Add radish and continue simmering for at least another hour, until meat is very tender and the broth is milky. Skim off the fat and any more foam that rises to the surface.

3   Combine the salt, pepper, 2 minced garlic cloves, and chili powder in a small bowl. Sprinkle each bowl of soup with a generous amount of green onions.

Serve hot with the seasoning mix on the side, rice, and *kimchi.*

Beef Noodle Soup

Sullong Tahng

 This hearty soup is made with just a little bit of rice noodle for added texture. Even though there are noodles in the soup, it's usually served with a side of rice. MAKES 5 TO 6 SERVINGS

1 medium Asian radish

1 pound beef shank

Water

5 garlic cloves, minced

$^1/_4$ pound thin rice noodles

1 green onion, chopped

Salt

Black pepper

1 Cut the radish in half. Add to large stockpot with the beef and about 16 cups (1 gallon) water. Bring to a boil. Reduce heat and let simmer for about 1 hour, until the meat is very tender.

2 Remove the beef and radish from the broth and let cool. Skim off any foam or fat from the broth. Slice the meat into thin, bite-sized pieces. Slice the radish into thin $^1/_4$ circles about $^1/_4$ inch thick.

3 Return the meat and radish back into the pot. Add the garlic and bring to a boil again. Add the noodles and let simmer for about 3 to 5 minutes, until noodles are cooked. Add the green onion and salt and pepper, as needed. Serve immediately.

Rice Cake Soup

Dduk Gook

 Eaten especially during Korean New Year (*Soll*), *Dduk Gook* can also be made with dumplings. (*See Mandu Gook*, page 135). MAKES 5 TO 6 SERVINGS

Water

12 cups Beef Stock (page 11)

2 (2-pound) packages of Korean rice cake ovalettes

2 eggs, yolks separated from whites

1/4 pound *Boolgogi*, cooked (page 23)

2 to 3 green onions, thinly sliced on the diagonal

2 to 3 sheets of seaweed (*gim*), cut into small, thin strips

Salt

Black pepper

1   Soak rice cakes in cold water for approximately 1 hour.

2   Scramble the yolk and whites of the eggs separately. Fry the yolk into a thin omelet. Fold or roll the omelet about an inch wide. Slice into thin strips. Repeat with egg whites. Set aside.

4   Bring the beef stock to a boil. Add rice cakes. Boil until ovalettes have softened, approximately 10 minutes.

Serve hot in large bowls garnished with egg whites, egg yolks, *boolgogi*, green onions, and seaweed. Add salt and pepper as needed.

Soon Dubu

Korean restaurants are generally specialty eateries. When my friends ask me to recommend the best Korean place to eat in any given city, I always ask them what kind of food they enjoy. A place that specializes in barbecue won't even have noodles on their menu.

One wintry night, I took my friends to eat their first bowl of hot tofu pot (*soon dubu*). Although it was pouring rain, the restaurant was doing a brisk business. Bundled-up customers huddled under their umbrellas, trying to keep dry from the rain dribbling down from the eaves. When we arrived, the umbrellas parted like the Red Sea. As usual, the Korean customers were surprised to see a group of non-Koreans approach.

The waitress was visibly relieved to see me and even more relieved that I spoke Korean. People make the mistake of thinking that Korean waitstaff are impolite. Not that I haven't had my share of grumpy waitresses, but I've noticed that they sometimes treat foreigners different from Koreans. It wasn't because they were rude, but rather because they were embarrassed about their own lack of English skills. They are usually curt to Americans because they're afraid to become engaged in a conversation they might not understand. As with anyone, just a little respect and politeness goes a long way.

Our waitress that night took special note of one of my friends, talking to me at length about his beautiful eyes and handsome looks. When she ducked back inside, my friends wanted to know what we talked about. With a mysterious smile, I pointed to the menu on the wall and told them to decide what they wanted. "Menu" was a generous word for the list of five or six types of *soon dubu* available. Underneath the list, it just said mild, medium, or spicy.

Although everything was translated into a decent English, my friends were still puzzled until I explained to them that this restaurant really only had one thing on their menu, tofu hot pot. The list was really just a matter of what you wanted in it and how spicy you may like it.

As we were deciding, the waitress came back out to take our orders. She leaned over and whispered to me like an excited schoolgirl, glancing over at my friend with the pretty eyes. She said she'd give us the next available table although there were people who had been waiting longer. By this time, he became suspicious.

"What did she say to you?" he nudged me.

"She said we'll get the next table," I smiled. "Lucky for us, she thinks you're cute."

"What?" my friend shrieked in disbelief, while trying to hide his blushing cheeks behind his umbrella. "You're lying."

"Oh yeah?" I raised an eyebrow. "See all these people waiting here. How much do you wanna bet that we get seated before them?"

Sure enough, the waitress returned and ushered us in just as the last syllable left my lips. I touched my friend's arm on the way in as he gave me a funny look I couldn't quite decipher.

We were soon squeezed into a corner table and served the usual array of *kimchi* and *mit banchan*. When the bubbling stone pots arrived, everyone became unusually quiet, as we buried our faces in the steaming goodness.

We got the best service that night. My friends were pleasantly surprised, having previously encountered less friendly staff. I'd like them to believe it was my wonderful Korean language skills that won over our waitress. Secretly, I know better. The next time I go to that place, I'll have to take my nice friend again—you know, the one with the pretty eyes.

Tofu Hot Pot

Soon Dubu

Soon dubu is made from very soft, silky tofu, usually in a stone pot (*ddook baegi*). If you don't have a stone pot, a metal one will work fine but the presentation won't be the same. *Soon dubu* can be made with beef, seafood, *kimchi*, or really anything you'd like. It can be easily made into a vegetarian dish by using vegetable stock and adding things like Korean zucchini and onions instead of meat or seafood. MAKES 2 TO 3 SERVINGS

4 teaspoons chili powder

2 garlic cloves, minced

2 teaspoons salt

2 teaspoons sesame oil

9 ounces soft tofu

6 clams

1 cup Beef Stock (page 11)

4 ounces squid, sliced into about 1-inch pieces

6 shrimp

2 green onions, cut into about 1-inch lengths

1 egg

1   In a small bowl, combine the chili powder, garlic, salt, and sesame oil. Set aside.

2   In a stone pot or other pot, add the tofu, clams, and 1 cup beef stock. Bring to a boil and add squid, shrimp, and seasoning. Let simmer another few minutes until the seafood is cooked. Add the green onions and cook for about another 1 to 2 minutes.

Serve bubbling hot with a raw egg to add to the broth immediately. Serve with rice and *kimchi*.

Kimchi Hot Pot

Kimchi Jjigae

When you have too much ripe *kimchi* on hand, this is a great recipe to make. The more fermented the *kimchi*, the tastier the *jjigae*. My dad perfected this dish when he was in the Korean military. All Korean men are required to do three years of service and seeing how good my dad makes this dish, I came to believe that all he did was sit around making *kimchi jjigae* for the other uniformed boys. My dad's secret is to cook up the pork with some sesame oil and chili paste. This is one of those down-home foods that you don't serve to guests but you like to eat at home. Made in a stone pot, *jjigae* goes right from the fire to the middle of the table, still bubbling over from the heat. You can make this dish vegetarian, but the pork works so well with the stewed *kimchi* that it's difficult to imagine doing without it. Any kind of pork will do. Boneless pork is easier to eat, but the cuts with bone taste a little bit better in this dish. MAKES 4 TO 6 SERVINGS

1/2 pound pork

2 cups traditional *kimchi*

1 tablespoon sesame oil

1 tablespoon chili paste

3 garlic cloves, sliced

Water

4 shiitake mushrooms (optional)

1 (12-ounce) package of medium or soft tofu

2 green onions

1   Cut pork into bite-sized pieces. Cut the *kimchi* into 1-inch pieces, making sure to save any liquid that may be lost.

2   In a stone pot, add the pork, sesame oil, chili paste, and garlic. Stir and cook over a medium-high heat until the pork is nearly cooked through.

3   Add the *kimchi*, some *kimchi* liquid, and 3 cups water. Bring to a boil.

4   In the meantime, cut the optional mushrooms, tofu, and green onions. Lower the heat, and add the remaining ingredients. Let simmer for 1 to 2 minutes until the tofu is heated through. Serve immediately.

Fermented Soybean Paste Hot Pot

Dwenjang Jjigae

This hot pot can easily be made vegetarian by omitting the pork. As with most *jjigae*, this is a salty dish meant to be shared by everyone at the table.

MAKES 4 TO 6 SERVINGS

$^1/_4$ pound pork

2 green onions

1 (12-ounce) package of medium or soft tofu

1 onion, sliced

1 medium Korean zucchini, cubed

2 tablespoons fermented soybean paste

Water

2 garlic cloves, minced

1   Slice the pork into thin pieces about an inch long. Cut the green onions on the diagonal into $1^1/_2$-inch lengths. Slice the tofu into rectangles about $^1/_2$ inch thick.

2   Arrange the pork on the bottom of a stone pot or other cooking pot. Add the sliced onion, Korean zucchini, and tofu. Dissolve the soybean paste in 3 cups water and add to the pot. Bring to a boil and add the garlic. Lower the heat and let simmer for about 5 to 10 minutes, until the pork is cooked and the Korean zucchini has cooked through. Add the green onions and let cook for 1 to 2 minutes.

Serve immediately with rice, *kimchi,* and other side dishes.

Seafood Hot Pot

Haemul Jungol

Hot pots are made from any variety of shellfish and fish, usually whatever is seasonally available in the region. This is a basic recipe with a variety of seafood. Feel free to add and subtract whatever seafood you like.

MAKES 4 TO 5 SERVINGS

1/2 onion, sliced

5 to 7 shiitake mushrooms, sliced

1/2 pound Napa cabbage, sliced into about 2-inch-long pieces

2 (2-inch) pieces of ginger, sliced

2 garlic cloves, minced

3 cups Beef Stock (page 11) or chicken broth

1/4 pound squid, cleaned and sliced into thin strips about 2 inches long

1/4 pound scallops

1/4 pound fresh oysters, shelled and cleaned

4 medium clams, shelled and cleaned

1 tablespoon chili paste

1 tablespoon chili powder

3 green onions, cut on the diagonal, about 2 inches long

3 or 4 stalks chrysanthemum leaves

Salt

Black pepper

1　In a large heavy pot, add the onion, mushrooms, cabbage, ginger, and garlic. Add the stock and bring to a boil. Add the seafood, chili paste, and chili powder. Reduce to simmer and let cook for about 5 to 10 minutes, until all the seafood is cooked through.

2　Add green onions and chrysanthemum leaves and let simmer for another 1 to 2 minutes. Add salt and pepper, if necessary.

Serve by placing the boiling pot in the middle of the table for everyone to share.

HOT POT

Wizard's Stew (or Wizard's Barbecue)

Shin Sul Lo *or* Jungol

$^1/_2$ head Napa cabbage, chopped into $1^1/_2$-inch pieces

1 medium onion, sliced into $^1/_4$-inch-thick pieces

1 medium Korean zucchini, sliced into $^1/_2$-inch-thick semicircles

1 (12-ounce) package of medium firm tofu, cut into $^1/_2$-inch-thick rectangles

2 medium carrots, thin sliced on the diagonal into 1-inch pieces

1 cup white mushrooms, sliced into $^1/_2$ or $^1/_3$, depending on size

3 to 4 green onions, sliced on the diagonal into 2-inch pieces

$^1/_4$ pound *Boolgogi* meat, marinated but uncooked

3 hard-boiled eggs, quartered lengthwise

1 package of (pink and white) fish cake, sliced into $^1/_4$-inch-thick pieces

12 cups Beef Stock (page 11)

Salt

Black pepper

1   In a shallow, tabletop electric pot, arrange the cabbage, onion, Korean zucchini, tofu, carrots, mushrooms, green onions, *boolgogi*, hard-boiled eggs, and fish cake radiating into three sections from the center of the circle. Stack the ingredients with the more colorful pieces on top, while putting the less colorful pieces on the bottom. Set aside any leftover ingredients.

2   Pour the beef stock slowly and carefully over the arrangement. Turn on the heat and allow to simmer for about 8 to 10 minutes, until *boolgogi* is browned and cooked thoroughly. Add salt and pepper if necessary.

3   Add the leftover ingredients throughout the course of the meal, as needed.

Noodles and Dumplings

FIGHTING FIRE WITH FIRE

In Seoul, temperatures can top 100 degrees Fahrenheit, but the killer is the humidity. Going into a summer in Korea is like being invited to the devil's sauna. Koreans have devised many ways to cope with the brutal weather. There are two opposing theories: On one side are the people who believe that you can fight fire with fire. They think that if you eat hot and spicy food, you get more energy and can combat the listlessness that summer brings. Not only will you sweat more, but in contrast to the hot and spicy food you just ate, the outside temperature will also make you feel cooler. • My dad and his friends belong to this first camp. They take hot baths and eat the most fire-burning, chile-filled hot pots, dabbing beads of sweat from their brows as they do. I've seen some of the most fervent ones emerge from steaming saunas on sweltering days. The other side believes that you should combat the heat with cold. They take cool baths, eat dishes drowned in

ice, and stay away from the more spicy foods. • I belong to the latter group. On any given summer day in Los Angeles, I can be found with my portable ice shaver in one

My nephew, Benjamin, eating noodles

hand and an ice pop in the other, running to the nearest climate-controlled shelter. Not that I'm afraid of heat, mind you, but I'm no glutton for punishment.

When I'm feeling extra-lazy and irritable (i.e., I don't feel like getting anywhere near a stove), I hop into my car, air-conditioner blasting me in the face, and head down to Koreatown to look for the familiar banners advertising *naengmyun* and *pot bingsoo*.

There are two major types of *naengmyun*—*mool naengmyun* (which means "cold water noodles" in Korean) and *bibim naengmyun* (which is a spicy mixed noodle dish with pieces of raw skate).

Naengmyun was originally a winter food, eaten by those from the cold northern provinces of Pyongyang and Hamgyong. People in Pyongyang province ate the predecessor to *mool naengmyun*. Their buckwheat noodles were served in beef stock with cold pheasant meat.

The *bibim naengmyun* from Hamgyong province was made with hot spices mixed with *hamhung* (flounder). The raw fish was salted and seasoned, then eaten, bones and all. Today, *bibim naengmyon* is prepared with skate, which is easier to get. Because of its refreshing coolness, *naengmyon* eventually evolved into the national summertime dish.

When Koreans speak of *naengmyun*, they are generally referring to the soup type. Usually served in large metal bowls with ice cubes clinking inside, *mool naengmyun* consists of noodles in a beef-based broth. It is garnished with cucumbers, pickled daikon, and hard-boiled eggs. The crunchiness of the cucumber and pickled daikon complement the chewy consistency of the noodles. Since the noodles can be so elastic and difficult to eat, the waitress will come and cut them for you with scissors. The cold metal of the dish feels wonderful against your palm as you lift it up to drink that wonderful broth.

Another popular chilled noodle dish is *kohng gooksu*—which is made with somen or other noodles in a beautiful white soy-based broth. A subtler flavor than *naengmyon*, *kohng gooksu* is another one of the joys of summer eating.

You can top off a cold meal with an order of *pot bingsoo* if you'd like. Found in most cafes and bakeries throughout Koreatown, it is simply a pile of shaved ice mixed with sweet red beans, fruit cocktail, cooked rice powder and with a variety of brightly colored fruit syrups added for flavor.

Even though it may be a clash of fire and ice when my dad and I sit down for a summer meal—my cold noodles and his spicy soups—the one thing we can agree on is what we're going to have for dessert: a nice bowl of ice cream shared between us.

Cold Noodle Soup

Naengmyun *or* Mool Naengmyun

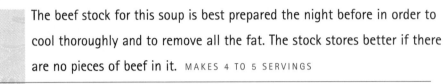

The beef stock for this soup is best prepared the night before in order to cool thoroughly and to remove all the fat. The stock stores better if there are no pieces of beef in it. MAKES 4 TO 5 SERVINGS

2 pounds beef brisket

2 pounds beef bones

1 (1-inch) piece of ginger

10 to 12 whole brown peppercorns

1 teaspoon bonita-type soup stock (*dashida* or *hondashi*), optional

Water

4 tablespoons rice vinegar

1 tablespoon salt

Asian hot mustard (or hot mustard oil), optional

1 (24- to 26-ounce) package Korean buckwheat noodles

2 small Korean cucumbers, sliced into thin strips (similar to julienne)

1 Asian pear, peeled, cored and thinly sliced

4 to 5 eggs, hard boiled and halved lengthwise

1   For beef stock: Combine brisket, bones, ginger, peppercorns, and optional soup stock in a large pot. Fill with about $2^1/_2$ quarts water. Bring to a boil, then reduce heat and simmer for 2 to $2^1/_2$ hours (until water reduces to about 2 quarts). Remove beef and bones. Set aside beef and discard the bone. Then strain the liquid through cheesecloth or a very fine mesh strainer. Refrigerate the beef brisket. Refrigerate beef stock, place in freezer, or cool over ice water until fat solidifies. Remove all fat from stock.

2   Combine rice vinegar, salt, and optional hot mustard in a bowl. Add to the beef stock.

3   Take the cold beef brisket that was set aside and cut into thin slices (approximately 1 × 2 inches).

4   Bring 1 quart of water to a boil, add buckwheat noodles. Boil for about 3 minutes. Remove noodles from the heat and rinse thoroughly in cold water to cool. Drain. Separate the noodles into 4 to 5 large bowls.

5   Distribute the beef stock evenly between 4 or 5 bowls. Add ice if required or desired to keep the dish cool throughout the meal. Garnish with cucumber, pear slices, and hard-boiled eggs. Serve immediately with Asian hot mustard, if desired.

Cold Noodles in Soybean Soup

Kohng Gooksu

For different flavors, sesame seeds can be substituted with peanuts or cashews. All nuts or seeds used should be roasted, to add that nice nutty flavor. If you can't find dried soybeans, you may use Asian soy milk to make the broth. MAKES 5 TO 7 SERVINGS

30 ounces dried soybeans (*maeju*)

3 tablespoons toasted sesame seeds (page 3)

3 tablespoons perilla seeds, toasted

3 teaspoons salt

Water

About 20 ounces somen noodles (7 bundles)

2 small cucumbers, sliced into thin strips

1 tomato, sliced into wedges (optional)

Black sesame seeds for garnish

1   Wash beans, then soak them in hot water for at least 2 hours. Rinse and remove peels. Place the beans in a large pot and add water to cover about 1 inch above the top of the beans. Bring to a boil. Reduce heat and simmer for 35 to 40 minutes. Occasionally skim foam from the top. Remove beans from heat, rinse thoroughly in cold water, then drain.

2   In a food processor, puree the beans, toasted sesame seeds, and perilla seeds in water until liquefied. Process the beans in stages (about 1 cup of beans with 2 cups of water). Strain the liquid through cheesecloth or a fine-mesh strainer. Add salt.

3   Refrigerate the soy liquid until thoroughly cool or chill over a bowl of ice water.

4   Bring 5 to 6 cups of water to a boil. Loosen the bundles of somen and add to the water. Boil for 2 to 3 minutes. Remove from heat and rinse thoroughly in cold water. Drain.

5   Distribute the noodles into 5 to 7 large bowls. Carefully pour cold soy soup over noodles. Garnish with cucumbers, 1 to 2 optional tomato wedges per bowl and then sprinkle each serving with black sesame seeds.

Serve with *Traditional Napa Cabbage* or *Asian Radish Kimchi*.

Tae Kwon Do

Like most developing countries, men over eighteen in Korea are required to do military service for three years, unless they have a medical reason, or their family can afford to buy them out of the obligation. In the army, the young men learn how to carry a gun and other military skills that may not necessarily come in handy during daily life later on. They also learn some useful things like tae kwon do, how to cook, and how to do their own laundry. Since women aren't required or even very welcome in Korea's military, learning martial arts is mainly a male phenomenon.

So, when I signed up for Seoul National University's tae kwon do class one summer, I had to put on a tough demeanor to prove that I wouldn't be some sissy girl, who would wince at a good roundhouse kick or would be afraid of the sight of her own blood. It also helped that my friend Anna enrolled in the class with me. When we got there, we were surprised that there was actually another woman in the class. However, we were not surprised when she didn't show up the following day.

The days were hot and oppressive. With grunts and aggressive yells, we would punch and kick, do our stretches and spar with one another, as our bare feet squeaked their sweaty complaints on the hardwood floor. Although we kept up our tough gal image the entire duration of a class period, afterward we would melt into soft puddles in the girls' locker room. We would run down the stairs, to feed the vending machine our 100 won coins, in exchange for slim cans of Pocari Sweat, a sports drink the name of which prevented us from discovering its refreshing qualities for rehydrating our exhausted bodies. Down in one gulp, we would fish for more coins as we wiped the beads of sweat from our brows. When we were relieved of our thirst or out of change, Anna and I would be able to catch our breaths.

We would be the only two people in the locker room as we laughed and talked over the shower water, apologizing for having to kick the crap out of each other in class. Freshly showered and back in our street clothes, sometimes the boys in the class would give us puzzled looks, trying to figure out where they knew us from. An eventual look of recognition and surprise would wash over their faces as they surveyed our long flowing hair and girly skirts. We would give them a nod and smile, secretly knowing we could do a front lateral kick as well as the rest of them.

Our instructor was a shy young guy, about twenty-one years old, although he looked like he couldn't be a day over sixteen—so young, he didn't need to shave that often. I appreciated the fact that he and the rest of the guys in the classes treated us like equals in the classroom. Outside, it was a different story. The traditional gender roles would be assumed again once we left the tae kwon do studio.

After a couple of hours of intensive physical training, we would be dying to stuff our mouths with whatever food we could find. Impatiently, we could hardly wait to find a gourmet restaurant to quell our hunger, settling for whatever hole-in-the-wall happened to be convenient and open. Anna loved to get spicy sautéed squid over rice, while I opted for some sort of noodles. Any fresh bowl of chewy noodles swimming in a wonderful broth was enough to revive my body's energy. I especially like the simplicity of "knife noodles" (*kal gooksu*) with chicken or clams.

We would finish our respective meals like two people who hadn't eaten in days, barely being able to breathe between gobbles. Once, a woman in the restaurant asked what we had been doing that we were so hungry. When we told her that we just got out of tae kwon do practice, she eyed us suspiciously.

"What sort of woman learns tae kwon do?" she raised an eyebrow as she muttered under her breath on her way back to the kitchen.

Anna and I just smiled at each other, exchanging the looks of two tomboys sharing a meal together.

Knife Noodles with Chicken

Dak Kal Gooksu

Knife noodles (*kal gooksu*) noodles can be found in the refrigerated section of Korean groceries. They are thick, soft, and chewy. *Kal gooksu* can be made with seafood, beef, chicken, or anything. The ingredients determine the base of the broth. MAKES 5 TO 6 SERVINGS

1 pound chicken breasts or thighs

Water

3 tablespoons chili powder

3 tablespoons soy sauce

1 tablespoon sesame oil

2 green onions, chopped

4 garlic cloves, minced

1 pound knife noodles (*kal gooksu*)

1 medium Korean zucchini, shredded or cut into thin strips

Salt

Black pepper

1 sheet toasted laver, for garnish (optional)

1   Boil the chicken in 1 gallon water and let simmer until thoroughly cooked, about 45 minutes. Remove the chicken and reserve the broth. When both have cooled, skim the fat from the broth and remove any bones and skin from the chicken.

2   Shred the chicken meat by hand and place the pieces in a medium bowl. Add chili powder, soy sauce, sesame oil, green onions, and garlic. Mix well until all the chicken is seasoned.

3   Bring the broth to a boil. Add the noodles and Korean zucchini and cook until noodles are chewy (about 5 minutes). Remove from heat and add salt and pepper as needed.

4   Pour noodles and broth into a large serving bowl or individual bowls. Add the seasoned chicken. If you wish, top with shredded or crushed toasted laver.

Serve hot with Seasoned Soy Sauce (*Yangnyum Ganjang*, page 4) on the side.

Sweet Potato Noodles

Japchae

> This dish is usually made for special occasions or for guests. Although it is usually part of an elaborate meal, I sometimes like to have *japchae* as a light snack. Be careful not to overcook the noodles or they will lose their flavor and chewy texture. The noodles should be translucent but still slightly firm.
>
> MAKES 10 TO 12 SERVINGS

1 (1 1/2–pound) package sweet potato noodles

10 to 12 dried *pyongo* or shiitake mushrooms

Vegetable oil for sautéing

1 pound sliced rib eye or *Boolgogi* beef, sliced into strips

4 garlic cloves, minced

1 tablespoon plus 1/2 cup soy sauce

2 teaspoons plus 2 tablespoons sesame oil

2 teaspoons toasted sesame seeds, crushed (page 3)

2 bunches of spinach, thoroughly washed with roots trimmed

2 teaspoons salt

2 medium onions, sliced

2 carrots, shredded or cut into thin strips

1 small green pepper with seeds removed, cut into thin strips

1 bundle green onions, cut into 1-inch pieces

1 tablespoon toasted sesame seeds, whole, plus additional for garnish (optional)

1/2 cup sugar

1   Cook the sweet potato noodles in boiling water for about 4 to 5 minutes. Immediately drain and rinse thoroughly in cold water. Cut the noodles with scissors into roughly about 6- to 7-inch lengths for easier eating.

2   Soak the mushrooms in cold water for about 1 hour. Squeeze the liquid from the mushrooms and slice. Heat vegetable oil in a skillet. Add the mushrooms, beef, 2 cloves minced garlic, 1 tablespoon soy sauce, 1 teaspoon sesame oil, and 1 teaspoon sesame seeds and sauté until beef is cooked (about 3 to 4 minutes). Remove from heat and set aside.

3   In boiling water, blanch the spinach. Squeeze the water from the leaves and cut in half. In a bowl, combine spinach, 2 cloves minced garlic, 1 teaspoon salt, 1 teaspoon sesame oil, and 1 teaspoon crushed sesame seeds and mix. Set aside to marinate.

4   Heat vegetable oil in a skillet. Add the onions, carrots, green pepper, and 1 teaspoon salt and sauté for about 3 to 4 minutes. Add the green onions and stir-fry for about a minute more. Remove from heat and set aside.

5   In a large bowl thoroughly combine noodles, beef mixture, spinach, onion mixture, 1/2 cup soy sauce, 2 tablespoons sesame oil, 1 tablespoon whole toasted sesame seeds, and 1/2 cup sugar.

Serve warm, sprinkled with whole sesame seeds if desired.

Humble Beginnings

When my family first moved to Los Angeles, we moved into a small one-bedroom apartment in the middle of Koreatown. Our story was not unique. There were thousands of Korean immigrants in the late seventies who came to the states for a better opportunity for their families. We didn't speak any English. We sold most of our belongings and brought whatever money we could to strive for that ever-elusive "American dream."

My parents slept in the bedroom while my siblings and I slept on mattresses in the middle of the living room. My mom got a job sewing in a sweatshop downtown. Because she got paid by the piece, she was always bringing her work home so that we could help by cutting patterns and such. My dad got a job working at a service station, figuring if he could fix airplanes, he would be able to fix a car. They worked long hours so my siblings and I were often left to fend for ourselves.

The first person I met was a little girl named Sunny Ye, who was five years old. I was seven. She was sitting on the steps of our apartment building when we became friends. At the time, I didn't know that her parents were the ones who got my folks their jobs. She had an older brother, Pyong-uk (Mike), who was several months younger than I was. Since our parents worked together and we played together in our urban playground, our families became good friends.

Although we later moved to different parts of town, we would get together on weekends, squeezing into my folks' Lincoln Continental for trips. Somehow we'd get all nine of us in that car with rice and *banchan* packed in the trunk. Although we were poor, we were happy and carefree, not feeling deprived in any way. We had a roof over our heads, food to eat, and clothes to wear.

As years went by, our lives got busier, and friends came and went, but our families remained close. Sunny would come spend summer nights at our house, sleeping in bed between my sister and me. Even in college, we would visit each other in our dorm rooms, making each other ramen with *kimchi* when we were too poor to go out to eat.

Even now, I can still call Sunny and ask her to come make me a meal, usually her specialty *sujaebi*, a simple soup made with dough flakes. The dish has a humble history like ours. When Korea was poor and people couldn't get rice, they could still make this soup. Sharing this meal is a way of reminding us of our past, while celebrating our present and future. Besides, Sunny makes a mean bowl of *sujaebi*. When we eat together, we know that our friendship is worth more than all the riches in the world.

Spicy Dough Flake Soup

Kimchi Sujaebi

Sometimes considered "poor man's food" in Korea, *sujaebi* originated when the country saw less prosperous times. This is the basic recipe with no bells and whistles. MAKES 5 TO 6 SERVINGS

4 cups flour

Water

10 cups Anchovy Stock (double the recipe on page 10)

4 garlic cloves, minced

1 tablespoon chili paste

1 cup *kimchi* plus extra *kimchi* liquid

3 green onions, cut on the diagonal into about 2-inch pieces

Salt

1   Combine the flour and $1^1/_2$ cups water, adding the water about $^1/_4$ cup at a time, until the dough clumps together in one piece. Knead into a dough. Form into a ball and wrap in plastic or place in a plastic bag and refrigerate for about an hour.

2   In the meantime, bring the anchovy stock to a boil and add garlic. Add the chili paste, *kimchi,* and *kimchi* juice. Rip the dough into thin pieces about roughly $1^1/_2$ inches in size and add to the boiling stock.

3   When the dough begins to float and becomes slightly translucent on the edges (about 5 to 7 minutes, depending on the thickness of your dough pieces), add the green onions. Remove from heat and add salt.

Serve immediately so that the broth is still steaming and the dough flakes don't become waterlogged.

SUNNY MAKING DOUGH

Dough Flake Soup with Potatoes

Gamja Sujaebi

 This is the Ye family recipe my friend Sunny makes for me. The clear broth soup makes a simple but deliciously satisfying meal. The refreshing broth works well with the chewiness of the dough flakes. MAKES 2 TO 3 SERVINGS

2 cups flour

Water

5 cups Anchovy Stock (page 10)

2 garlic cloves, minced

1 potato

1 Korean zucchini

1 green onion, cut on the diagonal into about 2-inch pieces

1 egg, scrambled

Salt

1 Combine the flour and $1/2$ cup water, adding the water about $1/4$ cup at a time, until the flour clumps together in one piece. Knead into a dough. Form into a ball and wrap in plastic or place in a plastic bag and refrigerate for about an hour.

2 In the meantime, bring the anchovy stock to a boil and add garlic. Cut the potato and Korean zucchini into flat cubes about $1/2$ inch thick. Add the potato cubes to the stock and let cook for about 2 to 3 minutes. Add Korean zucchini and cook another 2 to 3 minutes. Rip the dough into flat, bite-sized pieces by pulling and stretching the dough and add to the boiling stock.

3 When the dough begins to float and becomes slightly translucent on the edges (about 5 to 7 minutes, depending on the thickness of your dough pieces), add the green onions and the egg. Remove from heat and add salt as needed (don't make it too salty because you will be adding seasoned soy sauce when you eat it).

Serve immediately so that the broth is still steaming and the dough flakes don't become waterlogged. Serve with *kimchi* and Seasoned Soy Sauce (*Yangnyum Ganjang*, page 4).

NOTE When Sunny makes me this dish, she likes to mince a small green pepper or jalapeño to the seasoned soy sauce. The extra kick is a nice touch to the dish.

Dumpling Friends

Some friendships are like deep frying—hot and quick, good while it lasted, but probably not healthy for you. Others are like good winter soup—taking a long time to get just right, but hearty and fulfilling. One of my oldest friendships is like eating dumplings.

My friend Yunju and I met in Korea when we were just about four years old. Our older sisters were attending the same kindergarten and it was easy for us to become friends. When my family moved to the states, I remember exchanging gifts with her as we said good-bye. To an adult, they may have seemed like mere trinkets, but they were the treasures of six-year-olds—a small coin purse, in the shape of an animal's face and a little notebook, the kind you can stow away in your back pocket after you've written down some little secret.

Growing up, we sent each other letters. My Korean worsened as her English improved over the years. Since then, I've learned more Korean and she's learned more English, so that we both switch back and forth in our rapid

Eating lunch with Yunju

conversations, when we have the opportunity to get together. When we had some extra cash during our teenage years, we'd send each other gifts like New Wave T-shirts and pictures of rock stars, whose posters we're now too embarrassed to admit we liked.

The first time we saw each other again, more than ten years had passed. Still, we stayed up all night, sharing our adolescent trials and tribulations, giggling over current crushes and future fantasies. It was almost as if we had just seen each other yesterday. But we knew our maturing lives were different. We looked to each other's experiences and reflected on where our roads diverged. Yunju wondered if her life would have been like mine had her family immigrated to the states. I wondered if I

SINGING FOR OUR CLASS ON YUNJU'S BIRTHDAY

MY LAST SUMMER AT THE BEACH WITH YUNJU
BEFORE MOVING TO THE STATES

would have the same values as hers had my family stayed in Korea. Yet, even as we lived our separate lives on distant continents, we've managed to stay friends.

Last year, I had the fortune of having her not only in the same country, but also in the same city as me. We had the luxury of having a normal friendship for a while, with leisurely walks, long talks in cozy cafes, and invitations to each other's homes for dinner. Sometimes, I would make her favorite meal, dumplings. She, in return, would make me dumplings. The last time we saw each other, we shared a simple meal of dumplings, too.

She's trying to come live in America now. INS (Immigration and Naturalization Services) willing, we'll be able to share the same city again. This time, I'll be able to make her dumplings to her heart's content and we will talk well into the dark hours.

Fresh Dumpling Skins

Mandu Pi

Nothing beats the flavor and texture of homemade dumpling skins. Although it is more labor intensive, dumpling skins aren't difficult to make. If you must buy them, look for them in the refrigerated sections of most supermarkets. Round skins are preferred for Korean dumplings, but square ones will do if you have no other options. MAKES 50 SKINS

3 cups flour

$1/4$ teaspoon salt

Water

1   Sift together the flour and salt. Pour $2/3$ cup water in a bowl and add the flour a little bit at a time, mixing with each addition. Continue mixing until the dough is completely mixed and stiff. Wrap in a damp cloth and let sit for about 30 minutes.

2   To roll out the dough, prepare a lightly floured surface. Pinch off small pieces and make them into round balls to roll out flat with a rolling pin. Alternately, roll the dough into small, sausage-shaped rolls and slice them before rolling them into flat circles. Each circle should be about $2^1/2$ to 3 inches in diameter.

3   Use to making dumplings. If you are preparing the skins in advance, store by stacking each circle with a little bit of flour between each skin, wrapping the whole stack tightly with plastic wrap. Refrigerate for no more than a week. You may also freeze the skins, but be sure to defrost in the fridge overnight before using.

Fried Meat Dumplings

Twigim Mandu

Mandu make a nice light lunch, appetizer, or snack. Although you can really fill them with anything you want, the traditional way is to make them with pork. To make a vegetarian version, substitute the meat with tofu. The secret to getting nice, crisp dumplings is to make sure all the ingredients are as dry as possible, so that the filling doesn't make the skins soggy and cause extra splattering when frying. Still, to be safe, use a frying screen (they are screens stretched over metal circles with handles that fit over frying pans). If you can talk a friend, sibling, or spouse into helping, it's much more fun and the work goes faster. MAKES 50 DUMPLINGS

1 cup mung bean or green bean sprouts

$^1/_2$ pound ground beef or pork

$^1/_2$ medium onion, chopped

2 green onions, chopped very fine

3 garlic cloves, minced

1 tablespoon ginger, minced

1 egg

1 teaspoon sesame oil

$^1/_2$ teaspoon salt

$^1/_2$ teaspoon white pepper

50 homemade or store-bought dumpling wrappers (*see* page 129)

Vegetable oil for frying

1   Blanch the mung bean sprouts by dunking them briefly in boiling water. Rinse in cold water to stop cooking. Squeeze out as much water as you can from the sprouts, chop them, and put them in a bowl.

2   In the same bowl, add the remaining ingredients (except the dumpling wrappers) and combine until mixed.

3   Before you begin filling the dumplings, prepare a large tray or other flat surface for laying down the dumplings as you make them. Also, pour some cold water in a small bowl for dipping.

4   Place a wrapper on the palm of your hand. Then, spoon enough filling into the middle of the circle to leave about $^1/_2$ inch of empty skin (about a tablespoon). Dip your finger into the cold water and wet $^1/_2$ of the edge of the dumpling skin. Fold the skin in half, sealing the filling inside, making a semicircle.

5   To make a fancy presentation, make small ridges on one side of the edge as you seal, using your finger and thumb, making about 5 or 7 ridges on each dumpling. The dumpling will curve naturally as you do this. This takes some practice, so don't worry if the first one doesn't come out stellar.

6   Repeat with each wrapper until all the filling or wrappers are used.

7   In a frying pan, pour enough vegetable oil to cover the bottom surface of the pan and heat over medium heat. Carefully, place the dumplings in the pan, filling the pan, but not crowding them so much that they touch and stick to each other. Fry until golden brown and crispy on one side. Flip them (long wooden chopsticks work best), cooking all sides until they are golden and crispy all over. Continue until all the dumplings are cooked, adding more oil as needed.

Serve warm with Vinegar Soy Sauce (*Cho Ganjang*, page 4) for dipping.

N O T E If you have any leftover filling, you can form them into tiny meat patties, and fry them up. If you have any leftover skins, cut them in half and deep fry them with the dumplings. Each time you make *mandu*, you will get better at portioning each dumpling as well as making them look beautiful. Instead of frying them, for a healthier dish, you can steam them. See the instructions on the following page for how to cook dumplings in different ways.

There are many ways to cook dumplings. Here are the most common ones:

- To fry the dumplings, pour enough vegetable oil to cover the bottom surface of the pan and heat over medium heat. Carefully, place the dumplings in the pan, filling the pan, but not crowding them so much that they touch and stick to each other. Fry until golden brown and crispy on one side. Flip them (long wooden chopsticks work best), cooking all sides until they are golden and crispy all over. Continue until all the dumplings are cooked, adding more oil as needed. Serve warm with Vinegar Soy Sauce (*Cho Ganjang*, page 4) for dipping.

  Alternatively, while frying the dumplings, when one side has cooked, turn over the dumplings. Then carefully add about $1/2$ cup water and cover the pan with a lid. Be careful as the water will cause the oil to splatter. Lower the heat and steam for about 3 minutes. Repeat until all the dumplings are cooked. Serve as usual.

- To steam them, get a large broad steamer (preferably one with several layers). Lay a wet cloth on the bottom of the steamer to prevent the dumplings from sticking. Add a single layer of dumplings, making sure that they aren't touching each other. Steam over boiling water for about 10 to 15 minutes, until the filling is cooked through and the skins become slightly translucent. Serve immediately with a side of Vinegar Soy Sauce (*Cho Ganjang*, page 4).

- To boil the dumplings, bring a large pot of water to a boil. Add the dumplings one at a time. Do not fill the pot or the dumplings will stick together. Let the dumplings cook for about 8 to 10 minutes, or until the filling is cooked through and the skins become slightly translucent. Fish them out with either a slotted spoon or long wooden chopsticks. Serve immediately with a side of Vinegar Soy Sauce (*Cho Ganjang*, page 4).

- To make dumpling soup, follow the recipe on page 135.

T I P To freeze dumplings before you cook them, lay them out on a tray or baking sheet and put the entire tray into the freezer for about 20 to 30 minutes. Once the dumplings have hardened somewhat, you can put them in a large plastic bag or container with a tight lid. This way you can freeze them for later use without having them stick together.

Kimchi Dumplings

Kimchi Mandu

Any sort of dumplings can be steamed, fried, boiled, or cooked in soup. Although dumplings are always best fresh, this recipe can be made in advance and frozen a few days before eating. There's no need to defrost the dumplings before eating, because defrosting them would just make the skins soft and unmanageable. Be careful when frying frozen dumplings, because ice crystals can cause hot oil to splatter. You can substitute any ground meat for the tofu. MAKES 50 DUMPLINGS

2 (10-ounce) packages of firm tofu

1 cup *kimchi*

2 green onions, finely chopped

2 garlic cloves, minced

1 egg

1 teaspoon sesame oil

1 teaspoon salt

$^1/_2$ teaspoon black pepper

50 homemade or store-bought dumpling wrappers (*see* page 129)

1   Wrap each brick of tofu in cheesecloth or a flour towel. Squeeze out as much water as you can. If there are big chunks of tofu, crumble into smaller pieces and add to a large bowl.

2   Chop the *kimchi* and place in a fine sieve or cheesecloth, pressing out the *kimchi* juice. Save the liquid for another use (such as to add liquid in other recipes such as Kimchi Hot Pot, page 112, or Spicy Dough Flake Soup, page 125). Add the *kimchi* to the tofu. Add the remaining ingredients (except the wrappers) and combine until mixed.

3   Before you begin filling the dumplings, prepare a large tray or other flat surface for laying down the dumplings as you make them. Also, pour some cold water in a small bowl for dipping.

4   Place a wrapper on the palm of your hand. Then spoon enough filling into the middle of the circle to leave about $^1/_2$ an inch of empty skin (about a tablespoon). Dip your finger into the cold water and wet $^1/_2$ the edge of the dumpling skin. Fold the skin in half, sealing the filling inside, making a semicircle.

5   To make a fancy presentation, make small ridges on one side of the edge as you seal, using your finger and thumb, making 5 or 7 ridges on each dumpling. The dumpling will curve naturally as you do this. This takes practice, so don't worry if the first one isn't stellar.

6   Repeat with each wrapper until all the filling or wrappers are used. Cook by following one of the methods on page 132.

Vegetarian Dumplings

Yachae Mandu

Here's a vegetarian version of the old standard. Although my *Kimchi Mandu* recipe on the preceding page doesn't contain meat, *kimchi* usually has some sort of fish or fish sauce. This way we can enjoy the tasty treats with our vegetarian friends. MAKES 50 DUMPLINGS

2 (10-ounce) packages firm tofu

1 medium onion, finely chopped

1 bunch of Korean leeks (*baechu*), chopped

2 green onions, finely chopped

2 garlic cloves, minced

2 teaspoons sesame oil

2 teaspoons salt

1 teaspoon black pepper

50 homemade or store-bought dumpling wrappers (*see* page 129)

1   Wrap each brick of tofu in cheesecloth or a flour towel. Squeeze out as much water as you can. If there are big chunks of tofu, crumble into smaller pieces and add to a large mixing bowl.

2   Add the remaining ingredients (except the wrappers) and combine until mixed.

3   Before you begin filling the dumplings, prepare a large tray or other flat surface for laying down the dumplings as you make them. Also, pour some cold water in a small bowl for dipping.

4   Place a wrapper on the palm of your hand. Then spoon enough filling into the middle of the circle to leave about $1/2$ an inch of empty skin (about a tablespoon). Dip your finger into the cold water and wet $1/2$ the edge of the dumpling skin. Fold the skin in half, sealing the filling inside, making a semicircle.

5   To make a fancy presentation, make small ridges on one side of the edge as you seal, using your finger and thumb, making about 5 or 7 ridges on each dumpling. The dumpling will curve naturally as you do this. This takes some practice, so don't worry if the first one doesn't come out stellar.

6   Repeat with each wrapper until all the filling or wrappers are used. Cook however you like, by following one of the methods on page 132.

Dumpling Soup

Dumplings with any sort of filling can be made into soup, although the meat-filled dumplings are most commonly used. Although any shape can be used, dumplings made for soup can be made into half circles, with the ends attached to each other—sort of like the dumpling is hugging itself. They look more fun this way, but it's totally not necessary for taste. You can also add dumplings to Rice Cake Soup (*Dduk Gook*, page 108). MAKES 5 TO 6 SERVINGS

12 cups Beef Stock (page 11)

25 to 30 dumplings

2 eggs, scrambled

2 to 3 green onions,
thinly sliced or julienned

Salt

Black pepper

2 or 3 sheets of toasted laver
for garnish (optional)

Bring beef stock to a boil. Add the dumplings and boil until dumplings are cooked through. You'll know the dumplings are cooked when their skins become translucent and they float to the top. Add the eggs and green onions. Add salt and pepper as needed.

Serve immediately with some crushed or shredded laver on top, if you wish.

Seafood

YOUNG PEOPLE DON'T KNOW FISH
I used to think that my mom's godmother was the shortest woman in the world. Everyone just calls her "Godmother," which may be a little odd, but a definite step up from our childhood name for her: "Third-Floor Grandma." In the Korean language, the word "grandmother" (*halmuhni*) is used to describe all old women across the board, regardless of any direct bloodlines involved. I'm not sure how tall Godmother is exactly, but definitely less than five feet. But when we met her friend at Seoul's Kimpo Airport, I realized that there were at least two women vying for the "Shortest Woman in the World" award. Competition was fierce, depending on how high their hairstyles displayed at any given moment. • That weekend, though, I learned that neither height nor age had anything to do with stamina. As we followed them on our vacation to Jeju Island, my then-boyfriend (now-husband), Tim, and I quickly learned that short little grandmothers were a force to be reckoned with. By the trip's end, we were to

declare that grandmas ruled the world. • Jeju Do, what Seoul travel agents call the "Hawaii of Korea," is located off the south-western coast of the peninsula. A popular destination

TIM IN JEJU DO
WITH DIVER STATUES

for honeymooners, the island does have many similarities to Hawaii. A volcanic island, Jeju's climate is very similar to Hawaii's tropics—surrounded by warm, turquoise waters in the summer and assaulted by Pacific storms and high winds in the winter. The thriving tourist industry hides well the island's turbulent past. Throughout its history, the island has been a horse-breeding ground for Mongolians, a penal colony, and a home to banished political scholars. Now, however, Korea's largest island was enjoying the economic benefits of being Korea's prime vacation destination with over four million visitors a year.

We stayed for free in some luxury hotel owned by the Korean military. Godmother's friend's son was some official of significant enough ranking that relatives got to enjoy certain perks. The first night we arrived, the old ladies unwrapped some dried anchovies (*myulchi*), chili paste (*gochujang*), and some Korean rice wine (*soju*) from out of nowhere and proceeded to teach us crazy card tricks. When they saw how Tim was enjoying the fish and chili paste with such relish, they declared him an honorary Korean between rounds of *soju* and outbreaks of sixties Korean tunes.

There was no stopping these grandmas. Even after drinking all night, they were up the next morning before the crack of dawn, dragging our lazy butts out of bed to climb some extinct volcano or other. There was no arguing with them, as they were already decked out in their visors and hiking gear. We somehow managed to get our sleep-deprived selves up to speed with the old ladies. Despite all our grumbling, we eventually arrived at the edge of the crater. Godmother and her friend blended right in with the rest of the visor-wearing tourists making their way to the top of the volcano, but people gave us more than a passing glance as Tim stood out like a sore thumb amongst vacationing Koreans. Eventually, though, the spectacular view stole the spotlight from my curly-haired American boyfriend.

By the time we made our way down, a bus to who-knows-where (young people weren't supposed to question the authority of the elders) was waiting at the foot of the mountain. We climbed aboard obediently and took our seats behind their seats. As we tumbled along rough roads, a hand would appear in front of us holding an orange orb as the grandmas produced tangerine after tangerine from their purses, until we feared that orange was leaking from our ears. If you've ever wondered why little old Korean women carry such large purses, it's because they weren't evolutionarily graced with the voluminous cheek pouches of our chipmunk cousins. Their enormous purses are concealing a bag of local tangerines, puffed rice, toasted chestnuts, or some other treat for those inevitably long Korean bus rides.

In the meantime, our bus wound around rural island roads. We passed stone walls stacked around traditional houses and passed forests lush with tropical green. One last bend, then we were greeted by the foamy white spray of a wonderfully rocky coast.

As we were stepping across the jagged rocks, we noticed women, some in their late fifties, dressed in black rubber suits passing us by. Some were carrying nets and spears, while others had hoes and baskets slung over their shoulders. I watched these middle-aged women dive into the rough seas and resurface quite a time later with shellfish in their baskets.

Did I mention that they weren't using any sort of breathing apparatus? Somehow, they were able to hold their breath for up to four minutes without passing out. We also noticed the complete lack of male divers in the area.

The women of Jeju, who have been diving since the sixteenth century, were known as the Haenyo divers. For some reason, the women were better skilled than their husbands and sons. Their amazing skills were passed down through the maternal lineage. Mothers taught their daughters and daughters-in-law how to hold their breath for a long time and dive to the bottom of the ocean floor for mussels, abalone, and other shellfish. Unlike the women on the mainland, the women of Jeju Do were the breadwinners in the family, while the men farmed, or now worked in the thriving tourist industry. Sadly, this tradition is in danger of being extinct as more and more women divers give up their trade as pollution and illegal fishing cause havoc on their livelihood.

Farther down the coast, we arrived at a restaurant, floating right on the water. As we approached, a man was pulling a net full of shimmering fish, flipping about and gasping for water in the glistening sunlight.

"Just in time for lunch," one of us said, as our mouths began to salivate and we climbed into the tiny boat-cum-restaurant.

The first course was raw fish (*hwae*). Never before or since have I had fish so sweetly fresh. Sliced as soon as it had been taken out of the ocean, we dipped the fish in the seasoned chili paste and wrapped it in lettuce leaves, stuffing the whole mess into our eagerly waiting mouths. I didn't even know what kind of fish it was and didn't bother to ask. We were too busy gobbling up every morsel to waste any energy with idle talk.

By the time the second course arrived, our stomachs were sated enough for some conversation. The grandmas were worried that Tim might be taken aback by seeing the whole fish, eyes and all. But they didn't know about our long history with whole fish.

Many years ago, we were celebrating a friend's birthday at a Chinese seafood restaurant. When they brought the live fish out for approval, I was the only one at the table who could discern its desirability. Since I was sitting on the far end of the table, the waiter tipped the bucket a little too far and the feisty creature nearly landed on the birthday boy's lap. Once the rock cod arrived at the table, some of our friends were a little disconcerted by seeing its ugly mouth and face.

I was relating to Tim about how my siblings and I used to fight over the eyeballs when we were kids, not because they were such culinary delights, but because anytime there were only two of one thing, one of us missed out. A fish's eye isn't much of a delicacy. In fact, it hardly has any flavor at all. It's a little gooey on the outside with a chalky but chewy center.

I turned to Tim and said, "Do you want to watch an entire table full of adults turn into a bunch of squeamish little children?"

With his enthusiastic response, I waited for a pause in the conversational flow and reached over for the eyeball with my chopsticks. A sudden wave of silence washed over the table as all eyes were watching me as I chewed. Then I reached into my mouth and pulled something out and placed in on my plate.

"Wh-what was that?" one particularly worried diner asked.

I continued chewing, pausing for effect and swallowed before answering in the most nonchalant tone I could muster, "The eyelid."

Indeed, the entire table was transformed instantly into five-year-olds. Tim and I laughed between ourselves amidst cries of "Eeew!" and "Gross!" Of course, fish don't have eyelids. It was just some sort of gill or fin that I pulled out for added effect.

After an experience like that, the old ladies didn't have to worry about Tim and his delicate sensibilities. Our gracious hosts had taken what was left of the filleted fish, salted them lightly, and grilled the rest of the meat over an open flame. The whole fish was so simple in presentation, yet so delicious that we picked the bones clean of every bit of meat.

"You young people don't know fish," Godmother chided us, as we were preparing to rest our chopsticks.

Puzzled, Tim and I looked over at each other. We had heard the same thing just a few days earlier when we went to visit my great[3] aunt. Four generations ahead of me, she was the elder on my mom's side of the family. I wanted to pay respect to her before I left the country. Although her advanced cataracts had left her half blind in both eyes, she insisted on making us lunch that day. Another unstoppable old lady, she had a huge feast already waiting for us when we arrived at her house.

Her eighty-some-odd-year-old husband was also thrilled to have visitors. He pulled out his best bottle of expensive liquor, still unopened in its gift-wrapped state, and got two shot glasses for him and Tim. Tim, who doesn't drink at all, was trying to refuse, but I had to surreptitiously let him know that this was an excuse for my great³-uncle to drink. Tim thought that if he downed the shot as quickly as possible, he could get it over with, but it just meant that his glass would get refilled faster.

After a couple of drinks, my great³-uncle launched into an elaborate story about the olden days and his first trip on a plane. After a few sentences of my translating the story, I realized that this was the same story he told me the last time I saw him, some six or seven years ago. I wondered if he had been telling the same story all this time, or if he saved it for special occasions.

The meal, of course, was fantastic. As we were nearing completion, my great³-aunt brought out two little salted fish and laid them on the already full table. Her husband immediately began chiding her for bringing us the salty fish we supposedly didn't want. On the contrary, we devoured those fish, not just to make my great³-aunt feel better, but just because we enjoyed salty fish so much.

Ah, but her husband looked over at their bony remains, then over to us and said, "You young people don't know fish." And then he poured himself another shot and forgot to tell us why, launching back into the story of his first plane trip.

So, finally here on Jeju Do we were going to solve the mystery of the fish.

"You're leaving the best part," Godmother said as she reached for what I'd call the "cheek meat" of the fish, in that area between the fish's eyes and the gills. There is just a morsel of meat right there where the bone dips in.

She was right. There's something about the way that part of the fish tastes. It really was the best part. Maybe it was psychological, because it was like you had found a little secret out about the fish. Whatever it was, it was pretty damn tasty.

Just as we were savoring the delicious mystery, the third course arrived—a bubbling hot pot of the remainders of the fish (*mae-un tahng*), full of vegetables and creatures of the sea. The hot pot was a great topper to any meal, full of spicy chili paste, sliced Korean peppers, and fish meat flavorfully balanced by the coolness of the daikon cubes. I loved the way not even the bones of the fish were wasted to create such a medley of a meal. It was definitely the highlight of our Jeju Do trip.

Years later, we were out with my family celebrating at a Korean seafood restaurant. As we were eating the grilled fish (*saeng-sun gui*), I reached over for the cheek meat and put it on my dad's rice.

"Don't forget the best part," I said to him, as he looked up at me with a mixture of pride and surprise. I knew he was thinking: "How does she know about the best part of the fish?" Although his look betrayed his thoughts, his mouth slowly enjoyed the fish in silence.

Then, he reached over and placed an eyeball on my plate. "Remember how you kids used to fight over these?" he said with a slightly amused but loving paternal tone.

I didn't say anything either, but just put the eye in my mouth and chewed it quietly with a smile he would never quite understand.

WITH GREAT[3]-AUNT, GREAT[3]-UNCLE, AND TIM

Raw Fish

When buying raw fish for *hwae*, be sure you get the fish the day you plan to eat it. No matter what type of fish, ask for sushi grade and ask your fishmonger to slice it for you. *Hwae* is an excellent first course for an elaborate meal or special occasion. MAKES ABOUT 6 TO 10 SERVINGS, DEPENDING ON WHAT ELSE IS BEING SERVED WITH THE MEAL

2 pounds of assorted raw fish (tuna, salmon, yellowtail, halibut, etc.)

1 head of red curly leaf lettuce

10 garlic cloves, sliced (optional)

Vinegar Chili Paste (*Cho Gochujang*, page 9)

1   If you are slicing the fish at home, be sure to use a very sharp knife and cut fish into bite-size pieces. Reserve the rest of the fish to be used for stock or in a hot pot (*see* recipe on page 114).

2   Thoroughly wash and dry lettuce leaves. On a serving platter, lay the lettuce leaves flat as a garnish. Save the rest of the leaves for eating. Then place the raw fish in rows, arranging by color. (You may also use long strands of shredded daikon in place of the lettuce, although I find that lettuce is much less time consuming.)

Serve the fish with optional garlic slices with individual servings of Vinegar Chile Paste on the side. To eat, place a leaf of lettuce in your hand, then a slice of fish, a piece of garlic (if you like) and some chili paste. Wrap the whole thing and stuff it in your mouth.

N O T E   Rice and soup or a hot pot (*jjigae* or *tahng*) are generally served with the next course following the raw fish.

Seasoned Hairtail Fish

Galchi Jolim

Jolim can be made from any number of fish, but hairtail prepared this way is very popular. Sometimes called cutlass, hairtail fish are very thin and long, silvery with no scales. Fresh or frozen, they can be found in most Asian markets.

MAKES 6 TO 8 SERVINGS, DEPENDING ON HOW MUCH OTHER *BANCHAN* IS PREPARED

1 hairtail fish

1 tablespoon vegetable oil

3 tablespoons soy sauce

1 tablespoon water or rice wine

2 garlic cloves, minced

1 green onion, thinly chopped

1 tablespoon chili powder

1   Clean the fish and cut it into pieces about 4 inches long. Discard the head and tail. Pat dry with paper towels.

2   In a large saucepan, heat the vegetable oil. Add the fish pieces and cook through on both sides (about 5 to 7 minutes on each side).

3   Combine the soy sauce, water or wine, garlic, green onion, and chili powder. Lower the heat and spoon the sauce over the fish. Cover and cook for another 8 or 10 minutes, until the fish is infused with the seasoning.

Serve immediately with rice, *kimchi,* and *banchan.*

Stone-Faced Fisherman

In some ways, I was the son my father always wanted. It's true—even though he does actually have a son. It's even more true that my brother looks just like a younger version of my dad—a tall, dark-skinned man whose body is topped by a prematuring bald head. They have the same love of red meat, the same intolerance for bad food, and the same love of drinking with good friends. Genetics are a strange and fascinating thing.

Still, my brother hated doing most things my dad loved. I was the one in the backyard planting vegetables and mowing the lawn, while my little brother was indoors playing video games or glued to the television set. I was the one who fol-

MY DAD FISHING

lowed my dad to the driving range, as he taught me the basics of golf and tried to get me to take up the sport. And as much as he loves to golf now, he loved to fish even more back then.

He would want to take all of his children along for early morning adventures to waters, either salty or fresh. There was no hope for my sister who inherited my mom's tendency toward late-night activity and corresponding early morning inactivity. My brother inherited the same sequence of DNA, or rather, lacked what my dad called the "early morning" gene. I, on the other hand, would find myself taking in the crisp morning air while the still gray sky betrayed the actual wee hours.

Don't get me wrong. I'm not completely a morning person. I like to lounge around under soft blankets, hitting the snooze button as much as the next gal does. Yet, there's something so enervating and meditative about experiencing a city waking up—it's as if I'm sharing some nonverbal, close-friend secret with the universe.

Whenever my dad decided to go on some impromptu fishing trip, I was the only one of his offspring that would succumb to his early morning gruffness.

My dad's the type of guy who can catch a fish in a tiny trickle of water. He has been off on a fishing expedition with several of his friends and returned the only one with dinner in his hands. He didn't catch merely one or two fish, but half a dozen, while his embarrassed companions would make excuses while sheepishly scratching their heads in wonder. He knew which bait worked on which fish, which lakes had the best fish, and all those other fisherman tricks that are still as mysterious to me as the reasons why certain men spit on sidewalks and the intricacies of quantum physics.

So, one drizzly morning my dad got me out of bed. I was grumpy and disapproving, but not surprised that my normally stone-statue of a dad was visibly excited to go catch some special fish, which came closer to the surface during rainy weather. The prospect of sitting in the rain waiting impatiently for improbable fish was not a promising idea. Sitting in that rain next to one of the least conversational men I knew wasn't an exciting thought, either. I tried to convince my siblings that we were going to have a raucous good time, but one look at the dripping windows was enough for both my siblings to burrow deeper under the covers. I grabbed my jacket, a book, and transistor radio as I followed my dad into the misty dawn.

My first task was digging around in the moist earth for worms, trying to wiggle free from my grasp in their blind vanity. Wrapping my raincoat tighter around me, I cursed the raining sky, shaking my earth-stained fist at the gods above, playing such a cruel joke on me as to give me a father who couldn't buy normal bait from the tackle store like other fathers. Next, I cursed my two siblings, glaring at the quiet house as they slept, snug in their dry beds. As I gave the evil eye toward our house again, the only light was emanating from the kitchen window where my dad was preparing some magic bait, which looked all the world to me like round packs of dirt rolled in perilla seeds.

At the fishing spot, we were greeted by the quacking of invisible ducks and the pleasant rhythms of rain falling on lake water. As my dad walked around wordlessly, looking for the perfect place to fish patiently, I could tell that this was going to be another one of those quality quiet times spent between daughter and father. As I was taking it out on a muddy rock, my dad found a not-so-dry spot on the south side of the lake. I helped him put up a makeshift shelter with some poles and tarp, then watched as he began preparing our fish-tricking poles with bait.

Once we were cozy underneath the tarp, I scanned the radio dial, listening between static lines, trying to catch the scores of the prior night's ballgames.

If I could get those hours back, I would've spent them in wiser pursuits. I would have actually talked to my dad, pressing him with questions about his thirteen brothers, about the family farm, what happened during the war. I may have known a little more about the bald man in the faded, sepia-tinted photograph, the grandfather who died long before I saw light in this world, the grandfather whose nose and lips I inherited. I may have gotten to know more about the bald man, who sat silently next to me for so many hours during countless fishing trips—the ever elusive conversationalist, my father.

Instead, I buried my young girl nose in my paperback novels, voraciously devouring someone else's made-up stories, while my dad sat looking out over the waters in quiet meditation. With my father, the spaces between words were long and full. Sometimes, we would go for hours without so much as a sound between us.

Even still, I managed to absorb things from my dad. I learned that patience is a wonderful trait to have in fishing, in conversation, and in other manners of life. He taught me that it's good to go after what you want in life and even better to catch an opportunity when it presented itself with minimal effort.

When the tip of the fishing pole dipped slightly, I felt the pole in my hand lurch a little. I jerked it back, feeling a tugging resistance underwater. I jumped on my feet and let the line out, giving the fish a false sense of freedom before reeling the sucker in. It was a pretty large fish. Even as I struggled to pull it up out of the water, my dad didn't infringe on my independence. He stood by with a sense of pride, which I would see in his eyes only a handful of times again in later years.

Between the two of us, we caught over a dozen fish that day. Our ice chest was full of our bounty when we pulled up in our driveway. My dad pulled out the largest fish and said that I caught that one first thing this morning. When I saw the looks of envy on my siblings' faces, I didn't regret a minute of missing early morning sleep. I knew that my dad was going to have three children accompany him on his next fishing outing.

Inside, my dad and I gutted and scaled the fish, while my mom prepared rice and the rest of the *banchan* for dinner. That night, we enjoyed the gifts of the freshly caught fish, savoring the moist meat unsurpassable by its store-bought cousins. As I ate, everything tasted a little bit more delicious and a whole lot sweeter, knowing that I had contributed to the bountiful table.

Grilled Mackerel

Ggongchi Gui

Although I'm using mackerel for this recipe, you can substitute any number of fish. A very basic way to prepare fish, it is a delicious dish. If you don't want to bother with a grill, cook the fish in a broiler, watching carefully to keep it from burning. MAKES 2 TO 4 SERVINGS, DEPENDING ON HOW MUCH OTHER *BANCHAN* ARE BEING SERVED

1 mackerel

About 1 tablespoon salt

2 lemon wedges

Cucumber slices or parsley (as optional garnish)

1   Scale and clean the mackerel, removing the entrails. Depending on the size of the fish, put 6 or so slits on both sides of the fish. If you prefer not to present the whole fish, you may cut the fish into 4 or so pieces each, leaving out the heads and tails.

2   Sprinkle the fish with salt and let stand for about 15 minutes.

3   Meanwhile, heat and oil a grill. Cook the fish on the grill until both sides are cooked.

Serve on a long plate with lemon wedges and optional garnish (cucumber slices or parsley), with white rice, various other *banchan,* and *kimchi.*

VARIATION   You can also serve mackerel (or any other fish) grilled, topped with Seasoned Soy Sauce (*Yangnyum Ganjang,* page 4).

Grilled Eel

Jang-uh Gui

A favorite in Korean barbecue joints, this slightly sweet flavor is a wonderful seasoning for eel. Choose fresh, live eels if possible. Otherwise, use frozen, thawed eels. You can make a spicy version by adding a couple of tablespoons of chili paste to the seasoning. As with all grilling recipes, you may use the broiler to cook the eel. But watch carefully since eels cook very quickly.

MAKES 6 TO 8 SERVINGS, DEPENDING ON THE OTHER *BANCHAN* AND *KIMCHI* SERVED

5 tablespoons soy sauce

2 green onions, chopped

2 garlic cloves, minced

1 tablespoon ginger, minced

1 1/2 tablespoons sugar

1 tablespoon rice wine

1 tablespoon sesame oil

Black pepper

2 eels

1   In a small stockpot, add the soy sauce, green onions, garlic, ginger, sugar, rice wine, sesame oil, and black pepper and bring to a boil. Reduce the heat to medium and, stirring occasionally, simmer for about 10 minutes, until the sauce thickens slightly.

2   Meanwhile clean the eels, removing the heads and entrails. Halve the eels lengthwise, removing the bones. Then cut the halves into about 2- to 3-inch widths.

3   Grill the eel pieces on an oiled grill. Baste the eels with the seasoning and grill again. The fish should be white all the way through and slightly charred and browned on the edges.

Serve with several leaves of red curly leaf lettuce or just with rice, *banchan*, and *kimchi*.

Playing with Your Food

Sometimes, I feel like my life is a series of cartoons. I inherited my mom's propensity to attract crazy people, her magnetism for absurd situations, and the same ability to laugh when we both find ourselves in the middle of any of the above. When just the two of us are hanging out, we're just like characters in an animated film.

The day we went to the seafood market was no exception. As a general rule, I try to avoid getting in the car when my mom is driving, but this was a special occasion. Fresh crabs were in season and they were on sale. A herd of wild horses or my mom's driving couldn't keep me away.

FISH IN TANKS AT THE MARKET

Driving with my mom is like getting in a car with Mr. Magoo, that lovingly bald and myopic cartoon man who wanders through perilous situations oblivious to near-death dangers every few seconds. I envied my mom's natural ability to be completely unaware of falling debris, swerving trucks, and burning cars, mindlessly driving down the road while chatting away happily about something or other. It was all I could do to keep from having a heart attack every minute, while I wished for the comfort that naiveté might bring.

As usual, though, we arrived at the seafood market unscathed. As we were getting out of the car,

SEAFOOD AT THE MARKET

my mom gave me a brief sidelong glance, muttering quietly to herself why I would prefer that bristly hairstyle that made my hair stand up so funny. Some things are best not mentioned.

The sight of bubbling tanks and large metal buckets calmed my nerves. We made our way amongst the sparkling shellfish, glistening mussels, and rows and rows of every type of fish imaginable. The mountain of fresh crabs was a sight to behold. Distracted by a lobster fight in a nearby tank, I felt a squirt of water hit my exposed calves from behind. When I turned around expecting to find a small child pointing a water pistol, I was greeted by the teasing bubbling of aquariums with no child in sight. I turned my attention back to the lobsters when it happened again. This time, I turned around and found a huge pile of clams sitting innocently in their water. When I peered down to get a closer look, I got a face full of clam spit. I felt like Yosemite Sam, feeling all red faced with clenched fists as I wiped the water from my face. I thought better of stomping around with my two pistols shooting, ricocheting off the fish tanks and decided to direct my attention to the task at hand—the crabs.

Meanwhile, my mom had already selected enough live crabs to fill a case and some big guy was nailing the top of the case shut to keep the clanking crustaceans from escaping their inevitable fate. With his Popeye arms and dopey expression, he

A NICE ARRAY OF SEAFOOD AT THE MARKET

could have been a dead ringer for Baby Huey, the overgrown Harvey Comics duck in large diapers. Every once in awhile, a claw would break free and try to pinch anyone who dared to come too close. I pointed and laughed at them, getting my revenge on sea creatures everywhere, my ego not fully recovered from the spit-happy clams.

Back home, it was already a full house. News of fresh crabs had leaked somehow and my sister was already waiting with her son and husband. My brother had invited several of his friends and my dad was on the horn getting more people to come.

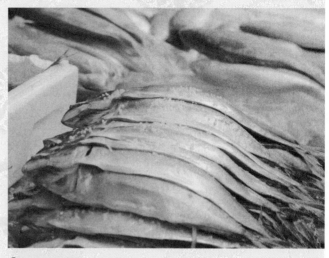

SALTED FISH AT THE MARKET

I put on a pot of water to boil immediately as we prepared to steam the whole lot for a fabulous feast. While we were chatting around the dining table, waiting for the water, we heard a scream from the kitchen, followed by the familiar clickety-clack of critter claws on kitchen tiles. What we saw still makes me laugh at the memory. My little nephew, about two or three at the time, was being chased by a frisky crab, which somehow managed to escape the boiling pot.

My mom is generally afraid of all animals, with an especially strong distrust of birds and snakes. She doesn't even like stuffed animals. But when it comes to crabs, she turns into a caricature of a French chef (that is, if you replace the French accent with a Korean one), wielding her cleaver and chasing sea creatures around the kitchen. So grabbing this runaway crab was an easy task for her, much to my nephew's relief. Whenever we have crab, my nephew pictures my mom wrangling them in the kitchen and I picture the terrified look on his face as the creature chased him sideways around the kitchen floor.

Spicy Raw Crabs

Gyae Jang

Be sure to get really fresh, live crabs for this dish. Blue crabs work best. Use care when handling live crabs because those pinchers really do pinch. As a young girl, I used to love taking the back shell off the crab, filling it with fresh, hot rice and mixing it in the raw crab and seasoning. Somehow, eating out of a crab shell tasted much better than from a bowl or plate. Although I washed the shell out, my mom eventually made me throw the shell away. MAKES 6 TO 12 SERVINGS, DEPENDING ON HOW MUCH OTHER *BANCHAN* ARE SERVED WITH THE MEAL

---

3 crabs

5 tablespoons soy sauce

2 tablespoons sugar

2 tablespoons sesame oil

2 tablespoons sesame seeds

2 tablespoons red chili powder

2 garlic cloves, minced

2 green onions, sliced on the diagonal into 1 1/2-inch pieces

1 tablespoon ginger, minced

4 red and/or green small chilies, seeded and thinly sliced on the diagonal into about 1 1/2-inch pieces

1   Place crabs in cold water. Scrub the shell and legs with a wire brush to clean. Rinse and drain.

2   Remove the back shell and cut the crab in half. Then cut each half into 2 or 3 pieces with parts of the body attached to the legs. Repeat with the remaining crabs.

3   Mix the soy sauce, sugar, sesame oil, sesame seeds, chili powder, garlic, green onions, ginger, and peppers in a medium-sized bowl.

4   In a container large enough to hold all the crabs, put one layer of crabs and sprinkle soy sauce seasoning evenly. Repeat with each layer until all the crabs are seasoned. If there is any seasoning left, pour the rest over the crabs. Cover and refrigerate for a day or two to marinate.

Serve chilled with steamed rice and other *banchan*.

Spicy Stewed Crab

Gyae Jjigae

When choosing crabs, get live seasonal crabs that feel heavy for their size.

MAKES 6 TO 8 SERVINGS

3 crabs

1 medium onion, chopped

4 green chile peppers, sliced on the diagonal into about 1¹/₂-inch pieces

2 tablespoons soy sauce

2 tablespoons chili paste

2 tablespoons soybean paste

1 tablespoon garlic, minced

1 tablespoon ginger, minced

2 Korean zucchinis, cut into ¹/₂-inch cubes or triangles

Water

4 green onions, cut on the diagonal into 1- to 2-inch pieces

4 stalks crown daisies (or chrysanthemum leaves), cut into 1-inch pieces

1   Place crabs in cold water. Scrub the shell and legs with a wire brush to clean. Rinse and drain. Remove the back shell and cut the crab in half. Then cut each half into 2 or 3 pieces with parts of the body attached to the legs. Repeat with the remaining crabs. Set aside.

2   Put the onion, peppers, soy sauce, chili paste, soybean paste, garlic, ginger, and Korean zucchinis into a large pot. Mix until well combined. Then add 2 cups water and crabs. Cover and cook over medium heat until the crabs are cooked, about 10 to 15 minutes. (The crabmeat should be white and the shells slightly softer.) Reduce heat and add the green onions and crown daisies, letting simmer for another couple of minutes.

Serve immediately with steamed rice, assorted *banchan* (opt for less spicy varieties) and your choice of *kimchi*.

Going to the beach is like visiting an old friend. The Pacific Ocean has been my playmate ever since I could barely waddle up to its taunting waves. Although we lived in the city, my family would find any excuse to get to the coast.

Our family albums are filled with photos of us splashing around in our bathing suits and inner tubes. I remember one particular image of my dad looking all cool in his seventies shades as he pulls along a long string of kids in inner tubes, linked like cars on a train. Page after page reveals images of us as children, wearing our bikinis and smiling our toothless grins. Sandy bottoms would be wiggling into more sand as we splashed and tanned during those seemingly endless summers.

EATING WITH FRIENDS AT THE BEACH IN KOREA

Korea is graced with a wide range of beaches. The selection varies from open sandy beaches to pebbles rounded by years of surf to sheer cliff faces with foaming white waves crashing below. So, it's no wonder that South Korea is one of the world's major harvesters of seafood. Even during the most economically difficult times, there would usually be some gift from the ocean on the table.

Throughout the centuries, Koreans have found dozens of different ways to prepare anything that is edible from the sea. Even the lowliest of kelp and the smallest of shellfish is not just made to be tolerably edible, but transformed into a dish fit for a king. Salted seafood is given an honorable place in society with its own annual festival in Gangayeong, an inland port town.

One summer day, we ended up on some coast somewhere on the western shores of the Korean peninsula. There was an open, sandy beach, stopped abruptly by the sheer face of a rocky cliff. The cliff cast a large shadow that grew larger and more ominous as the afternoon wore on. Someone had made a campfire in the middle of the beach. Some of the kids were finding twigs and pieces of driftwood to throw into the blaze.

When you're a kid, you don't think about how long it takes for your swimsuit to dry, the sand that crawls into your crevices, or anything else that impedes your sense of frivolity and fun. You eat when you're hungry and drink when you're thirsty, not thinking about how the food got there, who prepared it, or any number of practical, boring things.

WITH MY FAMILY AT THE BEACH IN KOREA

That afternoon was no different.

From thin air, a large net full of squid miraculously appeared. Most likely, some of the parents bought them from one of the many small fishermen nearby. I didn't care where they came from, but the anticipation of eating fresh squid cooked over an open fire was enough to get me to drop whatever trouble I was getting into and begin collecting wood with the rest of the well-behaved children.

The miracles produced by our parents never ceased to amaze me. The moms had managed to bring rice, *banchan,* sauces, drinks, chopsticks, bowls, and all the things you need to have a comfortable meal on the beach. How did they get them to this beach? Just like the spontaneous appearance of the seafood, the spread was just accepted, even expected, by the kids.

I can now appreciate how much work our mothers put into making our beach outings seem so effortless and enjoyable. During my younger years, I never knew how much went into packing up all that food to feed an army of children. It's a wonder my mom had the presence of mind to pack along seasonings to prepare a delicious meal outdoors, all while wrangling her toddlers into their clean clothing and getting them to the bus on time.

When I prepare for a beach outing with friends, it takes me hours to make the food, get the cooler packed, pack the towels and chairs, and still remember the sunblock. I did take a page from my mom's book, though, making it seem so effortless that even my husband wonders how I manage to prepare such delicious meals for a dozen friends on some desolate beach somewhere. I think it's best to let the men believe we women still have some superpowers they'll never quite master.

Grilled Baby Octopus

Jjukkumi

If you've never had baby octopus, grilling them is a wonderful way to try them. The onion adds a nice sweetness to this spicy dish, a great addition to any outdoor meal. MAKES 5 TO 6 SERVINGS

2 pounds baby octopus (16 to 25 pieces), fresh or thawed if frozen, cleaned

Salt

$^1/_2$ onion, minced

$^1/_2$ red bell pepper, minced

3 to 4 garlic cloves, minced

2 tablespoons soy sauce

1 tablespoon Korean sesame oil

1 teaspoon Korean red chili powder

$^1/_2$ teaspoon black pepper

1   Sprinkle octopus with salt to taste and rub on for about a minute. Rinse in cold water. Drain. Repeat. Pat dry with paper towels.

2   Combine onion, bell pepper, garlic, soy sauce, sesame oil, chili powder, and pepper in bowl. Coat octopus generously with seasoning.

3   Grill over medium-high heat, moving around grill so octopus cooks evenly, 3 to 4 minutes.

Spicy Stir-Fried Squid

Ohjinguh Bokkum

This spicy dish is a delicious way of serving squid. Although this dish is already spicy, like most Korean *banchan*, it's usually served with a side of *kimchi*. MAKES 5 TO 6 SERVINGS

3 fresh squid

2 tablespoons soy sauce

2 tablespoons chili paste

1 tablespoon sugar

1 tablespoon chili powder

1 tablespoon sesame oil

1 teaspoon ginger, minced

$^1/_2$ carrot

2 green onions

1 tablespoon vegetable oil

1 garlic clove, minced

1 medium onion

1 bell pepper

Toasted sesame seeds (page 3), for optional garnish

1   Clean and slice the squid into thin pieces about 2 inches long. Set aside.

2   In a small bowl, mix the soy sauce, chili paste, sugar, chili powder, sesame oil, and ginger. Set aside.

3   Slice the carrot into thin flat pieces about 2 inches long. Cut the green onions about the same size, on the diagonal into about 2-inch lengths.

4   In a large skillet, heat the vegetable oil. Add the garlic and cook for about a minute. Then add the squid, onion, carrot, and bell pepper. (Save the green onions to add later.) Cook until the squid is cooked. The meat will turn opaque and the pieces will curve. Add the green onions and cook for another minute.

Serve immediately, sprinkled with toasted sesame seeds, if you wish. Serve with rice (or over a bed of rice for informal meals), *kimchi*, and other *banchan*.

NOTE This recipe can also be made with octopus in place of squid. The rest of the recipe is the same. In that case, the dish would be called *Nakji Bokkum*.

Meats and Poultry

One Sunday morning, I was awakened by the sound of pounding. Bang! Bang! Bang! It was my father, but he wasn't hammering nails into wood. He was tenderizing the meat for the barbecue.   •   I peered outside the window at the dawn-gray sky, moaned slightly and buried myself deeper under the covers. Even pulling the pillow over my head wasn't enough to muffle the noise.   •   The sound my dad was making was magnified by the clattering of dishes and my mother's voice listing all the things that needed to get done before we left. Soon, with my father yelling at us to get up and throwing the covers off our beds, sleep was no longer an option.   •   Although early morning wake-up calls were never welcome, I knew even in my drowsy state that this time these sounds signaled the beginning of summer—endless days in the sun, no homework and the great taste of Korean barbecue.   •   Soon, the house bustled with activity. Someone had to put on a pot of rice. Someone else had to marinate all the meats. Still another of us had to pack up the *kimchi* and other pickled things that would be the *banchan* to accompany our meal. Once our friends arrived,

WITH MY FAMILY AT THE PARK

things got even busier. Trunks needed to be loaded, blankets needed to be taken, and kids needed to be sorted into their respective families' cars. Once everything and everyone was packed with maybe a trip or two back for the icebox, or some other essential-but-easily-forgotten thing, we were off to the park.

As we unpacked our *kimchi, banchan,* marinated meats, rice, soup, chopsticks, beer, soda, and everything else, I became aware that we were attracting a lot of attention. There were so many of us, being noisy and speaking loudly in Korean, that passing joggers and bicyclists kept staring and glancing over their shoulders at us. But my self-consciousness didn't prevent my stomach from growling as we started preparing the grill.

Soon, a group of Mexican families set up at tables nearby. Their group was equal in number and din to ours. My embarrassment waned as I realized that we were no longer the only noisy crowd in the park. We sized up their meal as they began unpacking and unwrapping their meat. They, in turn, took several glances at our containers of food.

PICNICKING WITH MY MOM ON THE LEFT, MRS. YE, MY AUNT NO. 7, ROSABEL, HER MOM, AND MRS. KIM

An especially burly man in a white undershirt began preparing their coals. He looked over and gave a little nod to my dad, who was pouring lighter fluid all over his already roaring blaze. As our short ribs (*galbi*—a specific cut of beef ribs) started smoking and giving off a delicious aroma, we imagined they must be salivating with envy. Yet, when their meat hit their grill, their stuff smelled pretty good, too.

My mom, being the open and generous person that she is, offered a plate of *galbi* to our neighbors. They, in return, shared their *carne asada* with us. Of course, this made them instant friends with my dad, who couldn't turn down a plate of barbecued red meat to save his life. The next thing I knew, my mom was holding someone's *bonita* baby, we were all eating *galbi* and *salsa, carne asada* and *kimchi,* and we broke out in a not-so-unmelodic rendition of "De Colores." Just another day at the park in Los Angeles, with good eats for everyone.

Koreans plan an elaborate balance with any meal, even a picnic barbecue. The flavors of grilled meat complement the spicy coolness of the *kimchi* (providing the same counterpoint to the meat that salsa does). Of course, there is steamed rice with every Korean meal, but there have to be several types of *banchan* and some sort of soup to wash it all down.

The traditional way to eat Korean barbecue in a restaurant is to take a piece of red-leaf lettuce (*sangchu*), place in it a piece of smoking meat, a slice of garlic (grilled or raw), a small dollop of chili paste (*gochujang*) or fermented soy paste (*dwenjang*), wrap the whole thing up and shove it into your mouth. In lieu of the *gochujang* or *dwenjang,* you can dip the "wrap" into a light sauce that the restaurant has provided for you. The vast array of *banchan* (ranging from spinach to tangy radish) completes the meal.

Koreans have been barbecuing since time immemorial, but *galbi* originated in restaurants only in the 1950s. Although *galbi* is now served in homes, eating it in a restaurant is still a special treat. Not that the marinade is particularly complicated. Actually, it is really just a good blend of some basic ingredients. But most of us aren't equipped with tabletop grills and ceiling vents at home, so we have to pack it up and take it outdoors. It's a nice excuse to have a barbecue. Besides, you can become the envy of any passerby with a nose.

Beef Short Ribs

Galbi

Korean short ribs come in two types of cuts. You can get the more popular kind for home cooking that is sliced through the bone with three rib eyes on the edge of a slab or meat. Alternatively, you can buy the kind with the big chunk of bone, which you'll have to slice thinly into a long beef "tail" attached to the bone (this type being more popular in restaurants). Use a very sharp knife when doing this. This marinade works for either type. If you don't have access to a Korean grocery and can't find the specific cuts, regular beef back ribs will work as well. Just be sure to separate the ribs before marinating. MAKES 10 TO 12 SERVINGS, DEPENDING ON WHAT OTHER *BANCHAN* ARE BEING SERVED

5 pounds beef short ribs

1 medium onion, minced

1 garlic bulb, minced

1/3 cup soy sauce

1/4 cup sugar

1/2 cup Korean malt syrup (*mool yut*)

2 tablespoons sesame oil

1 teaspoon black pepper

1 Wash the meat thoroughly in cold water and tenderize with the blunt edge of a knife or a clean hammer; or soak in a basin of cold water for about an hour. Drain and blot dry with paper towels.

2 Combine the onion, garlic, soy sauce, sugar, malt syrup, sesame oil, and black pepper in a medium bowl. Marinate the meat by layering, pouring the soy mixture between layers. Or mix the meat with the soy mixture in a large bowl. Cover and refrigerate for at least 3 hours, but preferably overnight.

3 Cook over a hot grill until well done. (Cooking time will vary depending on the intensity of the fire.)

Serve with leaves of red curly leaf lettuce, steamed rice, *kimchi*, and your choice of *banchan.*

Grilled Chicken

Dak Gui

If you have a tabletop grill at home, you can have your guests cook their own chicken on the table with other marinated meats. For a more elegant presentation, be sure to remove the meat from the bone and cut the chicken into more manageable, bite-size pieces. MAKES 10 TO 12 SERVINGS, DEPENDING ON WHAT OTHER *BANCHAN* ARE BEING SERVED

5 pounds skinless bone-in chicken

1 onion, minced

1 garlic clove, minced

1 (1-inch) piece ginger root, minced

$1/3$ cup soy sauce

$1/4$ cup sugar

$1/2$ cup Korean malt syrup (*mool yut*)

2 tablespoons sesame oil

1 teaspoon black pepper

1   Rinse chicken in cold water. Drain and blot with paper towels. Score chicken pieces on both sides with sharp knife, making a few shallow cuts on each piece.

2   Combine onion, garlic, ginger, soy sauce, sugar, malt syrup, sesame oil, and black pepper in large bowl. Rub marinade all over chicken. Cover and refrigerate for at least 3 hours or preferably overnight.

3   Grill chicken over medium-high heat until cooked through, about 30 to 40 minutes, turning occasionally.

Campfire for Adults

There's something magical about summer nights. Those nights spent inside canvas tents, wiggling around in sleeping bags as we bumped into the warm bodies of siblings and friends were especially memorable. An unusually heavy sleeper, I would slumber through crying babies, earthquakes, fires, and veritable train wrecks. I was usually the first one to fall dead asleep, kicking my way out of even the best-zipped sleeping bags, snoring my heart out as the other kids rolled me around to shut me up.

Yet, this particular night was different. I awoke with a start and found myself wide awake, surrounded by the soft breathing of the rest of the kids. I lay there for awhile, watching the giant shadows flicker by the campfire, imagining monster myths as I strained to figure out bits of the adults' conversations. When I finally tired of my imagination and the moths flitting about, I tumbled over the pile of bodies to make my escape into the night with the quiet "zzzzz, zzzzz" of two zippers opening in succession.

Rubbing the last remnants of sleep from my eyes, I found my parents in the campfire circle and made my declaration, "I can't sleep."

The adults' faces looked over at me, some with vague smiles, others indifferent. I half expected my folks to tell me to go back to bed. But without as much as a blink of the eye, they scooted over on the bench they were sitting on and let me squeeze my young girl body in between them.

I was elated, feeling as if I had just been admitted to some secret society by accidentally blurting out the password. I was being allowed to stay up with the grown-ups while the rest of the kids were having their silly childish dreams.

The parents were drinking beer and eating dried cuttlefish that they were roasting over the fire. Anything eaten with an alcoholic beverage is called *anju*. It can be peanuts, dried fish, rice crackers, beef jerky, anything really, but is usually something salty (if you've ever had cookies or cake with beer or Korean rice wine (*soju*), you'd understand why). My dad was especially fond of his *anju*. I don't think I've ever seen him have even a casual drink without making me bring him something to go along with it.

While my dad was enjoying his beer, my mom was getting everyone to play some crazy game. She was very fond of crazy games, always remembering even the most complicated rules and getting even the stodgiest of fathers laughing along. I was having a great time laughing and slapping my knees with the rest of them, especially since none of my friends was around to be embarrassed or roll their eyes up at their oh-so-unhip parents.

It seemed like hours had passed and the raucousness ran its course. Besides, we had run out of cuttlefish. As long as the beer was still cold and the logs were still burning, the fun wasn't going to stop. Someone suggested we cook up some of the marinating pork ribs (*dwaeji galbi*) left over in the icebox. I, being the youngest member in the bunch by far, was happily relegated to getting the ribs.

There are very few things in the world that taste better than charred meat cooked over a roaring fire on a summer night. If that meat is marinated just right, eaten late at night with a couple of swigs from your dad's beer, it's even better.

Once the games ended, the parents became serious adults again. Their subdued conversations, my full stomach, and the beer all conspired against my newly laid plans to stay up all night with the grown-ups. I tried really heard to combat the drowsiness, even pinching myself surreptitiously under the blanket I was sharing with my folks. Yet, nothing could lift the heaviness from my eyelids.

I don't know when I drifted off to sleep, but the last thing I remembered was a particularly beautiful spark that floated higher than the others, surrounded by the dancing curls of the wood smoke into the star-speckled sky.

The next morning, I considered boasting to all the kids that I had stayed up way late with the moms and dads, but something stopped me from cheapening my experience. I later whispered my night's adventures to my sister while we were alone by the river on dish duty.

"What did they say? I mean, what were they talking about?" she asked, her eyes all wide with curiosity.

I answered with authority and an air of mystery, not quite pulling off my nonchalant distance, "Stuff. Y'know, just stuff."

"Like what? What kinds of stuff?" she persisted.

"I don't know. Grown-up things. Boring stuff, really," I evaded her questions. "But we ate the rest of the *dwaeji galbi*!" I said, as I grabbed my share of the dishes and began running back to our campground.

"Aw man . . . " I heard my sister say. "I wanted to eat some today . . . " her voice trailed farther and farther behind, my sister not being much of a runner.

Relieved, I kept on running. I didn't want her to know that I was a really bad kid spy. When the real conversations began, I was falling asleep and couldn't remember much of what they were talking about. Even after one late night with the parents, the mysteries of the adult world would continue to elude me for a bit longer.

Spicy Pork Ribs

Dwaeji Galbi

This is one of my dad's favorite dishes, and it was also one of the Top Ten Recipes of the Year for 2000 in the *Los Angeles Times*. The chili paste and ginger add a nice kick to this dish. MAKES 10 TO 12 SERVINGS, DEPENDING ON WHAT OTHER *BANCHAN* ARE BEING SERVED

5 pounds pork back ribs

1 (1-inch) piece ginger root, minced

1 garlic clove, finely chopped

1 cup chili paste

$^1/_2$ cup Korean malt syrup (*mool yut*)

$^1/_2$ cup sugar

2 tablespoons soy sauce

3 tablespoons sesame oil

1 teaspoon black pepper

1   If ribs are not separated, separate by cutting meat between the bones. Place in large bowl.

2   Combine ginger, garlic, chili paste, malt syrup, sugar, soy sauce, sesame oil, and black pepper in large bowl. Rub marinade generously over meat. Cover and refrigerate 3 hours or preferably overnight.

3   Grill ribs over medium-high heat until done, about 5 to 6 minutes per side.

Fire Meat

One of the most popular Korean dishes of all time, *boolgogi* ("*bool*" means fire and "*gogi*" means "meat"). It is also fast and easy to make. Although it can be simply eaten as part of a meal, it is also an essential ingredient for such dishes as Mixed Rice Bowl (*Bibim Bap*, page 23) and Sweet Potato Noodles (*Japchae*, page 123). MAKES 5 TO 6 SERVINGS, DEPENDING ON WHAT OTHER *BANCHAN* ARE BEING SERVED

2 pounds sliced rib eye or *boolgogi* beef

1 tablespoon soy sauce

2 teaspoons sesame oil

2 teaspoons sugar

1 tablespoon Korean malt syrup (*mool yut*; optional)

1 garlic bulb, minced

Salt

Approximately $^1/_2$ teaspoon black pepper

1 green onion, sliced into $^1/_2$-inch pieces as optional garnish

1   Marinate the sliced rib eye in soy sauce, sesame oil, sugar, optional malt syrup and garlic, approximately 30 minutes.

2   Stir-fry meat until thoroughly cooked, usually about 5 to 7 minutes. Add salt and black pepper. Garnish with green onion if desired.

Serve with traditional Napa cabbage *kimchi*, steamed rice, and a variety of *banchan*.

Spicy Sliced Pork

Dwaeji Boolgogi

If you can't find thinly sliced pork sirloin at the Korean market, you can slice it yourself. Just use a very sharp knife and slice the sirloin as thinly as you can.

MAKES 5 TO 6 SERVINGS, DEPENDING ON WHAT OTHER *BANCHAN* ARE BEING SERVED

2 pounds sliced pork sirloin

3 tablespoons chili paste

3 tablespoons sugar

3 garlic cloves, minced

1 (1-inch) piece of ginger, minced

1 tablespoon soy sauce

1 tablespoon sesame oil

Black pepper

2 green onions, chopped (optional)

1   Combine the sliced pork with the chili paste, sugar, garlic, ginger, soy sauce, and sesame oil. Let marinate for approximately 30 minutes.

2   Stir-fry the meat until thoroughly cooked, usually about 5 to 7 minutes. Add black pepper as needed. Garnish with green onion if desired.

Serve with your choice of *kimchi*, steamed rice, and a variety of *banchan*.

Sliced Roast Beef

Roseh Gui

Low-fat sliced beef is available from any butcher shop or sometimes prepackaged in the meat section of Korean and Japanese supermarkets. You can also eat sliced pork this way. MAKES 4 TO 5 SERVINGS

1 pound sliced beef

Seasoned Green Onions
(*Pa Muchim*, page 9)

Red-leaf lettuce

1   Arrange the beef on a plate. Place an electric frying pan in the middle of the table and let the diners cook their own beef.

Serve with red-leaf lettuce and Seasoned Green Onions on the side.

N O T E   The best way to eat the beef is by first taking a leaf of lettuce (or half a leaf if it's large), placing a slice of beef, and adding some of the seasoned green onions. Wrap the whole thing and stuff it into your mouth.

Stewed Beef Ribs

Galbi Jjim

This recipe works best with the cut of beef that has the thick bone in the middle with the chunks of meat attached. Because the meat is simmered for a long time, it becomes very tender and falls off the bone. I like to think of this as Korean "down-home" comfort food, like meat loaf, although, like all meat dishes, *galbi jjim* is usually prepared for guests on special occasions. For a fancier recipe, you can add any combination of chestnuts, dried red dates, and gingko nuts. MAKES 6 TO 7 SERVINGS, DEPENDING ON WHAT OTHER *BANCHAN* ARE BEING SERVED

3 pounds beef short ribs

1 Asian radish, cut into large cubes

2 to 3 carrots, cut into large cubes

1 cup soy sauce

3 tablespoons sugar

2 tablespoons sesame oil

1 (2-inch) piece of ginger, sliced

3 garlic cloves, minced

Water

Pine nuts for garnish

Red pepper threads for garnish (optional)

1   Trim any excess fat from the ribs and score the meat to allow the flavor to seep in. Rinse the ribs in cold water to get rid of any excess blood or bone chips.

2   In a medium-sized pot, combine the ribs, radish and carrot cubes, soy sauce, sugar, sesame oil, ginger, and garlic. Add 2 cups water and bring to a boil. Reduce heat and let simmer for about 30 minutes. The beef should be well cooked and tender; if it isn't, cook for a few more minutes. Since short rib meat tends to be fatty, be sure to skim the fat.

3   Remove the ginger slices and discard. Serve immediately, nice and hot, garnished with pine nuts and optional red pepper threads.

Serve with rice, *kimchi*, and your choice of *banchan*. Refrigerate any leftovers for up to a week, heating before serving.

Korean Stuffed Sausage

Soondae

Sausages in Korea originated in the mountainous areas of the northern part of the peninsula. Originally, the intestines of wild pigs were used. Now, you can get regular pig intestines from a Korean butcher or prepackaged sausage skins. The stuffing is made from rice, pork blood, and seasonings. You can substitute fatty ground pork for the pork blood, although the taste will be different. It makes a delicious snack with a cold glass of beer or Korean rice wine (*soju*). MAKES 6 TO 7 SERVINGS

1 pound small intestine pork casings (or other sausage skins)

2 cups pork (or beef) blood

2 cups rice, cooked but firm

6 green onions, finely minced

4 garlic cloves, minced

1 (1-inch) piece of ginger, minced

2 tablespoons sesame oil

1 teaspoon toasted sesame seeds, crushed (page 3)

1 teaspoon salt

$^1/_2$ teaspoon black (or white) pepper

1   Clean the intestine casings well in cold water. Then soak in cold water, sprinkled with a little salt for about 1 hour. This will make the casing easier to handle. Tie one end of each casing with kitchen string.

2   In a large bowl, combine the pork blood, rice, green onions, garlic, ginger, sesame oil, toasted sesame seeds, salt, and pepper. Mix well.

3   Put the mixture into a pastry bag and pipe the stuffing into the casing, loosely filling the casing. (Do not fill too tightly, because the rice will expand when cooking.) Every 5 inches or so, tie a tight knot with kitchen string to form sausages. You may also make individual sausages, but cut and tie both ends. Using a pin, prick the sausages to relieve the pressure while cooking.

4   In a stockpot or deep pan, coil the sausage links. Cover with water, sprinkle a little salt, and bring to a boil. Lower the heat and let simmer for about 20 to 25 minutes. You'll know when the sausages are done when you insert a toothpick into one and the toothpick comes out clean.

5   Slice sausage on the diagonal into about $^1/_4$-inch to $^1/_2$-inch pieces. Arrange on a platter and serve warm with tiny salted shrimp *(saewu jut)* or coarse sea salt.

N O T E *Soondae* can be frozen or refrigerated. Slice the sausages before freezing. To reheat, steam them until the sausages are heated all the way through.

Korean Shishkabob

Sanjuk

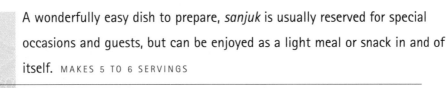 A wonderfully easy dish to prepare, *sanjuk* is usually reserved for special occasions and guests, but can be enjoyed as a light meal or snack in and of itself. MAKES 5 TO 6 SERVINGS

1 pound steak meat, rib eye, or other tender, thick beef, cubed into 1-inch pieces

1 tablespoon soy sauce

1 teaspoon sesame oil

1 teaspoon sugar

1 bunch of green onions, cut into 1-inch pieces

1 package of rice cake sticks

1 (8-ounce) package of white mushrooms (optional)

1   Marinate the beef in soy sauce, sesame oil, and sugar for approximately 30 minutes.

2   Spear beef, green onions, rice cakes, and optional mushrooms on two parallel hibachi sticks.

3   Grill until cooked thoroughly.

Korean Shishkabob, a variation

Sanjuk 2

If you're getting the beef at a Korean market, ask for the *sanjuk* cut and the butcher will precut it the right size for you. Slightly cooking the carrots beforehand makes it easier for you to pierce them with the toothpicks.

MAKES ABOUT 20 PIECES

10 to 12 shiitake mushrooms

$^1/_2$ pound beef round, sliced into about $2^1/_2$-inch strips

1 garlic clove, minced

1 teaspoon soy sauce

1 teaspoon sesame oil

1 medium carrot, cut into about $2^1/_2$-inch slices

3 green onions, but into about $2^1/_2$-inch pieces

About 20 wooden toothpicks

Flour

2 to 3 eggs

Salt

Black pepper

Vegetable oil for cooking

1   If the shiitake mushrooms are dried, soak in cold water for about 2 hours. Squeeze the water out of them and cut into about $^1/_2$-inch pieces.

2   Place the beef strips and mushrooms into a bowl. Add garlic, soy sauce, and sesame oil and mix well. Let marinate for at least 15 minutes.

3   Soften the carrots by placing them in a small pot of boiling salt water. Cook for about 2 to 3 minutes. Rinse in cold water and set aside.

4   Pierce the carrots, mushrooms, green onions, and beef onto each toothpick, alternating the ingredients for color and flavor. Leave enough room on the end of the toothpick so that you can still pick it up comfortably; repeat until shishkabobs are completed.

5   Pour flour on a plate. Whisk together the eggs and add some salt and pepper.

6   Add some vegetable oil to a skillet over medium to low heat.

7   Dip the speared ingredients in the flour, making sure that both sides are thoroughly dusted. Next, dip it in the egg batter and carefully place it on the skillet. Let cook on both sides for at least 8 to 10 minutes or until beef is thoroughly cooked. Taste the first one and sprinkle more salt and pepper on the *sanjuk* if needed.

The Chicken

My dad was a firm believer in raising his children to eat everything on their plates. He would put an unidentifiable piece of meat on our plate and make us finish every last scrap before he told us what we had just eaten. I have grown fearless after eating cow brains, sparrow, snake, deer, and fish intestines.

All those years of unusual foods still didn't quite prepare me for the day my father decided that I should learn how to kill my own chicken. As in most decisions regarding his children, he never got our consent. When it came to the actuality, as usual, I was alone. I peered into the coop and a ferocious-looking brown bird stared back at me. I was only saved from its pecking by the rusted chicken wire between us.

My dad had grown up on a farm, probably not too dissimilar to this one. He always lamented the fact that his city-grown children were so far removed from the soil and its mysterious gifts. I was the only one who even

A FARM IN KOREA

showed a glimmer of interest in gardening and agriculture, helping my dad plant packets of seeds that a friend or relative would bring us from the homeland.

I was also a tomboy. Growing up, I cursed my girl body, knowing that my gender was a disappointment to my parents when I was born. I wished I could be stronger. I wished people would stop buying me pink things lined with lace. I wished I were a boy.

So, when I stood there facing our lunch that had yet to be killed and plucked, I couldn't betray the terrified little girl inside. Instead, I summoned up all my strength and followed the farm woman into the coop. I studied the way she grabbed a bird with great gusto and broke its neck with the finesse of years of practice. She waited until the bird stopped flapping and began plucking, creating a huge cloud of feathers and down.

It was my turn. I looked around trying to find a chicken that would give me the least amount of resistance and grabbed its body with both hands. I tried to do what the woman had done, skillfully putting the bird under one arm. I managed to hold it and break its neck, but the creature got loose and began running around the coop. That was when I realized the true meaning of "running around like a chicken with its head cut off." Comical and deeply disturbing at the same time, I chased the bird and was able to get a hold of it again. I held it with both hands for what seemed like hours as I waited for the darn thing to stop flapping. The woman helped me with the plucking and I went over to the water pump to wash my hands while she took care of the rest.

When mealtime came around, my siblings were somehow visible again. If you've never had fresh chicken before, you'll not realize that the Styrofoam-packed pieces of flesh lined up under neon displays in supermarkets should be given a different name than the tender meat that you could savor fresh on a farm. It's like the difference between frozen fillets and a freshly caught fish, the flavor still untainted by hours of refrigeration.

Our meal was a simple country one with a few side dishes, rice, and the starring main course of chicken. I was as proud as a hunter who'd bagged a bear that morning, acting as if I had made the whole meal, while everyone raved about the delicious meat. As I enjoyed lunch, I almost forgot the insurmountable fear in my being as I faced the brown bird and the feeling of deep sadness as I watched the life leaving its body. I now had a deeper respect for the animals that had given their lives so that we could enjoy a wonderful meal.

I had forgotten about my chicken adventure until years later, when my parents came in possession of a couple of hens. Every morning, my nephew, Christopher, would go out with my dad to go feed the chickens, talking to them as if they were his friends. In return, the hens would reward him with lovely brown gifts, giving us the best eggs anyone could ever ask for.

One afternoon, my nephew had just taken my husband and me out to say hello to the birds. We came inside the house and sat on the sofa to tell each other ghost stories. When my mom showed up with a rotisserie chicken from somewhere, the look on Christopher's face broke my heart. He thought my mom had somehow killed his beloved hens and roasted them up for lunch. We had to take him out to look at the chickens once more before he could be placated enough to eat. I thought about the chicken farm and decided that some children may not need to kill their own food to appreciate the animals' sacrifices.

Soy Stewed Beef

Jang Jolim

This is one of those dishes I consider "down-home" Korean food—comfort food that isn't usually served to guests or on special occasions. Still, my husband loves this dish, special occasion or not. You can use beef brisket, flank steak, or a lesser grade of beef, since boiling the meat for a long time makes it tender. Beef leftover from making soup stock can be used here as well. MAKES ABOUT 4 TO 5 SERVINGS, DEPENDING ON WHAT OTHER *BANCHAN* ARE BEING SERVED

1 pound beef brisket

1 (2-inch) piece of ginger, peeled and sliced

Water

1 tablespoon soy sauce

1 tablespoon sugar

1 garlic bulb, peeled and trimmed

6 to 8 Korean mild green peppers (*ggoari gochu*)

2 eggs or a dozen quail eggs (*maechuli al*), washed (optional)

1   Place beef brisket and ginger in a medium-sized pot with about 5 cups of water. Bring to a boil, reduce heat and let simmer for about an hour. Remove the meat and let cool until it is safe to touch (about 15 to 20 minutes). Meat should be tender and flake easily. Skim the fat and foam from the broth and set aside.

2   Shred or slice the beef into pieces about $1^1/_2$ to 2 inches in size. Place the meat back into the broth, adding the soy sauce, sugar, and garlic. Simmer for about 20 minutes longer over low heat. Add the peppers and optional eggs and simmer, covered, for about 5 to 8 minutes longer, until the eggs are hard boiled.

3   Remove the eggs and run under cold water until they are cool enough to be peeled. Slice the eggs in half lengthwise.

4   Serve warm or cold as a side dish with the sliced eggs placed on top, if you wish. This dish (without the eggs) will keep in the fridge for about a week.

Seasoned Fried Chicken

Yangnyum Dak

Fried chicken is not a traditional Korean dish. In fact very few dishes are deep-fried in Korean cooking. After some discussion with my aunts, I decided to include this dish because it's an excellent example of how Koreans have incorporated Western fast food into their diet, but made it entirely their own. The chili paste adds a nice kick. MAKES 4 TO 5 SERVINGS

About 1 pound chicken, small pieces (about 3 inches each)

1/2 onion, grated

1 egg

Water

1 cup cornstarch

1 teaspoon salt

1 teaspoon black pepper

Vegetable oil for frying

3 tablespoons chili paste

5 tablespoons sugar

4 tablespoons ketchup

1 teaspoon lemon juice

1   Marinate the chicken pieces in the grated onion for at least 30 minutes, but preferably an hour.

2   In a medium bowl, combine the egg, 1 cup of very cold water, cornstarch, salt, and black pepper. Mix just until moist; do not mix well.

3   In a saucepan, heat enough vegetable oil at about 350° to 365°F to immerse the pieces of chicken.

4   Dip the chicken pieces in the cornstarch mixture and carefully place in the hot vegetable oil, repeating until the pan is mostly full. Cook until the chicken is crispy and golden brown and is cooked through, about 10 minutes. To test if the pieces are cooked, remove the largest piece and cut into the thickest part to the bone. The meat should be opaque throughout and the juices run clear. Remove the pieces and place on a plate lined with paper towels.

5   Repeat until all the pieces are cooked.

6   In a bowl, mix the chili paste, sugar, ketchup, and lemon juice. Add the chicken and mix until the pieces are well coated.

Serve immediately with a side of pickled radishes or *kimchi* and rice.

Chicken in Chili Sauce

Mae-un Dak

This dish is best made with fresh chicken. To get chicken in small pieces, have your butcher cut it for you. If you must cut it at home, use a sharp cleaver, being careful to wash out any bone chips. You may also use chicken that has been cut for frying. Just cook the pieces longer, making sure all the chicken is cooked through. MAKES 5 TO 7 SERVINGS

Water

About 2 pounds chicken, small pieces (about 3 inches each)

2 potatoes, cubed

1 medium onion, cubed

1 Korean zucchini, cubed

1 carrot, cubed

2 garlic cloves, minced

1 tablespoon ginger, minced

1 tablespoon soy sauce

5 tablespoons chili paste

2 green onions, sliced on the diagonal

1 tablespoon sugar

Salt

1 tablespoon toasted sesame seeds (page 3)

1   In a large pot or deep frying pan, bring 2 cups water to a boil. Add the chicken, potatoes, onion, zucchini, and carrot.

2   Add the garlic, ginger, soy sauce and chili paste and bring to a boil. Reduce heat and let simmer, covered, stirring occasionally until the chicken is cooked through, about 15 minutes. Add the green onions, sugar, and a little bit of salt. Cook for just about another minute. Remove from heat and sprinkle with toasted sesame seeds.

Serve immediately as a communal dish with rice and other *banchan*.

Stewed Chicken

Dak Jjim

This is a nice dish to make for an everyday meal. While the chicken is cooking, you can prepare other dishes or do something else. You may also use chicken that has been cut for frying. Just cook the pieces longer, making sure all the chicken is cooked through. MAKES 5 TO 7 SERVINGS

2 tablespoons vegetable oil

2 pounds chicken, small pieces (about 3 inches each)

4 garlic cloves, minced

1 tablespoon ginger, minced

2 medium onions, cubed

Water

$1/4$ cup soy sauce

2 carrots, cubed

2 potatoes, cubed

5 shiitake mushrooms

1 tablespoon sesame oil

4 green onions, sliced diagonally

1   In a deep pan or pot, heat the vegetable oil. Add the chicken and cook over medium heat for about 20 minutes. Add the garlic, ginger, and onions and cook for another 1 to 2 minutes, stirring constantly.

2   Add 1 cup water, soy sauce, carrots, potatoes, and mushrooms. Cover and let simmer over low heat for about 15 minutes. Add the sesame oil and green onions and cook for about 5 minutes more. The sauce should have reduced and become thicker.

Serve immediately with rice, *kimchi,* and a few *mit banchan.*

Desserts, Teas, and Snacks

Although I was born there, Seoul is not one of my favorite cities in the world. Cities in Asia tend to be overpopulated, noisy, and busy. Seoul, which is home to over ten million people (a quarter of the country's population), makes New York look like a rural town in comparison. It is a city of professional subway pushers, multilevel department stores, and open marketplaces brimming with people. There are some wonderfully onomatopoetic words in the Korean language to describe such crowds, like *bagul-bagul*. Its noises sound so much to me like the Korean word used to describe a boiling pot, *bogul-bogul*. • Shortly after college, I went back to my homeland to re-learn the language and get back in touch with my culture. There is no place for solace anywhere in the city. I wandered the concrete banks of the Han River late on summer evenings just to be confronted by the hordes. Parks, museums, libraries, and recreational areas were teeming with people. • For a semi-claustrophobic woman like myself, it didn't help that I was staying with family in what could only be called a closet. Lest you think I exaggerate, let me explain the layout of the "room." The twin bed that took up most of the floor space was butted up

OUTSIDE A TEA SHOP IN INSADONG

against two walls of the room. A tiny nightstand, just big enough for a dwarf, housed an even tinier lamp and my walkman. At the foot of the bed, there was just enough room for me to squeeze in my suitcase, which held all my clothes. Unpacking was not an option, so I pulled it out onto the bed to get dressed every morning. There was just enough floor space for the door to swing open and closed, barely missing the bed by about a millimeter.

Although I was grateful for a place to sleep, I rarely spent any time there, opting to wander the streets instead. I would browse in bookstores for long hours, watch movies in video rooms (*bideo bang*), squeeze my way between perm-haired ladies in open markets, or spend leisurely afternoons sipping cups of coffee in the city's countless but overpriced cafés.

RICE CAKES AND TEA

My only true salvation was Insadong, the arts district. Although it is now crawling with tourists, like Montmarte in Paris, it used to be a more genuine neighborhood. Populated by artists, musicians, craftsmen, and other layabouts like me, I felt at home there. I would gingerly caress handmade ceramics, bury my face amongst the fresh smells of rice paper reams, and gently run my fingers over bamboo brushes or the polished wood of musical instruments.

Once while walking down the street, I heard a raucous crowd. I quickly turned the corner to find a crowd of men surrounding something on a street corner. Imagining a game of dice, cards, or some other cheap thrill, I cautiously peered over the crowd. They were having a public calligraphy contest. As the contestants expertly swished their horsehair brushes leaving fluid ink lines on the paper, the admirers would hoot and holler as if they were watching a sporting event.

I strolled past their afternoon excitement as a cool breeze carried along the haunting sounds of the *gayagum*, a traditional stringed instrument played on the floor. While wandering through the back alleys, by chance I found what was to become my favorite tea shop. I was squinting up at the sunlight through the frosted windows of an unassuming building and was able to discern a paper lantern or two hanging from the second floor, which looked like it could be someone's workshop.

Curious, I tried the heavy metal doors and they yielded to my pull. I paused a moment at the bottom of the stairs, waiting for my eyes to adjust in the cool darkness. Looking around conspicuously, my footsteps echoed down the hollow staircase. Once upstairs, I let the faint inviting smell guide me to a most wonderful tea shop. There was a tiny bridge and a rock and bamboo garden flanking it on either side. I carefully walked over the stones and was welcomed by the overwhelming smell of cinnamon and ginger, washing over me like a warm shower.

The music of traditional bamboo flutes (*daegum*) floated out from the invisible speakers. The place was not crowded. Each table was placed far apart from surrounding tables, providing a sense of serenity and openness my thirsty soul had been seeking for months. A monk was meditating cross-legged on an embroidered pillow at a corner table. A couple of students were intently trying to decipher some ancient Chinese poetry at another. I sat down to spend a quiet moment alone with my thoughts and enjoy a cup of tea in a handmade cup.

Koreans have a long history with ceramics. The earliest traces of pottery were found during the Neolithic Era (over five thousand years ago), some fired in traditional ways and others simply made by drying the clay. Starting in the late ninth century and through the twelfth century of the Koryo Dynasty, celadon was produced on the peninsula. With the height of Buddhism's popularity and relative peace in the region, the art of celadon was perfected to heights never seen before or since. The Mongolian invasion during the thirteenth century unfortunately ended the period of celadon craftsmanship.

After the overthrow of the Mongols in the fourteenth century by General Yi, the Josun Dynasty (sometimes called the Yi Dynasty) saw further development in Korean ceramics. The Korean Punchong potters of this time were so highly regarded that many of the country's craftsmen and intellectuals were kidnapped by the Japanese in the 1590s, leading to the Pottery Wars and a huge influence on the development of Japan's own ceramic culture. With the loss of talented potters and the destruction of kilns, Punchong pottery all but disappeared in Korea.

Ceramics creation did not die out, however. Punchong pottery was replaced by White Ware, a simple but elegant white porcelain, which was often decorated with symbols and themes of the then popular Neo-Confucianism.

Even today, ceramic making is taken quite seriously by artisans and art appreciators. Walking down the street in Insadong, I met an old potter who was almost blind but was still wonderfully skilled with his hands. He caressed a bowl in his hand as if it were his child, lovingly showing off its beauty to me. It was indeed gorgeous, but there was a slight imperfection.

As if he was reading my mind, the man said to me, "Notice that slight pockmarked part here." He pointed it out with his thumb. "Just as nothing in nature is ever perfect, we make our pottery to be slightly imperfect. That's what makes it all the more beautiful." He smiled a toothless grin as he handed the bowl to me.

I smiled, too, feeling the roughness of the piece in my hand. "I, too, am imperfect," I muttered under my breath as I tried to give the bowl back.

"Keep it," he said, turning away from me to go back into his studio. I tried to give him money, but he refused. "Everyone should have a reminder of their mortality. It keeps us humble." Then, he disappeared into his dark studio.

I continued down the street to my favorite tea shop with the image of the potter's face floating in my mind. The owner lady (*ahjumma*) brought me my favorite beverage, Chilled Ginger Cinnamon Tea (*Soojong Gwa,* page 183). I examined the teacup in my hands and noticed that it was slightly lopsided, a gift from nature. Three small pine nuts were floating perfectly in the middle of the dark liquid. I thought about whoever made the teacup and felt an inexplicable connection to the earth, the sea, the wind, to humanity. I was almost ready to face the city again.

Sometimes, even now, when I try to get away from the hustle and bustle of daily living, I get some water boiling, put on a CD of traditional Korean music, light some lanterns, and pull out my embroidered pillows. I have dreams of creating a little rock garden in the entryway and building a little bridge to cross into the house. If my husband comes home one day to find a monk or two meditating in the corner, he should begin to worry.

Chilled Ginger Cinnamon Tea

Soojong Gwa

This drink is a perfect example of yin and yang, heat and cold. The fire (yin) of the ginger and cinnamon are perfectly balanced by the coolness (yang). This may sound crazy but boiling the ginger and cinnamon separately and combining the liquid later maintains their individual flavors. They can be boiled together, if you're trying to save time, space, or just don't want to bother. It is best enjoyed in a warm room during winter, but it makes a refreshing summer drink, as well. MAKES 15 TO 20 SERVINGS

Water

6 sticks cinnamon

4 to 5 inches of ginger

$1/4$ cup brown sugar

$1/4$ cup white sugar

Pine nuts for garnish

1 Add $1/2$ gallon of water each to two pots. Wash the cinnamon and add to one of the pots. Peel and slice the ginger. Add ginger to the second pot. Bring both pots to a boil. Reduce heat and let simmer for about 30 minutes.

2 Remove from heat and combine. Add sugars, stirring until completely dissolved. Chill in the refrigerator for several hours (or preferably overnight).

Sprinkle with a few pine nuts before serving.

VARIATION Traditional *Soojong Gwa* is served with dried persimmons. Freshly dried persimmons can be found in the late autumn or early winter. The better quality ones are covered with a fine white powder. After removing the hard stem and leaves, slice the persimmon into thin strips. Soak in a little bit of the ginger water for about 30 minutes. Add a few slices to the bottom of each cup or bowl before serving.

Citron Tea

Yuja Cha

If you're lucky enough to find fresh citron in the states, you may be initially put off by the odd shape (a certain variety is lumpy and looks like a hand with extra fingers), but you may fall in love with its fragrance. Although citron tea is readily available in Korean markets, it's easy to make your own at home. Some people like to use honey, but I think using sugar tastes better.

MAKES A POUND OF TEA

1 pound of citron

Salt

2 cups sugar

Pine nuts, for garnish
(optional)

1   Rub the citron skins with salt to clean. Rinse thoroughly in water and dry. Peel the citron. Slice the peel into thin strips.

2   Remove the white pulp from the citron and divide each fruit into sections.

3   In a medium glass jar, arrange a layer of peel. Sprinkle with sugar to cover. Next arrange a layer of fruit and sprinkle with sugar to cover. Continue layering peel and fruit alternating between them, but making sure to cover each layer with sugar.

4   Leave at room temperature until the sugar has completely dissolved, then refrigerate. It will be ready in about a week, but will keep in the refrigerator for up to a year.

5   To make tea, spoon out 1 tablespoon of sugared citron into a teacup. Add 1 cup of boiling water for each serving. Add a few pine nuts to each cup, if you wish.

Summer Ice

In Korea, there was no way you could ditch school. No matter what grade you were in, you had to wear a uniform. Just by the color of your uniform or even your haircut, everyone could tell what grade you were in. When the school bells rang, hoards of kids from all over could be seen overrunning the city's streets and subways with their loud chatter. In kindergarten, I looked forward to graduating from my chick-yellow skirt, white blouse, and white tights to the dark navy uniforms of my high school neighbors. The uniforms were bearable most of the year, but once the summers hit, the layers were like prison shackles on a young child's body.

Even before leaving the school grounds, I would pull off my tights and shove them into my school pack before running around with my friends. We would hop from shade to shade, scarcely getting any reprieve from the oppressive humidity as we tried to find some comfort. It wasn't long before my sister and I figured out a foolproof way to get home. We would find any air-conditioned building on the way home and temporarily relieve our sweaty bodies before we would run to the next air-conditioned haven. Bank lobbies were our favorite.

It was easy to spot a bank in Korea because they always planted gingko trees (also called *uenhaeng namu*, or "bank tree") all around. The trees' leaves turned a beautiful yellow in the fall, symbolizing the wealth and gold of the bank. Although the leaves were green in the summers, their distinctive fan shapes were easy to spot from even a mile away. We would nonchalantly enter a bank's lobby, sit in the waiting area until we'd stopped sweating, and walk out as inconspicuously as possible, leaving little sweat stains on the black leather seats. Between our air-conditioned oases, we found corner grocery stores from which we'd buy as much ice cream as we could afford. Our treks home were a series of bank lobbies and ice cream lickings.

SUMMER FUN WITH MY SIBLINGS AND MY COUSIN, SUN

By the time we got home, we were sticky from the summer sweat and sugary drippings from one too many frozen treats.

I loved anything frozen. We had these metal ice pop makers that I would fill with fruit juice each morning before leaving for school. When we got home, the homemade popsicles were waiting for us. Sometimes, some of the juice would have dripped out frozen along the side. You would think that I would've learned not to lick the frozen drippings from the first time my tongue stuck on the outside of those metal cylinders. But no. Each time, I would have to rescue my tongue from the metallic grip by running warm water from the faucet. Eventually, my mom got rid of those metal ice pop makers, so I began freezing everything else I could get my little hands on. I froze everything from cans of cola, which inevitably exploded all over making a frozen mess in the freezer, to slices of fruit. The one time I stuck a whole watermelon in the freezer was the last straw for my mom. I was banned from freezing anything that entire summer. Although I got in so much trouble, I have to admit there's something utterly strange and oddly beautiful about a 15-pound watermelon frozen solid.

That was the summer I learned to appreciate the simplicity of ice. I made iced coffees and teas for my mom's friends. I sucked on ice cubes while I jumped roped with my friends. My favorite thing of all was to make the sweet red bean ice dessert, called *pot bingsoo*. Although shaving the ice took a lot of elbow grease, the rewards were worth the labor.

Eating a bowl of *pot bingsoo*, I almost forgot the thrill of frozen fruit. Although, sometimes I still wonder what shaved watermelon ice would taste like. Now that I have my own freezer, I can find out. But this time, I'll cut the watermelon before freezing it.

Red Bean Paste

Pot

Although I'm not a huge fan of red bean, it is an essential ingredient in many Korean sweets. You can buy canned sweetened red bean paste, but as with all things, homemade tastes much better. MAKES 1 1/2 CUPS OF PASTE

1 cup dried red beans

3/4 cup sugar

A pinch of salt

1   Place the red beans in a bowl, cover with cold water, and let sit overnight.

2   The next morning, put the beans in a medium pan and add enough water so that the water level is about an inch above the beans. Bring to a boil, then reduce the heat to low and let simmer for about an hour.

3   Press the beans and the liquid through a sieve into a heavy skillet. Turn the heat up high and cook for about 30 minutes, stirring occasionally. Be careful when stirring, because the mixture will get very thick and sputter.

4   Add the sugar and salt and continue cooking for another 10 minutes, until the mixture gets thick.

5   Set aside to cool. If you're not using it right away, place in a glass jar and refrigerate for up to a week.

Red Bean Ice Dessert

Pot Bingsoo

A refreshing summertime treat, *pot bingsoo* is a wonderful alternative to your everyday snow cone. MAKES 4 SERVINGS

6 cups shaved ice

4 tablespoons Red Bean Paste (*Pot*, page 187)

4 teaspoons cooked rice powder (*misu gallu*)

1 (16-ounce) can fruit cocktail

Flavored syrup

Colored jelly candy, optional

1   In a small, round bowl, compact 1½ cups of the shaved ice. Place upside-down in a serving bowl to create a nice mound of ice. Repeat 3 more times.

2   Add 1 tablespoon of the red bean, 1 teaspoon of the rice powder, and 4 ounces of the fruit cocktail around the ice in each bowl. Pour flavored syrup on the ice and sprinkle with jelly candy, if desired. Serve immediately.

Ginger Tea

Saeng-gang Cha

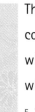

There's nothing like a steaming cup of ginger tea to help you fight off a cold. The warm feeling that coats your throat as you swallow is a comfort in winter weather. A spicy drink that warms up the entire body, don't drink it when you have a flu because ginger can aggravate fevers. MAKES ABOUT 5 TO 6 SERVINGS

1 (2-inch) piece of ginger, sliced

Water

Sugar or honey

Pine nuts for garnish

1   Add the ginger to 6 cups water in a medium pot and bring to a boil. Reduce heat and let simmer for about 10 minutes. Pour through a strainer. Discard the ginger.

2   Add sugar or honey to taste, or serve on the side for each person to adjust the sweetness.

Serve immediately, adding a few pine nuts to each cup for garnish.

Sweet Rice Drink

Shikeh

This sweet, chilled drink is usually made in large quantities for special occasions. The ginger isn't a necessary ingredient, but I think it adds a nice aroma and flavor. If you can get it, you can also garnish the drink with citron peel. A thin orange or lemon peel can make a fine substitute. The coarse malt flour can be found in the dry goods section of Korean markets. You may also substitute glutinous rice, but regular short-grain rice works just as well.

MAKES 15 TO 20 SERVINGS

Water

1 pound malt flour, coarse, not powdered

1 cup rice

1 cup sugar

1 (2-inch) piece of ginger, thinly sliced

1   Combine 16 cups (1 gallon) water and malt flour. Let sit for about 5 to 6 hours (or overnight), letting the malt soak into the water.

2   Using a fine-mesh strainer, strain the malt flour from the water. The water should be cloudy but not have any large malt pieces. Discard the malt flour.

3   Add the rice and $3/4$ cup water to the rice cooker and cook the rice as usual. Carefully pour the malt water over the rice. If there are any floating malt particles, remove with a small strainer. Stir in 2 tablespoons of the sugar and combine. Let sit with the rice cooker on "warm" for 5 hours.

4   Transfer the rice drink into a large pot. Add the rest of the sugar and ginger, making sure the sugar dissolves completely. Bring to a boil. Reduce heat and let simmer for about 8 minutes. Let cool to room temperature, then chill in the refrigerator. Remove the ginger and serve chilled, garnished with a few pine nuts in each serving.

Snack Attack

Growing up, we had our share of junk food. We weren't immune to the call of brightly colored packages beckoning us from store shelves. Yet, remembrances of candy and chips seem few and far between. Instead of the thrill of hearing the mangled jingles of ice cream trucks, we waited to hear the sound of the Scrap Man. He would either bang loudly on pots and pans or open and close a large pair of scissors in the air, calling in his deep and increasingly hoarsening voice for old scraps. With the rest of the neighborhood kids, my siblings and I would rush out with whatever scraps we could find and a bag of uncooked rice (*ssal*) in our hands.

The Scrap Man had this huge black kettle on his cart into which he'd pour in the white grains. Then the magic would happen. In a matter of minutes, our rice would be transformed into tiny little clouds of puffed rice. I always felt like we were pulling one over on that Scrap Man. All he got were some old pots and pans and we got to go home with an enormous bag as light as air, but full of tasty treats.

Once we got our treasure home, we would open the huge sack in the middle of the floor and the three of us would shovel huge fistfuls into our eager mouths, leaving a trail of little white puffs everywhere we went.

AT THE PLAYGROUND WITH
HAE-RAN AND SANG

The Scrap Man never came often enough, making each of his visits a neighborhood event. Most of the time, we got our snacks from the various vendors we'd run into on street corners and side alleys. Depending on the season, they were hawking different things. Sometimes, it would be sweet yams wrapped in newspaper, pulled out from large steamers. We would throw those yams back and forth between our hands as we impatiently tried to peel the pink skins off, revealing the sweet yellow flesh we couldn't wait to sink our teeth into even as we had to blow air to keep from burning ourselves. In the late autumns and winters, the vendors were selling roasted chestnuts, shiny and brown in wonderful brown paper bags, perfect for warming up your mittened hands and popping into your mouth between exhaling puffs of steamy condensation.

There were certain things that could be enjoyed year-round. Some vendors would be selling little red-bean-filled cakes shaped with a flower pattern or the occasional fancy fish shape. Every neighborhood inevitably had some toothless old lady making burnt-sugar candies from a small hot plate in some side street. She would squat in the same position for hours, melting sugar into perfect swirls and dramatically cracking the sugar circles into bite-size pieces. I was always afraid to buy too many candies from her, because I knew that all her teeth must have rotted off from one too many of those sugary sweets. All these treats were available for just a couple of coins that you could sneak out of your mom's purse or cajole from your dad's pockets as he unsuspectingly snored on the living room couch.

EATING SNACKS WITH MY AUNTS AND UNCLE

Despite all the temptations from the various aromas, my favorite snacks were the seasoned rice cake sticks (*dduk bokgi*). Sometimes, my mom would make them for us as an afterschool treat, but for some reason, the ones made by the street vendors or bought from the many covered food stands (*pojang macha*) lining Seoul's streets were tastier. Even if mom used the same ingredients, she could never duplicate the atmosphere of the streets in her kitchen. There were no crowds of uniformed kids swarming around the one dish that they could afford to share. There were no old men fanning themselves under the tarps of the covered stands, wearing the stools down with years of butt rubbing.

Seasoned Rice Sticks

Dduk Bokgi

This is such a popular snack in Korea, there is even an entire street in Seoul lined on both sides with only *dduk bokgi* stands. The name literally means "stir-fried rice cakes." Rice cakes to make *dduk bokgi* (which are cylindrical "sticks" about $1/2$ inch in diameter and about $1^1/2$ inches long) are available fresh, frozen, or refrigerated. If you buy the frozen kind, be sure to leave it out for a couple of hours to defrost before cooking. MAKES 5 TO 6 SERVINGS AS A SNACK

2 pounds rice sticks

1 tablespoon vegetable oil

1 onion, thinly sliced into strips

1 carrot, sliced on the diagonal into thin ovals

1 Korean zucchini, cut into $1/2$ slices, lengthwise

1 tablespoon chili paste

1 tablespoon soy sauce

1 tablespoon sesame oil

1 tablespoon sugar or Korean malt syrup (mool yut)

$1/4$ pound marinated *boolgogi* (page xx), (optional)

2 green onions, sliced on the diagonal into about 1-inch pieces

6 pyongo or shiitake mushrooms, sliced

1   If using refrigerated or frozen (thawed) rice cakes, separate and soak them in cold water to soften them for at least an hour before using. Drain the rice cakes.

2   In a large skillet, heat the vegetable oil. Add onion and carrot and sauté for a couple of minutes (until the carrot becomes a little soft). Add the rice sticks (separate them if they are not separated already), Korean zucchini, chili paste, soy sauce, sesame oil, sugar or malt syrup and optional *Boolgogi*. Continue sautéing for another 5 or so minutes. If the rice cakes are still extra hard, cover and let cook for a couple of minutes to soften.

3   Add the green onions and mushrooms and cook for another 2 or 3 minutes.

VARIATION Instead of the *boolgogi*, you can add fish cakes (which are available in the refrigerated section of most supermarkets). Slice them up and cook the same way as you would the beef.

A Bit of History of Rice Cakes

Rice cakes (*dduk*) have been around since ancient times. Grinding stones and mortars for making rice and other flours has been found dating back to the seventh and eighth centuries B.C. Steamers for steaming grains were discovered in use during the Bronze Age. Historically, rice cakes were eaten both as an everyday food and for ritual occasions. They were made from rice and other grains and varieties differed from region to region.

After the Three Kingdom period, rice cakes became associated with ceremonies and special occasions. According to records found from the Josun Dynasty, there were about 250 different varieties of rice cakes at that time.

Today, there are three major ways of preparing *dduk:* steamed, pounded and pan-fried.

SOME RICE CAKES READY TO BE EATEN

Regional Rice Cakes

GYONGGI PROVINCE

Thanks to the Han River (*Han Gang*), this region has fertile plains that produce wonderful rice and other crops. *Dduk* ingredients from Gyonggi Do can vary from mugworts, found in the fields, to oysters, which are from the sea to the west.

NORTH AND SOUTH CHOONG CHONG PROVINCES

Rice and barley are abundant crops in this region. Common *dduk* varieties in Choong Chong Do include pumpkin (*hobak*) *dduk*, potato rice cakes (*gamja dduk*), and even one called "cow's head" (*somuli dduk*).

GANGWON PROVINCE

Not a good region for growing rice, Gangwon Do's agricultural products include potatoes, corn, and other crops that don't require field flooding. *Dduk* from this region includes *song pyon* made from potatoes (*gamja*), buckwheat (*memil*) rice cakes, and cloud rice cakes (*goolum dduk*).

NORTH AND SOUTH JULLA PROVINCES

The largest grain-producing region in Korea, Jolla Do also produces edible wild grains, mushrooms, and bracken. Varieties of *dduk* include flower-shaped filled rice cakes (*ggot song pyon*), barley rice cakes (*boli dduk*), and those made from pumpkin (*hobak meshiri*)

NORTH AND SOUTH GYONGSANG PROVINCES

Gyongsang Do is a region plentiful in a variety of agricultural crops, including fruits. There are many local specialties that make use of the abundance. *Dduk* ingredients include arrowroot, vine leaf (from the mountains), and China grass leaves.

JEJU ISLAND

Although the island receives a fair amount of rain, lack of irrigation water and the poor quality of the soil makes growing rice a difficulty. Sweet potatoes, red beans, barley, and other minor grains are grown here. Jeju Do *dduk* includes those made from potato starch, buckwheat, and even foxtail.

HWANGHAE PROVINCE (NORTH KOREA)

With a vast area of fertile plains, rice from this area is well known and used to be provided as the rice of choice for royalty. Known for their hospitality, people in Hwanghae Do serve their *dduk* in large quantities. *Dduk* from this region includes wedding rice cakes (*honin jool pyon*), honey water rice cakes (*goolmool gyongdan*), and fried filled rice (*Song Pyon,* page 196).

PYONG AN PROVINCE (NORTH KOREA)

A largely mountainous region, Pyong An Do has small areas of farmable land in the west. Given its size, it produces surprisingly large quantities of rice. The area's *dduk* is very large and sometimes considered oddly shaped by Korean standards. Some rice cakes from this region include rainbow rice cakes (*mujigae dduk*), a variety made from corn (*golmu dduk)* and mung bean cakes (*nokdu dduk*).

Also a mostly mountainous area, this region has poor farming land. Rice does not grow well, so minor grains are farmed. Hamgyong Do's *dduk* are usually made from Indian millet and there are even some made from potatoes (*gamja dduk*) and a variety made from oats (*jool-pyun*).

Rice Cakes and Superstition

Traditional Korean toilets were actually separate outhouses that had two large footstools and a big, deep hole in between. I remember visiting my cousins in the countryside and listening to them tell ghost stories about the Egg Ghost. The egg-shaped apparition floated about inside the outhouse. If you were passing by and saw a glow of light from inside, it was said that a ghost was probably inside and that you should run away before it could get you. It lived inside the toilet and would sometimes get hungry and want a child to eat.

Listening to these stories always made me think that I would rather go in my pants than have to go to the bathroom in the dark shadows of the night. Usually, I could convince my sister or a cousin to accompany me to the toilet, which seemed to be located miles away from the house. These rural toilets were shaped such that children sometimes fell into the hole. As would stand to reason, it was considered bad luck for the poor sap that fell in. It must have happened often enough that there is a special rice cake made to exorcise the evil spirits from the misfortune. The family of the ill-fated child called in an exorcist and shared the rice cake with their neighbors to expel the child's (and the family's) bad luck.

Rice cakes were also used as a fortune-telling device. In olden times, all the people in the village gathered together to pound rice and make rice cakes. Each family wrote their name on a sheet of paper and put it under their share of the rice cakes. After the rice cakes were steamed, they examined them to tell their fortunes. Those with well-cooked rice cakes were said to have good luck, while those with undercooked or uneven rice cakes were said to have bad luck. The undercooked rice cakes were not eaten but dumped in the middle of a three-way street so that the unfortunate family could avoid bad luck.

Half-Moon Rice Cakes

Song Pyon

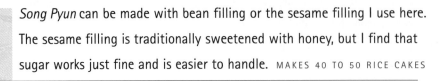

Song Pyun can be made with bean filling or the sesame filling I use here. The sesame filling is traditionally sweetened with honey, but I find that sugar works just fine and is easier to handle. MAKES 40 TO 50 RICE CAKES

Water

5 cups sweet rice flour

3 ounces toasted sesame seeds (page 3), crushed

$1/2$ cup sugar

1 teaspoon salt

Pine needles for steaming

1   Bring 3 cups water to a boil. Pour carefully over the sweet rice flour. Mix thoroughly with a wooden spoon. Set aside to cool.

2   In a small bowl, combine sesame seeds, sugar, salt, and 2 tablespoons water. Set aside.

3   Separate the pine needles from the branches, taking care to remove all the brown ends. Wash thoroughly in cold water.

4   Lay wet cloths to cover the bottom of a flat, shallow steamer. Layer pine needles on top of the wet cloth.

5   Once the dough is cool enough to touch, knead it for about 30 minutes. The longer you knead, the smoother and chewier the rice cake. Take a small piece of dough into your hands, knead it a few more times, then roll it around between your palms until you have a round ball about $1/2$ inch in diameter. Depress a part of the dough ball with one of your thumbs, continuing to turn and depress the dough until you have a bowl shape.

6   Spoon some of the sesame seed filling, compacting it into the rice bowl, but not filling it completely. Fold the lip of the bowl together and squeeze gently until it is sealed. Lay it on the pine needles. Repeat until you run out of dough and/or filling. When laying the *Song Pyon* on the steamer, make sure they aren't touching each other to prevent sticking when cooking. Cover the *Song Pyon* with another layer of pine needles and steam for about 10 minutes, or until they become slightly translucent in color.

Serve warm or at room temperature.

Flower Rice Cakes

Hwajun

Koreans say that chrysanthemums have the scent of autumn. The petals and the leaves are used in this dish for garnish and to add the smell and taste of autumn. Some people make *Hwajun* with red bean folded inside, but I prefer the simpler, subtler flavor without the filling. If you're fortunate enough, you may be able to find a bottle of chrysanthemum wine to drink with the rice cakes to experience the full flavor of the season. MAKES 20 TO 25 RICE CAKES

Chrysanthemum petals and leaves

10 to 15 dried red dates, sliced thinly lengthwise

2 cups sweet rice flour

Water

$1/8$ teaspoon salt

Vegetable oil for cooking

20 to 30 pine nuts

Honey, for dipping

1   Wash chrysanthemum petals and leaves and set aside to dry.

2   Pit the dried dates and slice into thin strips.

3   Combine sweet rice flour, 1 cup water, and salt. Make a dough ball about 1 inch in diameter and flatten into a 4-inch circle about $1/4$ inch thick.

4   Heat a little vegetable oil in a skillet and place several dough circles to cover the surface, but not too crowded that they touch each other and stick. Cook on one side for about 3 to 4 minutes over low heat. Turn over and cook the rice cakes on the other side for about another 3 minutes, pressing the flower pattern on the rice cake while it's hot. Press the date strips (skin side up) or chrysanthemum petals into the top of the rice cake to make a flower pattern. Press a pine nut in the center of the flower and a couple of chrysanthemum leaves on the outside of the flower.

Serve with honey on the side.

Soybean Powdered Rice Cakes

Injulmi

One of my favorite rice cakes. The basic recipe (before you coat the sticky rice cakes) is similar for all cakes made with sweet rice or sweet rice flour. Although this recipe calls for soybean powder, these rice cakes can also be coated with dried red date slivers, citrus zest, red bean paste, or a variety of chopped nuts. Toasted soybean powder can be found in the dried goods section of your Korean grocery. MAKES 30 TO 40 RICE CAKES

5 cups glutinous rice

1 tablespoon salt

1 tablespoon sugar

Water

1 cup toasted soybean powder (*kohng galu*)

Honey for dipping (optional)

1   Soak sweet rice in lukewarm water for 1 hour. Drain in a colander. Steam in a steamer for about 45 minutes.

2   Meanwhile, in a small bowl, dissolve the salt and sugar in 1 cup of cold water and set aside. During the last 15 minutes of steaming, sprinkle this solution over the rice to season it and help its cooking.

3   Transfer the hot rice to a work surface. Using a mallet, pound the rice into a dough. Flatten the dough into a $1/2$-inch-thick sheet, then slice it into small rectangles, about $1 \times 1^{1}/_{2}$ inches. Dip the rice cake pieces until completely coated in the soybean powder.

Serve as a dessert or snack with a bowl of honey on the side, if desired.

Sweet Rice Balls

Gyong Dahn

 Sweet rice balls are used in soups and porridges or can make an easy dessert or snack when coated with cinnamon, soybean powder, or sesame seeds. MAKES 2 DOZEN RICE BALLS

1 1/2 cups sweet rice flour

Pinch of salt

Water

1   In a medium bowl, sift together the sweet rice flour and salt. Add 1/2 cup hot water, a spoonful at a time, stirring constantly until the mixture has the consistency of cornmeal. Dust your hands with a little bit of rice flour and knead the mixture into a soft dough. Divide the dough into 24 little balls.

2   In a large stockpot, bring about 1 gallon of water to a boil. Drop the balls into the boiling water, one at a time, and cook for about 7 minutes. The balls will float to the top and become slightly translucent.

3   While the balls are boiling, prepare a cooling bath by adding ice to a medium bowl of water. As the balls are cooked, place them in the ice water to stop cooking.

Serve coated or add to soups and porridges.

VARIATION To coat the balls, prepare 3/4 cup of ground cinnamon, toasted soybean powder (*kohng galu*), toasted black sesame seeds, or finely sliced jujubes. Remove the balls from the ice water and roll them in any of the above. Serve with a side of honey.

Sweet Spiced Rice or Medicinal Rice

Yak Bap *or* Yak Shik

Yak Bap got its name from the variety of nuts and fruits that add nutrition to the dish. During the Shilla Dynasty, King Yuri was supposedly saved from a disaster by a crow, who delivered an important letter for him. To show his gratitude, the king honored the life-saving bird with a celebration of *Yak Shik* on the fifteenth of January every year. Most families also prepare this dish for *Choosuk* in September.

This is the first dish my mom learned how to make in sixth grade home economics. She was so fascinated with the process of cooking that she's been hooked ever since. You'll need a large steamer to make this dish.

MAKES ABOUT 40 TO 50 SMALL SERVINGS

5 pounds glutinous rice

1 (14-ounce) package of dried red dates, pitted

1 (14-ounce) package of raw chestnuts, peeled

3 cups dark brown sugar, firmly packed

1/3 cup soy sauce

3/4 cup sesame oil

1/2 cup pine nuts

1   Soak the rice in cold water for 4 hours. Drain and steam for 30 minutes.

2   Cut the dates and chestnuts in half, removing the pits of the dates if they are not already pitted.

3   Place the rice in a large bowl, being careful not to burn yourself. Add the brown sugar, soy sauce, sesame oil, dates, and chestnuts. Mix with a wooden paddle until the rice is evenly coated.

4   Put the entire mixture back into the steamer and steam for another hour. Try one of the chestnuts to make sure they are cooked. If not, steam another 10 minutes or so before removing from the heat.

5   Put a layer of the sweet rice onto square or rectangular casseroles or other serving dishes. Sprinkle with pine nuts. Repeat, making sure to sprinkle pine nuts on top. Let cool enough to slice into squares. Serve warm or at room temperature.

If not serving immediately, you can refrigerate *yak bap* in a covered dish for about a week. Microwave for a couple of minutes to soften the rice before serving.

VARIATION   If you like, you may add about 1 tablespoon of cinnamon to the dish.

Special Occasions

New Year Soll

Being Korean American, I get to celebrate the New Year twice: first the solar new year on January 1, and second the lunar New Year, which changes annually with the cycle of the moon. The Lunar New Year (*Soll*) is the first day of the year and the first day of a new beginning in Korea. It is a time to sweep away the misfortunes of the previous year and look forward to new endeavors. But the celebrations don't stop there. The traditional folk festival, *Jishin Balpgi*, is celebrated on the first full moon of the new year.

Jishin Balpgi, which literally translates as "stepping on the spirit of the earth," originates from a time when most Koreans lived in farming villages, according to the National Korean American Service and Education Consortium. It symbolized the collective ritual cleansing of the village and the chasing away of the bad spirits of the old year. The festival was a period of renewing personal ties and fostering a sense of community among the villagers.

During *Jishin Balpgi,* a group of musicians travel around the village playing the *poongmul,* or traditional Korean drums. They then visit individual homes to wish the residents peace and good fortune for the coming year through a combination of drumming, dancing and chanting. In return, the hosts offer rice cakes and wine to the musicians and donate money to be used for the betterment of the entire village. At night, people gather at the center of the village (*madang*) to celebrate under the full moon. As the villagers eat, drink, and play games together, they renew old friendships and reaffirm their bond as a community.

Traditional games against neighboring villages are another part of the *Jishin Balpgi* festival. These games can be as benign as a tug of war or as dramatic as stone fights and mock battles with torches. According to tradition, the winning village will be blessed with a bountiful harvest. This custom may have originated when neighboring villages shared a water source and had to determine priority for drawing water for their fields.

IN TRADITIONAL DRESS WITH MY SIBLINGS AND COUSINS

Traditionally, people stayed awake the night before New Year's Day. Ceremonies were performed to exorcise evil spirits (*narye*). Ten dancers in special masks (*choyong*) danced to music played by a live band. In rural areas, the farmers' music (*nong-ak*) was performed to also expel the bad spirits and bring good fortune to the village.

Now, with more than a quarter of South Korea's population living in Seoul and other cities, everyone tries to visit relatives in the country for the New Year. Many city dwellers have extended families living in farming communities, and they go not only to view the festival but also to pay respect to their ancestors. My father was one of those city dwellers who would pack his family off to some distant province in the dead of winter for the New Year. Because my father was one of 16 children, I never knew exactly which uncle's house we were going to visit.

I remember being forced out of bed in the darkness of the winter dawn, hastily dressing in the jolting cold to catch some crowded train out of the city.

The long trek to the countryside was always rewarded with plenty of snow in which to play and plenty of cousins to play with. My siblings and I would run around, ruining our new traditional Korean clothes (*hanbok*), falling and laughing in the dirty snow.

Around the New Year, people still love to fly traditional kites (*yon*) made from a stick of bamboo and rice paper. The adults and older kids had kite fights, wherein they tied small blades onto their kites and tried to cut through an opponent's string. In the old days, women and children also enjoyed playing on see-saws (*nol ddwigi*). Two people would stand on either side of a plank, taking turns jumping up and down, pushing their partner into the air on the opposite site. They would go back and forth, trying to see who could get their partners the highest in the air.

The best part of *Soll* for me was sneaking into the kitchen while the mothers were occupied and peering into the huge pot of Rice Cake Soup (*Dduk Gook*, page 108) boiling over the fire. I would climb onto something precarious and inhale the aroma of the steaming soup while salivating with anticipation until one of the women discovered me and chased me out of the kitchen.

Some people put *mandu*, Korean dumplings, into their *dduk gook*, but our family is full of purists. We always have the soup with rice cakes, untainted by the nontraditional *mandu*. Each year, when the women would serve up the hot bowls, either Uncle No. 3 or Uncle No. 5 (I forget which one) would inevitably say that we were "eating another year."

But before we could sit down for breakfast, we had to take care of our familial obligations. First, we would pay respect to our ancestors with ceremonial bows. Then we could eat. After breakfast, the younger generation paid respect to our elders with a ceremonial bow, called *saebae*. As the oldest members of the family sat cross-legged on the floor, the successive generations would take turns wishing them prosperity and good fortune. After all the bowing was over, the elders lectured the younger ones. Sometimes there was a pearl of wisdom offered, but more often than not it was a stern warning to do well in school.

Our rewards for being young and sitting patiently while the older folks droned on about this and that were the wads of cash, candy, and fruit generously placed into our outstretched hands. Later, the kids were free to play and the women were back in the kitchen, preparing for the next meal, several hours away.

During free time, my mom's favorite thing to do was gather everyone together to play *yut,* a game involving throwing sticks and advancing pieces on a game board. Four sticks, which were flat on one side and curved on the other side, were tossed into the air. The combination of flat and curved faces determined the number of spaces moved along a board. The first team to get all their pieces all the way around the board wins. Sometimes the grownups played for money, but often, my mom liked to devise some punishment for the losing team. For some reason, Koreans' favorite punishment for their opponents is to make the losers spell their names in the air with their butts. Nothing was more embarrassing than having to point your butt toward your relatives and gesture your name amidst howls of laughter.

This year, I'm far from the Korean village of my ancestors. And this year, as years before, I will be the one chasing the children away from the kitchen. I will be the one handing out lucky money to my bowing nieces and nephews. And when I sit down to that bowl of *dduk gook,* I will not only be another year fuller, but hopefully, another year wiser.

New Year's Food

No Korean holiday is complete without a variety of rice cakes. The most representative dish for the New Year is rice cake soup. Also, a variety of nuts, dates, dried persimmons, and other foods saved from the previous harvest are enjoyed. The *dduk gook* is a symbolic dish in many ways. Not only does eating it symbolize that you are getting a year older, but the nature of the dish itself holds many meanings. Eating rice cake soup is to wish for a year without illness. The round shape of the rice cake pieces symbolize the rising sun, strength. The *dduk* is cooked in a clear broth, which represents having a clear mind for the turning new year. You may wish to also put dumplings (*mandu*) in your *dduk gook.* And as with all Korean meals, nothing is ever complete without some *kimchi* on the side.

Rice Cake Soup (*Dduk Gook,* page 108)
Traditional Napa Cabbage Kimchi (*Baechu Kimchi,* page 41)
Various side dishes (*Mit Banchan,* pages 58 to 77)

Harvest Festival   Choosuk

"Younger generation people don't know how to bow properly! You've lost touch with traditions!" said one of my uncles in disgust as my cousins and I took turns paying respects to our ancestors. My parents nodded in agreement, muttering to themselves what a mistake it was to have immigrated to the states, that their children were nearly Americans, that we were losing our language, and so on.

They thought I wasn't listening, but I heard every word—so well, in fact, that their echoes were still ringing in my head when I returned to Korea as an adult to rediscover my language and culture. I thought it was because I was a first-generation immigrant (*gyopo*) that I had no sense of tradition. Or maybe it was because my family and I moved to the States when I wasn't quite yet seven that I had lost my sense of history.

When I got to Korea, I discovered that I was wrong. It wasn't just me. The entire country seemed to have lost some of the old-time ideals I remembered as a child. The loss of tradition was most apparent to me during *Choosuk,* Korea's harvest moon festival. The celebration happens on the fifteenth day of the eighth lunar month. It usually falls sometime in September. In the old days, you could tell that *Choosuk* was coming. Not just because of the shorter days and cooler nights, or the crisp leaves falling on the ground, but because newspapers and TV began advertising travel tickets. People were packing their traditional clothes (*hanbok*) and making plans to go to their hometowns to participate in the ritual. Everyone was getting ready for a big holiday.

The harvest festivities can be traced back to the time of the Three Kingdoms, specifically in the Shilla kingdom. The capital of Shilla was divided into six areas. The women from the different areas were grouped into two competing teams, each led by a princess, for a month-long weaving contest. This competition ended on the eighth full moon of the year when the king announced the winner. The losing team had to provide the food, drinks, and entertainment for the citywide celebration that ensued.

In later years, a game of tortoise (*gobook nori*) was introduced in the villages. In this "game," the tortoise (*gobook*) was created by two men on their hands and knees covered with a large "shell" made of straw or corn husks. The tortoise was driven like an ox from house to house by a group of men to entertain and to be entertained. The tortoise danced and performed antics for a bit and then, pretended to be tired and hungry. The household then treated everyone to food and drinks and joined in the singing and dancing.

In some villages in the southwestern part of the peninsula, a circle dance (*ganggang suwollaw*) was performed. It was supposedly developed by the regional women to trick

Japanese invaders in the sixteenth century. A large group of women sang and danced round the evening fires to make them believe that their target was well defended. The lyrics expressed the singers' desires for happiness, long life, and love, while describing typical household scenes.

With time, harvest festivities became more of a community and family activity, involving visits to the family tombs and an offering of food prepared from new crops to thank our ancestors for the bountiful harvest.

I was staying with relatives in Seoul and looking forward to seeing the colors of autumn while traveling through the Korean countryside to our distant hometown. I was already salivating in anticipation of the *Choosuk* feast—eating the fruits of the harvest and making *song pyon* (half-moon-shaped rice cakes filled with sesame seeds, beans, or chestnuts).

Traffic was bumper to bumper the whole way. It seemed the entire population of Seoul, was all on the road at once. The traffic problems have become so severe in recent years that the Korean government has extended the holiday to two or three days to accommodate travel. The painted lines on the highway were largely ignored as three-lane roads accommodated four or even five lanes of cars full of angry vacationers, crawling through the traffic with their horns blaring.

Somehow, I fell asleep. When I awoke, we had already reached our destination—a house of the relative who lived closest to the family tombs. I was disappointed to have missed the scenery on the way there, but even more disappointed to find that half of the relatives were too busy to even make it out for the *Choosuk* festivities.

Still, the house was brimming with activity. There were some people (related to me somehow; I could never keep track) watching a Korean soap opera in one room, others smoking outside, and a few of the older women cooking. After greeting everyone, I joined the women in the kitchen. They were just getting ready to set the special table to pay respect to our ancestors (*jesa*). One of my aunts ran out to grab a newspaper from the other room.

Just as I was wondering what she was going to use the paper for, she opened it to an article about *Choosuk*. There was a diagram of the *jesa* table, showing you where to put the piles of persimmon and dates, where the bowl of rice should go, and even which direction the fish should face. I had to laugh. I didn't even know there was fish on the *jesa* table. No one could remember where everything should go. They were all studying the diagram to make sure the table was set properly.

After the bowing and eating, we made our way to the burial mounds of our ancestors. The trek was not hard, but it was uphill the entire way. The whole family spent a little time, pulling up weeds, trimming the grass, and making the graves look respectable. There was another series of bowing and paying respect before we headed back to the house.

When we returned, my great-aunt pulled out the dough to make the *song pyon*. This was the part I looked forward to the most growing up. Every year, my mom and I would drive to a park to find pine needles to steam the *song pyon*. So imagine my disappointment when they started laying the *song pyon* in the steamer without any pine.

I got up to put on my shoes. The door closed behind me, but not before I heard someone say, "Hae-Jin's more traditional than we are. She's insisting we have pine needles." And I wished my uncle were around to hear that.

The last time I made *song pyon* was at my parents' house. My then-five-year-old nephew came into the kitchen to see what we were doing. I told him to pull up a chair so I could teach him how to make rice cakes.

"Christopher, do you know what they say about making *song pyon*?" I asked him.

"They say that if you make beautiful *song pyon*, you will have beautiful daughters. If your *song pyon* are ugly, your daughters will be ugly, too."

"It's a good thing your mom only had sons," I said louder to make sure my sister heard as she rocked her baby back and forth in the other room. "You should see her *song pyon*!"

My nephew didn't notice as he sat quietly for awhile, concentrating hard on the *song pyon* he was making. Finally, he looked up from the misshapen dough in his hands.

"*Imo* (auntie)," he said to me earnestly. "I don't think I'm going to have any kids."

Harvest Festival Food

The *jesa* table prepared for ancestors is distinctive for *Choosuk,* because all the food is made from the new harvest. There is also a certain way the food must be presented. The fish is always located to the east and the meat is placed on the west side of the table. Dates are placed to the east and chestnuts are placed on the west. Red-colored fruits (like apples) are placed on the east and white-colored fruits (like pears) are placed on the west. Of course, as with all traditions, there are slight variations depending on region or your family's customs.

The most representative food for *Choosuk* is *song pyon* ("*song*" derived from the Chinese for pine, and "*pyon*" means rice cake). *Song pyon* is traditionally offered to the ancestors during the fall. The pine needles not only add a wonderful fragrance to the rice cakes, but they are also considered nutritious and to have preservative properties. The rice cakes are shaped like half-moons instead of full moons, because the half moon symbolizes growth and progress. The full moon is said to be already filled up, so it symbolizes decline. Eating half-moon shapes is wishing for a good harvest the following year.

All the foods prepared for *Choosuk* are made with care, because Koreans believe that the ancestors will give the family good blessings. All the food that has been offered to the ancestors, is then shared by the whole family, as a symbolic connection between the ancestors and the descendants as well as among living relatives. The meal is an elaborate one with *jun*, meat, fish, as well as a variety of *mit banchan* made from seasonal vegetables. The usual rice with a bowl of soup is present. The meal is finished off with fruits and nuts from the *jesa* table.

Half-Moon Rice Cakes (*Song Pyon*, page 196)
Special battered foods (*Jun*, pages 81 to 97)
Seasonal side dishes (*Mit banchan*, pages 61 to 77)
Fruits, nuts, dates, etc.

Birthdays Saeng-Il

My first birthday in America was a complete disaster. It had been just over a week after our plane descended onto the Pennsylvania tarmac. My cousins, aunts, Uncle No. 7, siblings, parents, and I were temporarily crowded into my Uncle No. 5's home. Being the first one to celebrate my birthday in America was almost more excitement than I could bear. While the rest of the extended family slumbered away, I stayed up all night playing with my paper dolls, occasionally parting the bedroom curtains to peer out for the luminescent signs of morning.

My mom and aunts spent the day preparing a feast, spending hours in the kitchen while I played happily with the rest of the kids. Before long, the house was filled with the amazing aroma of a birthday feast.

There was *boolgogi, japchae, buchingae*, and no birthday could go by without the soothing liquid of seaweed soup (*miyuk gook*). We ate like we hadn't eaten for days.

After the meal came my favorite part—the cake. Earlier, I had snuck a peek at the pink box sitting majestically in the fridge. I imagined a beautifully frosted cake revealing a velvety chocolate with the first cut. Or maybe some moist yellow cake with banana cream. My imagination and taste buds went wild. I stood as still as I could as the singing happened, forgetting to make a wish. My aunt did the cutting honors while all eyes were on her hands skillfully doling out slices for everyone.

PHILIP YE, SUNNY'S LITTLE BROTHER, HOLDING RICE CAKES ON HIS FIRST BIRTHDAY

Naturally, I got the first piece. I took a huge bite of cake and realized my folly too late. Forgetting all my manners, I ran out of the dining room to spit out that awful bite into the trash can. Rum cake with raisins. What a terrible thing to do to a seven-year-old girl! It was the first time I missed my home country. Back home, I would have celebrated my birthday with stacks of colorful rice cakes and cake. I decided to stay in the kitchen alone and enjoy my dessert—a second helping of seaweed soup to wash away the bad taste of rum.

100-DAY CELEBRATION   Baeg-il

In past times, the death rate for babies was very high in Korea due to factors such as lack of medical advancement, extreme seasonal temperature differences, and childhood diseases. Many children died before they turned one. The first three months were the most critical, and once the baby reached the 100-day mark, the family celebrated on a small scale.

They first gave thanks to the three gods (*sam shin*), who take care of the child while he is growing up. The family then prayed for wealth (*jae-ak*), longevity, and good luck (*cho-bok*).

BENJAMIN, MY NEPHEW,
ON HIS FIRST BIRTHDAY

Although the food prepared for *Baeg-il* was less extensive than for the one-year celebration, there were still special dishes. Nowadays, *Baeg-il* is most often celebrated with a portrait photo for the baby.

FIRST-YEAR CELEBRATION   Dol

Although medical advancements and modernization has made the Shamanistic reasons for celebrating *Dol* no longer necessary, families like to celebrate *Dol* as a way to congratulate the parents and family. Friends and colleagues of the new parents often collected money together to buy a gold ring for the child. It wasn't meant for the child to wear; rather, it was saved for the child's education or other future needs.

The traditional celebration had four main components. First, the family prayed and gave thanks to the spirits and their ancestors. Next was the making and wearing of special birthday clothes.

Then the child's future was determined during the *doljabee*. During the *doljabee,* a special table was set out with particular items. Then the child was placed in front of the table. Whatever the child grabbed first and second were considered the most important in determining his destiny.

Traditionally, the items on the table were as follows:

Bow and arrow—the child will become a warrior.

Book, pencil, pen, brush, etc.—the child will become a scholar.

Thread—the child will have long life.

Dried red dates/jujubes—the child will have many descendants.

Money (usually a 10,000-won bill)—the child will be rich.

Rice or rice cakes—the child will have abundance (although rice cakes can sometimes mean that the child will not be very smart).

Ruler, needle, scissors—the child will be good with his/her hands.

Knife—the child will be a good cook.

In this day and age, the bow and arrow is never seen on the *doljabee* table. (Who wants a warrior kid these days?) Also, I have never been to a *Dol* where there have been any sharp objects on the *doljabee* table. Having a knife on the table seems like a sure way of ensuring the lack of longevity in the child's life.

After all the excitement, the *Dol* celebration concluded with eating, of course. When the guests are given the food, they are supposed to wish the child longevity and good fortune.

Four types of rice cakes were prepared for both *Baeg-il* and *Dol*: (1) White rice cakes (*baek-seogi*) represented a pure and clean spirit. It was also prepared for long life. (2) Rice cakes coated with red bean powder (*susupo dduk* or *susu gyongdan*) were made to ward off evil spirits. Koreans believed that evil spirits did not like the color red. (3) Sticky rice cakes with soybean powder (*Injulmi*, page 198) was made to give the child patience and tenacity, like the stickiness of the rice cakes. (4) Half-Moon Rice Cakes (*Song Pyon*, page 196) were to represent thought. Two types were made— one type was left empty and the other ones were filled. The empty *song pyon* was made to help the child grow a big heart and be generous. The filled one symbolized wisdom.

For the *Dol* celebration (*Dol Janchi*), over 12 different rice cakes were set on the table, as well as a nice array of colorfully arranged fruits. The fruits varied with the season.

CHRISTOPHER, MY NEPHEW, ON HIS FIRST BIRTHDAY

SIXTIETH BIRTHDAY   Hwan Gap

After *Dol,* the next important birthday celebration in a person's life happens 59 years later. For Koreans, having lived 60 years means completing one big circle in one's life and starting another one. At age sixty, a person will have lived through the entire cycle of the 12 lunar zodiac animals (Rat, Ox, Tiger, Rabbit, Dragon, Snake, Horse, Sheep/Ram, Monkey, Rooster, Dog, and Boar/Pig) and the five elements (water, fire, metal, earth, and wood). In Asian cultures, we are constantly reminded of the cyclical nature of time, rather than the Western perception of a linear time. Although not as significant these days, living to be 60 was a big deal back in the old days.

One of the determining factors of how successful your life has been up to 60 is the number of children and grandchildren one has. Luckily for my dad, my sister had her first child (his first grandson) the day before his sixtieth birthday. Although she couldn't attend his big bash, he was glowing like a Christmas tree, knowing that he was a proud new grandfather.

Every decade after the sixtieth is usually celebrated with a nice *janchi,* as well, but none as important as *Hwan Gap.*

Birthday Food

Birthday celebrations evolve around the usual piles of rice cakes and special battered food found in all Korean celebrations. For less formal birthdays, my mom always made us seaweed soup.

For special birthdays, such as *Dol,* the parents of the baby should prepare huge amounts of rice cakes to give out to relatives, friends, and neighbors. The rice cakes are given to ask for blessings for good fortune and health from as many people as possible. Different rice cakes are presented for different reasons. Some are supposed to give the baby bright minds. Others are supposed to make them brave. Still others give health, resilience or good luck.

For the sixtieth birthday (*Hwan Gap*), the rice cakes are piled as high as those for a wedding celebration.

BLOWING OUT MY BIRTHDAY CANDLES
WITH MY COUSIN SUN WATCHING

Seaweed Soup (*Miyuk Gook,* page 103)
Special battered food (*Jun,* pages 81 to 97)
Side dishes (*Mit banchan,* pages 61 to 77)
A variety of rice cakes (*Dduk,* pages 192 to 199)

Weddings   Gyeol Ohn

When my husband and I got married, I don't think any or our friends were quite ready for the ceremony that ensued. Not only were there over 300 guests, but there were also two distinctly different ceremonies. The first, a traditional Catholic affair, was a good example of two grown adults going through their filial duties for their traditionally religious parents. Donned in an out-of-character white gown and tuxedo, we were like two actors putting on a play during which the priest prompted us our lines. The luncheon, toasts, and cake business went on as usual.

Then the fun part happened—the traditional Korean ceremony. Well, part of it at least. No one actually goes through the entire event anymore, but a small portion of the ceremony is still performed. In Korea, marriage represents the joining of two families rather than the union of two individuals. The event is called a "Great

TIM AND I PERFORMING A GRAND BOW TO OUR GUESTS AT OUR WEDDING

Ritual" (*Daerye*) and, back in the old days, it was indeed great, if not just long and elaborate. The groom and his entourage traveled to the bride's family's house for the ceremony and stayed for three days before taking his new wife home. The actual ceremonies involved many small rituals, complete with tons of bowing and symbolic gestures.

MATCHMAKING   Eui Hon

Most marriages back in the old days were organized by professional matchmakers, who researched the family lineages of the single people in the area, their education, and social levels. Once they found a good match, they would organize a meeting with the elders of the two families. Frequently, they forgot to mention the ages of the bride or groom, causing grossly mismatched couples, e.g., a 35-year-old woman marrying a seven-year-old boy.

A fortune-teller was also consulted to determine if the match was suitable according to the four pillars (*gung hap*). Although no one gets married this way anymore, arranged marriages are still not uncommon in Korea. My mom loves to play matchmaker and has successfully set up several couples. When I heard about this at age 13, I made my mom promise me that she would never try to set me up with anyone.

My mom is a bundle of contradictions. When she was to get married to my dad, she consulted a fortune-teller, who warned her that her match to my dad was one of the worst ones she'd seen in years. Ignoring the clairvoyant's advice, my mom married my dad and has been happily living in that union for nearly 40 years. When I announced to my folks that I was getting engaged, my mom flew off to Korea to buy gifts for the groom's family, special-order traditional costumes (*hanbok*), and take care of other details I didn't want to know anything about. In the middle of her whirlwind trip, she managed to see a fortune-teller, who gave her good news about Tim's and my matrimonial plans.

DATE SETTING   Napchae

Once the bride's family has accepted the formal proposal from the groom's family, the planning would begin. First off, the groom's family would prepare a paper (*Saju*) with the exact date, time, etc., of the groom's birth and send it to the bride's family. The bride's family would then consult a fortune-teller to determine the best wedding date. When a date was chosen, the bride's family would send a message (*Yeongil*) to the groom's family that stated the wedding date and ask about the groom's measurements.

Tim and I just coordinated our dates by phone and e-mail. And when my mom needed the groom's measurements, she just came over with a tape measure.

EXCHANGING GIFTS   Nappae

Before the wedding, the groom's family sent presents to the bride and her family in a box called a *hahm.* It usually contained three things: (1) The *Honseo,* the marriage paper, which symbolized the dedication of the wife to only one husband. The wife was supposed to keep this paper forever, even having it buried with her when she died. (2) The *Chaedan,* red and blue fabric to make clothing. The two colors represented the *Eum/Yang* (Yin/Yang) philosophy. (3) The *Honsu,* a collection of other valuables for the bride.

Historically, gifts from the groom's side were delivered the day before the wedding. The *hahmjinabi* (the person who delivered the *hahm*) and some of the groom's close friends also took a pot of red bean rice cake (*bongchi dduk*). They would put on special costumes, paint their faces black with dried squid ink, and parade around in front of the bride's house with the *hahm.* They would approach, shouting that they had a "*hahm* for sale." The bride's family would rush out to greet them and to entice them with money and food. As time passed, the *hahmjinabi* and his friends would become more and more demanding, getting drunk, being raucous around town, and refusing to hand over the *hahm* unless the bride's family paid them. Usually, a maid from the house would have snuck the *hahm* away from them by this time, anyway. This tradition has been largely discontinued some time ago. It's a good thing, too, because if Tim's friends came around wearing funny clothes with black faces, I would think twice about letting them in, let alone offer them food or money.

Having married an "American" (i.e., white) man, I thought I could get away with avoiding the frenzied exchange of gifts that accompanies many Korean weddings. Still, when I went to pick my mom up from the airport, she managed to bring back sets of handmade satin blankets for everyone in Tim's family.

WEDDING PARADE   Chin Young

The groom usually rode a white horse or pony and his attendants would walk to the bride's family's house. The attendants often played musical instruments to make the mood more festive. The groom, however, had to remain serious and hide his emotions. This was often not very hard to do since he couldn't get too excited about marrying a woman he had never met.

PRESENTATION OF THE WILD GOOSE   Jeonanrye

This falls in the category of Korean wedding traditions I'm glad are no longer being practiced. During the procession, the lead person (*Gilugabi*) held a wild goose (*gilogi*). Upon reaching the bride's house, the *Gilugabi* gave the goose to the groom who then placed it on a small table. After the groom bowed twice to his future mother-in-law, she would take the goose into the house. The goose and duck were symbols of conjugal fidelity for a hundred years, since the birds supposedly keep only one mate for life. It was a way of saying, "I'm going to be faithful to your daughter," to the stern mother-in-law. Now, what would my mom do with a live goose? Today, thank goodness, live geese are substituted with wooden ones (called *gilogi*).

LOTS OF BOWING   Gyobaerye

Often, this was the first time that the bride and groom saw each other. The groom and bride each had two attendants who helped them throughout the ceremony. First, the groom walked to the east side of the wedding table; the bride to the west side. The helpers spread a carpet or mat out for the groom and the bride, respectively. The bride and groom then faced each other across the wedding table. The helpers then washed their hands, physically and spiritually cleansing them for the ceremony. With the aid of her helpers, the bride bowed twice to the groom. The groom bowed back once. The bride then bowed two more times to the groom, who bowed back once more. They finished by kneeling down and facing each other. The bowing represented the promise of commitment to each other.

DRINKING Hapgeunrye

The drinking part of the ceremony happened around a special table (*deresan*), set off by a screen with images of peonies. Depending on the region, the couple drank from the same cup or two halves of the same gourd (grown by the bride's mom). The drinking of the special white wine (*jung jong*) signified the destiny of the new husband and wife, as well as their union. Using the same gourd further symbolized that the bride and groom each made up one half and only together could they be considered whole. This was the wedding vow (*gunbere*).

First, one of the helpers poured alcohol into a small cup for the groom, who then drank it. Another helper poured for the bride who sipped it or only pretended to drink. (It would be considered unladylike to be a boozer on your own wedding day.) The groom's helper then poured again and the groom drank again. The bride's helper poured again, with the bride sipping or pretending to drink again. Finally, the groom and bride joined together and bowed three times: once to their parents, once to their ancestors, and once to the guests.

TIM AND I BOWING

BOWING TO HUSBAND'S PARENTS Pebek

Immediately after the wedding, the bride met her new parents-in-law. This ceremony took place in an area of the main living room sectioned off with a folding screen. The groom's father sat on the east side of the room, while the groom's mother sat on the west side. The bride bowed to them four times, showing her respect to her husband's family and his ancestors. This expressed her loyalty to the family. She often presented them with a small gift of food, usually dried dates or jujubes and chestnuts, symbolizing children. Her new in-laws offered her tea. At the ceremony's conclusion, the parents-in-law tossed the dates and chestnuts at the bride, who tried to catch them in her skirt. The more she caught, the more children she was to be blessed with.

At most Korean-American weddings, the *Pebek* is the only part of the lengthy traditional ceremony still performed. Ours was no different, except we paid respect not only to the groom's family, but also to mine. My mom was thrilled at the anticipation of grandchildren, grabbing a huge pile of dates with both hands and throwing them at us with great zest. With a small wink, Tim and I both ducked out of the way, letting all the dates fall to the floor, much to my mom's disappointment. Undeterred, she pelted more dates at us, hoping for future grandchildren.

BRIDAL ROOM   Shinbang

After the ceremony, the bride and groom would retire to one of the rooms of the house especially decorated for the occasion. Outside the room, relatives would use their fingers to poke small holes in the rice paper covering the windows so they could watch what happened inside. Ostensibly, they did it to make sure the bride did not run away in frustration, but I think they were all just a bunch of voyeurs. As the grooms were often much younger than the brides, they often did not know what to do. To help the young couple along, servants from both families started getting them undressed by removing the outer layers of their wedding costumes. The bride's servant began removing the groom's jacket, while the groom's servant removed the bride's jacket. After the servants left, the groom had to finish undressing his bride, while she was to offer no help to him.

BRIDAL PROCESSION   Wugwi

After three days, the bride and groom would go to the groom's family. The groom rode the same horse or pony that he brought to the wedding, while his servants carried his bride in a small palanquin (*gama*). Near the groom's house, neighbors scattered red beans, cottonseeds, and salt to keep away any evil spirits that might have followed the procession. Additionally, the groom's family placed sacks of grain and burnt straw at the threshold to the house that the bride had to cross. In addition to keeping out evil spirits, the practice also represented a wish for a good harvest brought on by adding a new family member.

INTRODUCTION TO HUSBAND'S FAMILY   Hyeon Gurye

Once in the groom's house, the bride was formally introduced to the groom's entire family. This ceremony resembled *Pebek,* but was less formal.

My maternal grandparent's
wedding

COSTUMES

Commoners usually wore white or subdued clothing except during special occasions and festivals when they wore bright, festive colors. As marriage represented the most important event in a person's life, even the most common of brides or grooms were allowed to wear clothes fashioned after those reserved for members of the court. In addition to the clothes, they also wore ceremonial headgear. The groom wore a black hat, while the bride wore a veil covering her face until halfway through the ceremony. Additionally, she wore a long hairpin.

BRIDE'S COSTUME   Wonsam *or* Hwalot

The bride wore an elaborate topcoat with flowing sleeves over her other clothes. Similar to the costume worn by queens and noblewomen of the time, a *wonsam* was made with blue silk on the inside and red silk outside. The front and back had embroidered flowers representing wealth, longevity and nobleness. The billowing sleeves had blue, yellow and red fabrics, with a wide strip of white at the cuffs, which also had colorful embroidery.

The *wonsam* replaced the *hwalot* during the Josun Dynasty and brides followed suit. Princesses wore green ones. The wide sleeves often had four or five colors, with wide white strips at the cuffs.

A belt of red woven silk with gold embroidery (*daedae*) was wrapped around the *wonsam* or *hwalot* and tied in the back. The bride also had simple makeup with three red circles on her face to ward off evil. In the old days, they made the circles out of dried chile peppers and pasted them on, but now the circles are painted on. Mine were drawn on with lipstick from one of the *ahjummas* helping me dress in the back room.

The ceremonial coronet (*Jokduri*) was fashioned after a cap used by Mongolian women when they went outside the home. The Korean version became smaller than the original size and is used mostly as an accessory. *Jokduri* worn by royal family members contained seven different jewels. During the reign of King Yeongjo in the Josun Dynasty, only black *jokduri* were permitted to prevent extravagance and the even more ostentatious headpieces, the *hwagwan,* were outlawed altogether.

GROOM'S COSTUME

The groom's *hanbok* (*samogwandae*) consisted of silk trousers, tied with straps at the ankles to fit under the boots, a shirt, a vest, and a jacket (*hyungbae*). The jacket, usually blue or maroon, had two red-crested white cranes embroidered on the middle of the chest. A belt (*gakdae*), similar to the bride's belt, tied the whole thing together. Topped off with a black hat (*samo*) with wings on the side and a pair of black cloth boots (*mokhwa*), the groom's attire was complete. His clothing was fashioned after the lowest ranking court officials from the Josun Dynasty.

Most people only celebrate a small, modernized portion of the elaborate ritual. Even in Korea, most people have Western-style weddings, complete with white dress and tuxedoes. To see an entire traditional wedding these days, you'd have to go to a Korean museum or cultural institute, which performs them to keep the cultural history alive.

Wedding Food

As with most Korean celebrations, special rice cakes are made for the occasion. Some are made for the grand ritual table (*daeryesang*), while another is made by the bride's family to give the gift-bearers from the groom's family. As usual, the exact foods placed on the *daeryesang* varied by region and by family. Always present on the table are chestnuts, which represent chastity and longevity, because chestnut trees have a single root that dies if replanted. Also on the table are jujubes, red dates, or *daechu*, which represent fer-

DAD'S OLDEST BROTHER'S DAUGHTER'S WEDDING

tility and the continuation of the blood lines. When jujubes germinate, almost every flower bears fruit. During strong winds, the jujubes are said to be more fertile and resilient.

During a traditional wedding banquet, feast noodles (*janchi gooksu*) are served. In olden times, instead of asking someone when their children were going to be married, they would ask, "When are you going to treat me to feast noodles?" As fancy as they sound, *janchi gooksu* is really a simple somen noodle in a clear beef broth, garnished with vegetables and eggs. A tradition imported from China, the noodles were a wish for a long and happy life for the married couple.

Also on the table was a duck, which symbolized peace, many children, and fidelity. People in poorer regions sometimes used a live chicken instead of a duck. The chicken was set free after the wedding. Whoever caught the chicken became its lucky owner.

Feast noodles (*Janchi gooksu*)
Various battered foods (*Jun*, pages 81 to 97)
Rice cakes (*Dduk*, pages 192 to 199)
Chestnuts, jujubes, and other fruits
Rice wine

Paying Respect to Ancestors   Jesa

Ever since I can remember, our family has honored our dead family members several times a year. We usually get together at the eldest son's house. All the women in the family gather in the kitchen and cook all day, preparing a special meal of more than twenty dishes. Everyone dresses up in their traditional Korean outfits (*hanbok*), although the men now wear suits.

Although my parents converted to Catholicism back in the mid-1970s, practicing *jesa* is still a big part of the family. During the time when missionaries were converting large groups of Koreans to Christianity, a Christian minister declared that ancestor worship was against the religious faith. Not only were his sentiments unpopular throughout the country, but he was eventually beheaded for his antinationalistic views. In essence, it's not really "worship." It's more like we're paying respect to our ancestors, asking them to take care of us. It's all an extension of the filial piety expected of younger generations of Koreans.

That familial pressure isn't as strong on younger sons as it is on the first-born.

In the states, we get together at my Uncle No. 4's house (since he's the oldest son in America) every year on the anniversary of my grandfather's death. Koreans also perform *jesa* ceremonies on the New Year (*Soll*) and during the Harvest Festival (*Choosuk*). There are several types of ancestral rituals. The ritual that takes place during the period of mourning is called *Esang jung*. The memorial service held on the ancestor's death is the *gi*. Memorial services on major holidays are called *charye* and the rituals performed in the memory of old ancestors are performed at the tombs (*myosa*) on the tenth lunar month. During *myosa*, the head of the household spent days performing and attending various rituals. In modern times, most people simply visit their family gravesite on *Choosuk* and skip the whole *myosa* altogether.

THE JESA TABLE OF MY GREAT UNCLE

The importance of paying respect to one's ancestors couldn't be stressed more as it is in Korean society. If someone escapes a car accident unscathed, people wouldn't say that they were lucky. They would say, "That person must have respected their ancestors well."

Everyone sets aside a great deal of time and money to return to the family gravesite, which can house up to four generations of the family's deceased, and prepare the necessary ritual foods.

Koreans traditionally buried their dead under grassy mounds in upright coffins made from six planks of wood. The planks represented the four points of the compass, and one each for heaven and for earth. The corpses were placed to either face south or a mountain or other important part of the landscape.

Special dishes were prepared for the ceremony, the women in the family usually having worked for hours the day before. In the autumn, for instance, fresh chestnuts were cut into jewel-like shapes and arranged in beautiful stacks on a tray. Stacking stones or food was considered a form of prayer. All food being offered to the ancestors had to be passed over burning incense. The *jesa* table had a special arrangement of dishes—five rows of different types of food and cups of rice wine (*chongju*). The number five was important in Confucian ideals and was repeated in many rituals. A cooked fish was placed on the east side with the head also facing east. Fish always meant good luck and the east symbolized eternal life.

On the morning of the *jesa* ceremony, a shrine was set up and the incense was lit. Offerings to the deceased were placed on a table in front of the shrine. This was followed by several ritual greetings (*gangshin*). The first entailed an offering of rice and wine to the spirits by the first son. A designated person would then recite a written chant. At the end of the first ritual, the eldest son would show his respects by bowing twice.

The second offering of wine was performed by the next eldest son. Following that, another offering was carried out by either one of the sons-in-law of the deceased or by the next oldest person.

Next came the dramatization of the symbolic arrival of the spirits. This set of rituals was to help the spirits accept the offerings. For example, the lid of the rice bowl would be uncovered and a spoon placed upon it to assist the spirits. A pair of chopsticks would also be placed on the meat. Then, everyone stood silently in respect for a few minutes while the spirits savored the food and wine.

When we were little girls, the idea of calling back our ancestral ghosts scared the bejeezus out of us. My sister and I would hold each other's clammy hands while peering out from behind my mom's *hanbok* skirt. One evening, after the chopstick tapping and wine pouring, we got so scared during the silent period that we looked over at each other with wide eyes and hair-raised goosebumps and ran out of the room, preferring the darkness outside to the supposed ghosts in the ceremonial room.

If we had waited a bit longer, we would have known the ceremony was almost over. After the food and wine, some soup was offered to the spirits, followed by another few moments of silence. When all the offerings were made, everyone bowed twice and the spirits were sent off to their business until the next year. The food and offerings were cleared off the table and the written prayer that was recited at the beginning of the ceremony was burned.

Eating the food and wine (*gumbok*) by the family members was an important part of the ceremony. It symbolized the receiving of blessings from the ancestors upon the living members of the family.

Although ancestral ceremonies have been transformed and simplified dramatically, it is still an integral part of the society. Some people hold ceremonies for only two generations of deceased ancestors. Still others, like my family, hold ritual for only their deceased parents. Although rituals are traditionally held in the early morning, many people hold their ceremonies in the evening when it's more convenient for their busy schedules. No matter how much the rituals change, paying respect to our ancestors reminds us of the cyclical nature of life and the long chain that links us to past and future generations.

Jesa Table

The ritual involved in paying respect to our ancestors is an old tradition that varies slightly by region and by family. Still, the basic rites are the same.

The foods prepared for the table include the following:

Basic steamed rice (*Bap*, page 15)
Soup (a simple *tahng*, pages 104 to 106)
Various seasonal vegetables (*namool*, pages 70 to 74)
Usually a white *kimchi* (page 43)
Rice cakes (*Dduk*, pages 192 to 199)
Dried, sliced fish (*Po*)
Sweet Rice Drink (*Shikeh*, page 189)
Rice candies
Fruits
Wine, etc.

A photograph of the deceased is placed at the back center of the table. A spoon, a pair of chopsticks, a bowl for wine, an incense burner, and a pair of candlesticks are also included. The use of chili powder or chili paste, garlic, or green onions is generally prohibited.

The rules for placement go as follows:

Dried sliced fish is placed to the left and the sweet rice punch (*Shikeh*, page 189) is placed to the right.

The fish is placed on the east with its head facing east; meat is placed on the west side.

Fruits and candies that are red are placed on the east side, while those that are white are placed on the west side.

Jujubes, chestnuts, peaches, and persimmons are placed starting from the west and going east, respectively.

The ritual begins with all participants lined up before the table with the oldest son at the center. He comes forward, kneels to light the incense, offers a drink, and bows twice. This is to welcome the spirit of the ancestor. Then everyone else bows twice. The head performer circles the wine bowl over the incense smoke. Another person reads the celebratory message out loud. After this reading the head performer bows twice.

Next, the second son offers a drink and bows twice. This ritual is also performed by the third son, if there is one. The head performer offers his second drink to the deceased,

Cutting food during the Jesa ceremony

after refilling his wine bowl with three drops. Then a spoon is put into the steamed rice and chopsticks into the *namool* or beef. At this time, everyone leaves the room and closes the door, symbolically allowing the deceased to eat in peace. After a couple of minutes, everyone coughs three times, rises to their feet and returns to the room.

The soup is then replaced with burnt rice water. A spoonful of steamed rice is put into the burnt rice water. Chopsticks are also placed over the bowl. The spoon and chopsticks are removed with the lid being placed back on the rice bowl. All participants bow twice to finish the ritual. The eldest son cuts a piece from each plate or bowl. The food is then removed from the table.

Afterward, the whole family eats the offered food on a different table. The food is called *eumbok,* which means "eating the ancestor's blessings."

Other Traditional Holidays and Celebrations

NOTE Most of these holidays are generally not celebrated any longer. However, a few of them are still celebrated in rural areas or just on a minor basis in the cities.

THE FIRST FULL MOON   Dae Borum

The first full moon falls on the fifteenth day of the first lunar month. Representing the beginning of the agricultural cycle. Traditionally, Koreans would get up at dawn and eat nuts, because they believed hard foods strengthened the teeth. They would also drink a cup of special cold wine, called "ear-sharpening wine" (*gwibalgi sool),* which was said to clear the ears for good news. A special Five-Grain Rice (*Ogok Bap*, page 17) was eaten with dried vegetables collected from the previous autumn's harvest. The meal is supposed to ward off heat in the coming summer. In rural communities, special rituals were performed to honor their local spirits and for hope of a good harvest. Kites with words saying "good riddance to evil" were flown to bring in good fortune throughout the year.

THE FIRST DAY OF THE SECOND LUNAR MONTH   Chungwha Chul

In rural communities, people made moon rice cakes and ate one for each year of their age. This tradition was created to motivate slaves at the beginning of the agricultural season.

THE THIRD DAY OF THE THIRD LUNAR MONTH   Samwol Samjinnal

Marking the beginning of spring, this day originated from the happiness of the people with the warming changes of the season. The swallows returned from their winter migrations and people performed traditional fertility rites. Rice cakes made from azaleas (*chindallae hwachul*) were eaten outside to enjoy nature and the new season.

COLD FOOD DAY   Hanshik

One hundred and five days after the winter solstice (around early April) is a day to eat cold food. This tradition started from an ancient Chinese story about a man named Gaejachu. His enemy chased him, so he hid at Mount Myeongsan. The villain, Jinmunggong, tried to get Gaejachu to return, but he refused. So, Jinmunggong set fire to the mountain and Gaejachu burned to death. *Hanshik* was a day to celebrate the stubborn man's loyalty. On this day, people went to their family's gravesite and planted trees, pulled weeds, or added sod, as well as performing a *jesa* ceremony.

BUDDHA'S BIRTHDAY   Chopa Il

The eighth day of the fourth lunar month was the celebration of the Buddha's birthday. Roses and sprouts in zelkova trees bloomed this time of year, so people made steamed rice cakes (*siru dduk*) using these ingredients. Even in Seoul today, people celebrate Buddha's birthday by lighting thousands of lanterns, definitely a sight to behold.

THE FIFTH DAY OF THE FIFTH LUNAR MONTH   Dano

Based on the philosophy of yin and yang, dates with the same number for the month and day (especially odd numbers) were believed to be good days to celebrate life and happiness. One of Korea's oldest holidays, *Dano* celebrations usually took place outside. Round mugwort leaf rice cakes were eaten, because mugwort was believed to have magical powers. The rice cakes were placed in front of the door to ward off evil spirits. Also, rice cakes with herbs (*surichi dduk*) and herring soup (*junchi gook*) were eaten. Women washed their hair in water boiled with flowers (*changpo*) and wore red hairpins to expel evil sprits. They rode standing on long swings made of hard boards tied with long ropes in their traditional clothes (*hanbok*). The men held wrestling competitions (*sshirum*), which eventually became a professional sport. *Dano* was also the day to pay respect to the village spirit and ancestors.

THE FIFTEENTH DAY OF THE SIXTH LUNAR MONTH   Yudu

On the day of *Yudu*, which meant "water greeting," people would get up early in the morning and make noodles, rice cakes, and fruit dishes to respect their ancestors. In rural villages, people bathed and washed their hair, believing this would wash away bad luck and prevent them from suffering during the coming hot summer. They also had ceremonies to wish for a good harvest. Special rice cakes made with flour mixed with alcohol (*sangwha byong*) and rice cakes wrapped in fried vegetables (*milcheun byong*) were made on this day.

THE THREE HOTTEST DAYS OF THE YEAR   Sambok

Sambok comprises the three days of *chobok, jungbok, and malbok*, marking the beginning middle and the end of the hottest period of the summer. People believed that eating hot meat dishes on this day would help boost their stamina. People still make chicken soup with a whole chicken stuffed with glutinous rice, ginseng, red dates and garlic (*Samgaetahng,* page 100) to help fight off the heat.

THE SEVENTH DAY OF THE SEVENTH MONTH   Chilsok

There is a Korean legend about two lovers, represented by the constellations of Altair and Vega (*Gyeonu* and *Jiknyo,* respectively). They were banished by the gods to opposite sides of the Milky Way, but would meet once a year by the grace of the birds. Birds would make a bridge in the summer sky for the two lovers to walk on so they could meet for a few fleeting moments. Rain in the evening meant the two lovers had met and were shedding tears of happiness. The next morning's rain was supposedly the lovers' tears as they were forced to leave each other again. Rural villagers made offerings of newly harvested rice at the local shrine. Women and children of the village cleaned the area around the communal well and lit candles as part of a ritual. Some people prayed for the well-being of their children on this day, while some young people also prayed to Altair and Vega for good luck. This was right in the middle of Korea's rainy season. Wheat pancakes (*milijun byong*) and rice cakes with red beans (*siru dduk*) were eaten on this day.

THE FIFTEENTH DAY OF THE SEVENTH MONTH   Baekjung

This day came after the busiest time of year for farmers. In rural villages, this marked a day of rest before the busy harvesting season began.

THE NINTH DAY OF THE NINTH MONTH   Jung Gu

Jung Gu, which literally means "double nine," was a day to enjoy the autumn. On this day, people ate chrysanthemum rice cakes and special dumplings and drank crysanthemum wine or Citron Tea (*Yuja Cha,* page 184). They would pack a picnic and hike up the mountains to view the fall colors. In traditional times, scholars would compose poetry or paint pictures to celebrate nature.

THE FULL MOON OF THE TENTH MONTH   Sang Dal

The tenth month and the tenth full moon of the year was called *Sang Dal,* which means "the moon shines the brightest in the year." This tenth full moon was considered sacred and ceremonial services were directed towards the sky. At home, people set the table with a steamed rice cake (*shiru dduk*) to calm the household god and bring peace in the household. They also replaced the grain jar of the tutelary spirit (of house sites) with newly harvested grain.

THE WINTER SOLSTICE   Dongji

Dongji falls on December 22 in Korea. Since this is the longest night of the year, people celebrated the beginning of the days getting longer again. It was believed that the sun got its life back on the solstice. The day is celebrated with a red bean porridge with small rice cakes inside (*Pot Jook,* page 35). In traditional times, people would sprinkle the porridge around the house and large tree nearby, because it was believed that the color red scared away evil spirits, who could cause more problems during the longer winter nights. Traditionally, people made new calendars to mark the seasonal divisions and agricultural dates. In modern times, people give each other calendars as year-end gifts.

NEW YEAR'S EVE   Jaesuk or Jeya

On New Year's Eve children and young men paid respect to their older relatives with "old year farewells." People stayed up all night with their doors wide open to receive the ancestral spirits. There was also an old saying in Korean that said, "If you fall asleep tonight, tomorrow, your eyebrows will be as white as snow."

Ingredients

Anchovies (*Myulchi*) Dried anchovies of various sizes can be found in Korean and other Asian markets. Although dried varieties are more commonly used in Korean cooking, salted anchovies found in jars (sometimes labeled anchovy paste or sauce) are also used in certain dishes. Korean brands are usually less salty and pungent than those of other Asian countries. Store both dried and salted varieties in the freezer and they'll keep for at least a year.

Asian Pear (*Naju Bae*) Also known as apple-pear, this fruit is found in Korean and Asian supermarkets (the best time of year to get them is in the fall when they're in season). They look like large brown apples with tough skins and have very crisp, juicy insides. They must be peeled for eating.

Bellflower Roots (*Dolaji*) White and crunchy with a slightly sweet flavor, bellflower roots are about 4 to 5 inches long. Fresh roots can be found in the produce section, preshredded roots are usually in the deli section, and prepackaged, preshredded dried roots are in the dried food aisle of Korean groceries.

Chile Peppers (*Gochu*) *See* Peppers.

Chile Pepper Threads (*Shil Gochu*) A traditional garnish, these hair-thin threads resemble saffron. They're machine-cut from dried red chile peppers and sold in small packages (1 ounce). They'll keep for several months in the refrigerator in a tightly sealed pack. They don't really serve much of a purpose except as a garnish. You can substitute chili powder as a garnish to add color to any dish.

Chili Paste (*Gochujang*) Found in Korean markets, chili paste is one of the staples of Korean cooking. Jars and containers of various sizes can be found in the condiment aisle or in the refrigerated section of the store. In the olden days, every household made their own. But since such delicious varieties are so readily available now,

CHILE PEPPERS SUN-DRYING
ON A MAT

such traditions only continue in rural areas or really traditional households. Store in a tightly sealed container in the fridge indefinitely. Still, I've included a recipe for the traditional chili paste, in case you want to try making it yourself (page 6).

Chili Powder (*Gochu Galu*)   Korean chili powder is made from thin red peppers sun-dried on woven mats or strung together and hung from eaves of thatch-roofed houses throughout the Korean countryside. Available in Korean groceries, they come in various degrees of coarseness and spiciness. Pay a little extra for the quality brands, because the flavor difference is worth it. Store in the freezer or refrigerator indefinitely.

VARYING GRADES OF CHILI POWDER AT THE MARKET

Citron (*Yuja*)   A citrus fruit with a tart and slightly bitter flavor, citron is similar to lemons in that both the rind and the juice are used. The trees begin fruiting in the spring, bearing green tangerine-sized fruits in the fall. They turn ripe and yellow in the fall. *Yuja* is difficult to find outside of Asia, but look for the fragrant fruits in Asian markets in the late fall or winter. Certain varieties look like hands with extra fingers. As with any citrus fruit, look for firm fruits that are heavy for their size. Substitute lemon or lime for the rind. For the juice, substitute equal parts lime and orange juices.

Crab (*Gwae*)   Koreans harvest blue crabs from waters around the peninsula from early May to mid-July and eat them either raw or stewed. Crabs are best bought live in Chinese or Korean stores or from seafood markets. Look for active crabs that are heavy for their size. The shells should be moist, not dry or flaky. Small baby crabs are also eaten whole, seasoned in soy sauce, garlic and chile pepper as a side dish.

Crown Daisies (*Soot* or *Sootgat*)   Edible crown daisy leaves, which resemble chrysanthemum leaves, are not the kind you find in your flower garden. They're specially grown for eating. Since the plants grow wild on Korean hillsides, you can always see older women crouching on the side of a hill gathering them into their aprons. Used mainly as a garnish, the leaves have a soft yet slightly stringy texture and a floral and musty fragrance. They are also used to flavor and color special rice cakes. When choosing the leaves, look for qualities you'd find in any fresh leafy vegetables—firm and crisp. Rinse them as well as you'd wash spinach because they grow low to the ground and pick up dirt.

Cucumbers (*Oi*) Unlike the large, seeded cucumbers widely found in American markets, the smaller, pickling varieties are used in Korean cooking. For dishes like Cucumber *Kimchi* (page 57), smaller, uniform cucumbers (about 3 inches long) are essential. If the cucumber will be sliced, the larger English or French cucumbers or Persian varieties can be substituted.

Dates or Jujubes (*Daechu*) Dried red dates are used often in Korean dishes, especially rice cakes, to add color. They can be found in the dried goods section of Korean markets. They are slightly wrinkled with deep red skins. Inside, the fruit is brown surrounding the thin seed.

Eggplants (*Gaji*) Contrary to popular belief, eggplants did not originate in the Mediterranean but are native to Southeast Asia. Long and thin, Asian eggplants grow soft quickly, so they should be prepared within a few days of purchase. Look for firm, smooth skins. Either the Chinese variety (with pale skin) or the Japanese kind with dark purple skin can be used in Korean cooking.

Fermented Soybean Paste (*Dwenjang*) Although quite often mistaken for Japanese miso, Korean fermented soybean paste is brownish yellow in color and chunkier in texture. Another one of the fundamentals of Korean cooking, jars and containers of soybean paste can be found in the condiment aisle of the refrigerated section of Korean groceries. Store in a tightly sealed container in the fridge indefinitely.

Fern Bracken (*Gosali*) This brown stem of the fern bracken (sometimes called fiddlehead fern), can be found in the dried goods section of most Asian markets. Fresh or reconstituted fern bracken is available in the deli section of most Korean groceries. When using dried fern, soak them in warm water for several hours or overnight. Drain and use in such dishes as Mixed Rice Bowl (*Bibim Bap*, page 23), Spicy Beef Soup (*Yookgaejang*, page 101), or make an easy side dish by sautéing them in sesame oil with a little garlic, soy sauce, green onions and sesame seeds.

Fish (*Mool Gogi*) If it comes from the sea and it's edible, Koreans have found a way to eat it. Fish are eaten every which way possible—raw, fried, battered, grilled, steamed, or boiled. You will find most fish whole (with heads and tails intact) in the seafood section of most Asian markets.

Garlic (*Manul*) Korean food can't be imagined without garlic. In fact, Korea is number one in the world for garlic consumption per capita. Originating from somewhere in Central Asia, garlic has made its way into the heart of Korean cuisine. There are three major types grown in Korea—*soinpyun*, which has about three or four large cloves, *dainpyun,* with many small cloves, and *jangsun*, grown mostly for its stems. The most widely used is the variety with smaller cloves, which is spicier and tangier than other varieties. Since garlic varieties are difficult to find in the States, use any fresh garlic. The freshest garlic is available in late spring, when the bulbs are in season; however, garlic is available year-round. In the early spring, young garlic is pickled (page 66). When choosing garlic, look for firm bulbs that are compact and not sprouting. Store garlic in a cool, dry, dark, and well-ventilated place. Although you can buy garlic preminced in jars, it is always best, flavorwise and nutritionwise, to peel garlic for immediate use. There really is no substitute for fresh garlic. Garlic powder isn't flavorful or pungent enough. For convenience, though, you can mince a bunch of garlic and freeze it tightly wrapped in plastic. Just thaw in the fridge for a few hours before using. To rid your hands of the lovely garlicky smell after peeling them, rub them with a cut lemon before washing with soap and water. (Incidentally, the lemon trick is great for getting rid of fishy smells as well.) When you go to a Korean barbecue joint, you may get a side dish of sliced raw garlic to eat with your meal. If you've ever tried it, you know that it's very spicy and pungent. I prefer to grill the garlic along with the meat for a milder flavor, but my dad likes his garlic raw. He'll come home with so much garlic on his breath, that my mom has made him sleep upside-down in bed, preferring his feet to his stinky breath.

Gelatin (*Mook*)   Jellies or curds in Korean cuisine are savory, not sweet. You can find them in the refrigerated section of Korean groceries. The semitranslucent white gelatin is made from mung beans. The brown-colored gelatin is made from acorns. They should be stored in the refrigerator in water and will keep for about a week.

Ginger (*Saeng-gang*)   When selecting ginger, select the hardest and the heaviest. The roots will be wrinkled and light if they have been stored too long. You can substitute powdered ginger, if you absolutely must, but I don't recommend it. The freshness and spiciness of ginger is lost when it's dried and powdered. Ginger keeps for about a week unrefrigerated, or longer in the refrigerator. Ginger can be frozen, but you'll lose the wonderful crispness and texture. For ginger juice, first finely grate the ginger. Then simply squeeze the grated ginger in your hand. Two tablespoons of ginger will make about a tablespoon of juice, depending on how fresh the ginger is.

Gingko Nuts (*Uenhaeng*)   Sold unshelled or shelled, gingko nuts are available fresh in late autumn (around October and November). Luckily for us, the nuts come to us already washed and cleaned of their stinky outer fruits, which can cause skin irritations. Canned nuts are available year-round, but they are of course not as fresh as those that are sold unshelled. To remove the soft, yellow nuts from their hard shells, crack them with the flat side of a knife or the back edge of a heavy knife. When cooked, they turn a bright green color. Buy your nuts fresh in Asian groceries. If you must store them, keep the unshelled nuts in a paper bag in a cool, dark place.

LADIES IN KOREA HARVESTING LARGE GREEN ONIONS (KEUN PA)

Green Bean Sprouts (*Sookju Namool*)   *See* Mung Bean Sprouts.

Green Onions (*Pa*)   Green onions are used to add color and flavor to many Korean dishes. Choose firm ones with dark green shoots and thin white stalks. Large green onions (*keun pa*) are often used in soups. Wilted leaves should be removed and trimmed.

Jellyfish (*Haepali*)   The edible part of the jellyfish, the skin, is sold either whole or dried in Asian markets. The skin is golden in color and the texture of plastic before it is soaked and prepared for cooking. The texture is crunchy but rubbery and the flavor is non-existent. Predominately eaten in China for the texture, Koreans prepare jellyfish with spicy mustard and cucumbers.

Jujubes (*Daechu*)   *See* Dates.

Kelp (*Miyuk* or *Dashima*)   Korean kelp is sold dried in bags in Asian supermarkets. Used for soups (recipe, page 103) and side dishes, *miyuk* can be reconstituted by soaking in water for about 10 minutes. As the seaweed soaks up the water, it will soften and expand, becoming slightly slimy and flowing. *Miyuk* is a little softer than the Japanese *dashima*, which is usually sold in large dried sheets in the same dried goods section of Asian groceries. *Dashima* can be eaten deep fried, sprinkled with some sugar (recipe, page 77).

Korean Chives (*Buchu*)   Found in the produce section of Korean markets, they look more like bundles of long grass more than ordinary chives, although they belong to the scallion family. A highly perishable green, buy them the day of use, or store them in the fridge wrapped in a paper towel for only a couple of days. Use in such recipes as flatcakes (*buchu buchingae*) and Cucumber *Kimchi (Oi Sokbaegi, recipe,* page 57).

Laver (*Gim*)   Sold in thin sheets, laver is actually a form of marine algae. To enhance its flavor and maintain its texture, the sheets are usually toasted before eating. Used for rice rolls (*see* recipe for *Gim Bap*, page 29), laver sheets are also eaten as side dishes (*see* recipe for *Gim*, page 61).

Malt Powder (*Yut Gilum*)   A beige-colored powder sold in bags in the dry goods section of Korean markets. Read the labels carefully, because it is difficult to distinguish amongst malt powders just by looking at the contents. *Yut Gilum* is a malt powder made from dried barley. Malt powder made from dried soybeans is called *meju galu*.

Malt Syrup (*Mool Yut*)   Barley malt, made from toasted barley sprouts, is used for sweetening and to add an appetizing gloss in some dishes. It can be found in Korean markets or health food stores. You can substitute corn syrup, but in lesser quantities, unless you like your dishes extra sweet.

Mugwort (*Soot*)   Resembles tiny chrysanthemum leaves. My brother and I used to call it "the weed." It's a little bitter in taste and very fragrant. Used in various dishes, most notably in rice cakes, to add a dark green color and a woodsy flavor.

Mung Beans (*Nokdu*)   Originating from India, dried yellow mung beans can be found in Asian and Indian markets. The mung beans are used to make flatcakes. (*See Nokdu Buchingae*, page 82).

Mung Bean Sprouts (*Nokdu Namool*) or Green Bean Sprouts *(Sookju Namool)*   Found next to soybean sprouts in Korean markets (and sometimes just labeled "Bean Sprouts"), mung bean sprouts and green bean sprouts are interchangeable. They are smaller than soybean sprouts and don't have the big yellow bean head. Check carefully that they are fresh and discard any with brown spots.

Mushrooms (*Busut*)   Most types of mushrooms found in Korea and other parts of Asia are not imported to the United States. For instance, pine mushrooms (*songi*) are harvested wild in pine forests in the fall and have a slight pine fragrance, hence the name. However, *pyongo* (also known as shiitake) mushrooms are easy to find in most Asian markets. Although fresh is always preferred, dried varieties can be mail ordered or bought in Chinese markets and pharmacies. They come in varying grades and are priced accordingly. The more expensive varieties have a meatier texture and better flavor. To rehydrate dried mushrooms, soak them in warm water (stem side down) for about 30 minutes. Use one cup of water for every two ounces of mushrooms and reserve the soaking water to make a vegetarian soup stock, if you wish.

Mustard (*Gyuh-ja*)   Spicy yellow mustard is used in Korean and Chinese cooking. Powdered mustard (i.e., Coleman's) can be found in regular supermarkets and Asian groceries.

Follow the directions on the package or mix the powder with enough water to make a smooth paste.

Napa Cabbage (*Baechu*)   Napa cabbage is the most popular vegetable used in traditional *kimchi* (page 41). When choosing a cabbage, look for a firm and heavy head with tightly packed, green leaves that are unblemished. When washing the cabbage, do not throw away too many of the darker leaves; they contain most of the vitamin A. If you cannot find Napa cabbages in your local market, bok choy can be substituted. These cabbages have a relatively long shelf life and will keep for a couple of weeks in the refrigerator, although I recommend buying them fresh just before use.

Noodles (*Gooksu*)   Knife-cut noodles (*Kal gooksu*) can be found refrigerated or frozen in Korean and Asian markets. Most other noodles, such as regular wheat noodles, sweet potato noodles, mung bean noodles, and buckwheat noodles, are all found in the dried goods section.

Octopus (*Nakji*)   Koreans eat octopus raw, grilled, stir-fried, boiled—pretty much any which way we can. Generally, octopus is prepared in spicy dishes or eaten with a side of Seasoned Chili Paste (*Yangnyum Gochujang*, page 8). Small baby octopus is great grilled (*Jjukkumi,* page 156) or in hot pots. For adult octopus, prices will vary depending on the size. I don't think larger ones taste better; they just look more impressive. The thing to look for in octopus is freshness. They should be slightly firm to the touch and have a glossy skin (which you should peel off before cooking). Most are grayish-white with a slightly translucent skin and will become opaque and purplish-pink when cooked. Be sure not to overcook your octopus, or it will become tough and rubbery, and not very good to eat.

Peppers (*Gochu*)   When the Portugese and Spanish traders introduced chile peppers to Asia in the seventeenth century, Koreans embraced them with a fervor that never let up. You will find several varieties in Korean groceries. First, there are the mild green peppers, called *ggoari gochu*. These tiny things are wrinkled and about 1½ inches long. They're great for dishes like Soy Stewed Beef (*Jang Jolim*, page 175). Next, you'll see long, thin green peppers, with smoother skin. Depending on the season, these can vary from mild to fire hot. Supposedly, the more crooked the pepper, the spicier they are, but I've had some killer ones that were straighter than a pencil. Sometimes, within the same pepper the spiciness increases with a vengeance as you venture closer towards the stem. These peppers are great just for eating raw, served with a side of Seasoned Fermented Soybean Paste (*Yangnyum Dwenjang*, page 5). When these peppers turn red in autumn, they are dried to make chili powder (*gochu galu*). You may also find some smaller red peppers (sometimes labeled "Red Jalapeños") in the produce section. These are usually milder than their color would suggest, albeit still not for the faint of palate, and make nice additions to hot pots, stir-fries, or as a garnish for other dishes.

Perilla (Wild Sesame) Leaves (*Ggaetnip*)   Originating from southern China, Perilla leaves have a fragrant, sort of mint-like flavor. Fresh perilla leaves are sold year-round in the produce section of Korean, Chinese or Japanese groceries. Larger leaves are sold together in bundles, sometimes packed in Styrofoam cases with plastic wrap. Smaller, less evenly shaped leaves are sold in open bundles. Look for fresh leaves that are unwithered with no brown spots. Highly perishable, buy them the day you'll use them. If you must, store them in the fridge for just a couple of days.

Perilla (Wild Sesame) Seeds   Perilla seeds are about the size of sesame seeds, but they are dark brown in color and round in shape. They're available next to sesame seeds in Asian markets.

Persimmons (*Gam*)   All varieties of persimmons are sold in markets. There are two types of persimmons that become available in the fall. The larger, acorn-shaped variety is extremely bitter and makes your mouth dry, unless it is allowed to ripen until very soft. They are called *hongshi* or *hongshi gam*. Hard, flat varieties are called *gam*; the flatter varieties can be eaten either firm or soft. These are the kinds used to make dried persimmons (used in Korean desserts or drinks), called *ggotgam*. They look like they are dusted with flour, but in fact it's a fine coating of sugar that appears during the sun-drying process. Fresh persimmons are found in Asian groceries and farmer's markets in autumn, while dried ones are available year-round. Fresh persimmons should be kept at room temperature or stored in the refrigerator for just a couple of days, if already ripe.

Quail Eggs (*Maechuli Al*)   Quail eggs are small, speckled brown and black and taste similar to chicken eggs. They taste better to me, but the difference is so minor that it may not be worth the extra expense. But you may want to decide for yourself. These cute little eggs are available next to regular eggs in Asian markets, and certain farmer's markets.

Radish, Asian or Daikon (*Mu*)   Koreans use a variety of radishes to make different types of *kimchi*, in hot pots and soups, as well as grated and used raw in salads or side dishes. Asian radishes are wonderful roots exemplifying the combination of yin and yang. They are both spicy and cool, crispy and juicy. When choosing radishes, look for heavy cylindrical roots with smooth skins. Cracks on the sides can indicate frostbite, which affect the crispness of the daikon. Ponytail radishes (*Yulmu*) should also be firm and smooth with leafy green tops. A variety of radishes can be found in most supermarkets, Asian groceries, and in some farmer's markets year-round, but the sweetest are available in colder months. Store in the warmer part of the refrigerator and use within a week of purchasing.

Radish Greens (*Mu Chong*)   The leafy parts of young radishes are said to be more nutritious than full-grown radishes (*mu*). Radish greens are sold by the bunch in the produce section of Korean markets.

Red Beans (*Pot*)   Red bean is most often cooked, mashed and combined with sugar for use in rice cakes or other sweets. Because of their bright color, they have been a symbol of good fortune and eaten during celebrations and festivals since China's Han Dynasty (206 B.C. to 220 A.D.). Red bean is also combined with other grains to make seasonal rice dishes, an alternative to ordinary white rice (Red Bean Rice or *Pot Bap,* page 16). Presweetened and cooked red beans are also available canned in most Asian markets.

Rice (*Ssal* or *Bap*)   Koreans eat short-grain rice, which may be found in most supermarkets and Asian groceries. The best rice is available in late autumn, when the new crops have been harvested. In Korean markets, you can buy rice in a range of 2- to 50-pound bags. Store rice in a cool, dry place for up to a few months.

Rice, Sweet (*Chap Ssal*)   Used mainly in making desserts, it looks like short-grain rice but is opaque and chalky. It turns clear and translucent when cooked and the texture is chewy and sticky (hence its other names "glutinous rice" or "sticky rice"). Sweet rice is steamed instead of boiled because of its stickiness. More expensive than short-grain rice, it's found in Asian and Korean markets.

Rice Cake Ovalettes (*Dduk Gook*)   Made from slicing large cylinders of rice cakes on the diagonal, rice cake ovalettes are used mainly for making Rice Cake Soup (*Dduk Gook*, page 108). Found in the refrigerated section of Korean markets, you can also find them fresh next to other rice cakes around the Lunar New Year. Or you can get the cylinders and slice them yourself. When using refrigerated ones, soak in cold water for at least an hour to soften them up.

Rice Cake Sticks (*Dduk Bokgi*)   These look like small white cylinders and can be found in the refrigerated section of Korean markets. Some groceries offer fresh ones, displayed with the other rice cakes. Sometimes used in Korean Shishkabob (*Sanjuk*, page 171), these rice cakes are mainly used to make the ever-popular snack, Seasoned Rice Sticks (*Dduk Bokgi*, page 192).

Rice Flour (*Ssal Galu*)   Made from ground short-grain rice, rice flour should be stored like regular wheat flour, tightly sealed in a cool, dry place or in a tightly sealed container in the refrigerator. It should be used within a year.

Rice Wine, Refined (*Chongju*)   There are three types of rice wine available in Korea—*makgulli*, a milky rice drink; *chongju*, a strained version of *makgulli*; and *soju*, a distilled version of *chongju*. Although wine is rarely used in Korean cooking, if any is used at all, it would be *chongju*. *Soju* (a clear rice wine similar to sake) is a widely popular drink amongst Koreans.

Salt (*Sogeum*)   Koreans use coarse sea salt (*goolgun sogum*) for making *kimchi* and certain sauces. Refined salt (*ggot sogum*, literally translated as "flower salt") is identical to kosher salt. Regular table salt can be substituted. Coarse sea salt can be found in Korean markets.

Salted Shrimp (*Saewu Jut*)   Tiny salted shrimp (or *krill*) are one of the vital ingredients in making *kimchi*. The best are considered to be sweet and pink shrimp caught in June (*yook jut*). Do not confuse Korean salted shrimp with the more salty and pungent Southeast Asian shrimp paste. Korean salted shrimp can be found in the refrigerated section of Korean groceries in 1- to 2-quart jars.

Seaweed   *See* Kelp, Laver, or Wakame.

Sesame Oil (*Chang Gilum*)   Korean sesame oil is darker and richer in flavor than many other Asian varieties, because the seeds are toasted before pressing. Look for dark, rich oil with a strong nutty aroma. Sesame oil has a lower temperature tolerance than regular vegetable oil, so take care not to burn it when cooking. Store in the refrigerator to keep fresh longer.

Sesame Seeds (*Ggae*)   Sesame seeds are widely available in most grocery stores, but in Korean markets, there are three types—uncooked, toasted, and crushed. The crushed varieties are sometimes called "Sesame Salt" (*Ggae Sogeum*), although there is no salt added. It's easy and tastes much better to toast your own seeds at home (see recipe, page 3). Store all sesame seeds in either the freezer or fridge to retain freshness.

Soybean Curd or Tofu (*Dubu*)   Bean curd was first made in China from a variety of beans, including mung beans. Because meat is expensive throughout Asia, soybean curd is a major source of protein for most Asians, including Koreans. In general, softer bean curds are used in soups and firmer varieties are used for frying. It's best to buy tofu fresh the day it's made out of large tubs in Asian markets. However, it is available packaged in most supermarkets and health food stores. Store bean curd in the refrigerator. If you change the water every day, it'll stay fresh for a couple of weeks.

Soybean Powder (*Kohng Galu*)   In the dry section of Korean markets, this yellow powder is found in one-pound bags.

Soybeans (*Kohng*)   Koreans have eaten soy and soy products for centuries. Tofu, sprouts, soymilk and *dwaenjang* are made from light-colored soybeans. Black soybeans (or just plain black beans) are also used in Korean cooking. Growing up, we used to sit on the floor and eat boiled soybeans as a snack, spreading out a newspaper to discard the casings, instead of popcorn.

Soybean Sprouts (*Kohng namool*)   These sprouts are longer and thicker than regular bean sprouts and are topped with a large yellow bean. They are sometimes just labeled "Bean Sprouts" in Korean markets. Available in Asian markets year-round, buy them fresh no sooner than a day or two before you need them. They will only keep for a few days in the refrigerator. In Korean slang, a tall skinny boy (like my brother) is called a "*kohng namool.*"

Soy Sauce (*Ganjang*)   Soy sauce is made from naturally fermented soybeans, which are processed in several steps and aged for up to two years. Some found in most supermarkets are made from quickly hydrolyzed vegetable proteins and aren't true soy sauces. The difference is in the flavor. True soy sauces are usually found next to the fake sauces in most supermarkets. Chinese have both light and dark varieties, depending on the region. You may use either light or dark varieties in Korean cooking, although a medium sauce is preferred.

Squash (*Hobak*)   There is a variety of squash in Korean cuisine. Korean summer squashes resemble Italian zucchini in size and flavor, although their skin color is a lighter green and some are plumper. Of course, Italian zucchini can be substituted if the Korean variety is not available. Other squashes are round and with dark green stripes on the outside. These have sweet orange insides that are best used for such dishes as Sweet Pumpkin Porridge (*Hobak Jook*, page 36).

Squid (*Ohjinguh*)   Koreans eat squid in a variety of ways: cooked, steamed, in hot pots, or dried. When you visit practically any seaside town in Korea, you can see long lines of whole squid hung out to dry. Dried whole squid is roasted and eaten as a snack or accompaniment to alcohol (*anju*). Processed squid strips, available in Asian markets, look similar to pulled-apart string cheese. When choosing fresh squid, look for firm, bright ones with slightly translucent, grayish meat. If they haven't been cleaned, wash and peel off the speckled skin before cooking.

Sweet Potatoes (*Goguma*)   A New World crop, sweet potatoes were introduced to the Philippines by the Spanish Conquistadors. From there, they traveled to China and spread throughout Asia. The skin of the sweet potato is purplish or pinkish and the insides a bright yellow. American sweet potatoes and yams are not as sweet and contain more water. They come in season in the late fall. Roasted or boiled, they make healthy and delicious cold-weather snacks. Look for sweeter varieties in Asian groceries.

Sweet Potato Noodles (*Dang-myun*)   Although there are dozens of noodles throughout Asia, sweet potato noodles are distinctly Korean. They are found with other noodles in Korean groceries. Sold in large, dried strands, they are slightly transparent and grey. They are sometimes used in soups and mostly used to make *Japchae* (page 123).

Taro Root (*Talong*)   Taro roots are found in Asian and Latino markets. Koreans generally use the smaller varieties in their dishes. They are hairy with brown skins and noticeable rings. The flesh is beige in color, sometimes with purple specks. Because the flesh has a serious skin irritant, which is destroyed by cooking, gloves are recommended when peeling them raw. Although they are sometimes compared to potatoes, they are very different. For instance, taro roots don't keep more than a week and turn a purplish grey when cooked. They also have a distinctively hearty taste that's different from their potato cousins. A delicious soup can be made from the roots during colder months (*Tolang Gook,* page 104).

Wakame (*Miyuk*)   These thin strands of seaweed are sold dried in Asian markets. In Korean cooking, they are used in soups (Seaweed Soup, page 103) and side dishes. Also, *see* Kelp.

Watercress, Korean (*Minali*)   It looks similar to Western watercress, but it has pale green leaves with a long, slender and knotty stem (similar to bamboo). It has an herbal fragrance, similar to celery or parsley. An important ingredient in *kimchi* making, *minali* is often used as a garnish in dishes. Sold in bunches in the produce section of Korean grocers, it's best to buy fresh, but can be kept for a few days in the refrigerator. There is no substitute for it in cooking for flavor, but Western watercress can be substituted as a garnish.

Tools and Implements

Bamboo Baskets   Inexpensive and versatile, bamboo baskets can be used for everything from straining noodles to cooling off flatcakes. They are flat and round and available in a wide range of sizes, from 6 inches to 3 feet in diameter.

Chopsticks (*Jut Galak*)   Koreans are the only ones in Asia who use metal chopsticks regularly. This practice goes as far back as the Baekje Period (18 B.C.–660 A.D.), when royalty used bronze implements, probably imported from China. During the Shilla Period (668–932 A.D.), royalty used silver implements because silver was said to tarnish with the presence of poison. Having grown up using metal chopsticks, I find them quite easy to use, but many of my friends have a hard time with their slippery grasp. To be honest, even my great aunt uses wooden chopsticks, because she finds the metal ones too heavy for her aging hands.

Electric Frying Pans   Although I generally prefer cooking over a gas flame, I've found that electric frying pans are useful for many things. Since Koreans like their meals to be communal, certain things like Sliced Roast Beef (*Roseh Gui,* page 168) taste best when cooked right on the tabletop. Besides, nothing beats sitting on the floor with an electric frying pan when a hundred *buchingae* have to be made. Available to fit any sized kitchen or budget, look for those with nonstick surfaces, variable temperature control, and heat-resistant handles for safe handling.

Glass Jars (*Hang Ali*)   Although clay pots are the optimal storage vessels for pickling vegetables or sauces, glass jars are easier to handle and more widely available. Gallon-sized jars are the best for storing large batches of *kimchi*. Smaller jars can be used for pastes and sauces.

Knives (*Kal*)   According to ancient customs, knives were considered bad omens, rarely seen outside the kitchen and never given as gifts. (Giving a knife as a gift was a symbol of cutting the relationship ties.) Old superstitions aside, good knives are not only essential in Korean cooking, but in any kitchen. You don't have to spend a lot of money to get decent knives, and keeping those knives well sharpened will make all the difference. A Japanese water stone is wonderful for giving your knife a good edge. If you're not sure how to sharpen knives at home, you can have them done professionally for a nominal fee.

Pans   You don't really need a huge variety of pans to make Korean food. Pans, like most kitchen equipment, should be purchased for quality, not low price. Once you have a superior pan, you'll use it for the rest of your life, rather than spending money every few years to replace crappy pans. A couple of large skillets (for cooking *jun*) and a medium-sized one, preferably with covers, are all you need to make great Korean food.

Pots   Pots, like pans, should be chosen for high quality. For Korean cooking, larger ones are used to make soups, cooking noodles, and such; medium-sized ones are used for hot pots; and smaller saucepans are used for heating small quantities of soup. As with pans, it's always best to get a larger pot that can be used for both large and medium-sized dishes, instead of having a bunch of different sized pots that are impractical. Although expensive, a good pot will last you a lifetime. Choose ones with thick bottoms for even heat distribution. A medium clay pot is nice for serving *jjigae*, but definitely not a necessity.

Rice Bowls (*Bap Geulut*)   Koreans use both ceramic and metal rice bowls with covers to keep the rice warm. Traditionally, metal ones were used in cold weather and ceramic ones during hot weather, but hardly anyone follows those customs anymore. As with the soup and dipping sauces, each person gets his own bowl of rice, while the rest of the food is communal. And in terms of Korean etiquette, don't ever pick up your rice bowl and eat out of it during a Korean meal. Leave the bowl on the table and eat the rice with a spoon.

Rice Cookers (*Bap Sot*)   Although it may seem like a luxury item, I couldn't imagine living without my rice cooker. When I went away to college, I even got an individual-size one for my dorm room. There are so many different ones on the market, it's difficult to choose. But like any kitchen appliance, spend a little extra money to get the features you want because you'll have the cooker for a long time. Features that I have found useful over the years are a nonstick surface, a lid with a hole allowing steam to escape (otherwise the steam bubbles up and escapes on the sides; it's not detrimental but definitely messier), and measuring lines so you don't have to use a measuring cup (although I always measure with my hands). I also prefer those that keep the rice warm after cooking because I don't always serve the rice immediately after it's done.

Spoons (*Soojuh*)   As equally important as chopsticks in a Korean meal is the spoon. Unlike most other Asians, Koreans eat both their soup and rice with a spoon. Korean spoons are flat and wide with a long thin handle. They acquired this shape during the early Josun Period (1392–1910 A.D.). During a meal, Koreans never put the spoon down to rest on the table. Instead, it is set in the rice or soup bowl until one's finished with the meal. There are also superstitions associated with the spoon. For instance, a person who holds their spoon too high up on the handle is said to be fated to marry far from home. Those who hold their spoons too low on the handle are considered to have poor etiquette.

Steamers   Both metal and bamboo steamers are great for quick steaming of vegetables, dumplings, and more. Wide-bottomed, multilevel steamers are available in many Asian household stores. These are wonderful for steaming large batches of dumplings (*mandu*, pages 129–134) or rice cakes.

Stone Pots (*Dol Sot* or *Ddook Baegi*)   Used for making a variety of dishes from hot pots to just plain rice, stone pots are most famous these days for Stone Pot Mixed Rice Bowl (*Dolsot Bibim Bap*, page 26), a mixed rice dish with vegetables and a bit of meat served in a heated stone pot. They are available in Korean and Chinese houseware stores in a variety of sizes. Medium-sized ones are the most versatile, used for both single-serving dishes and for making a hot pot to be shared. They should be tempered first before using. Place the stone pot in a pot large enough to hold it comfortably. Add enough water that the stone pot is completely immersed. Bring to a boil, remove from heat, and let cool before trying to remove the pot. Set the pot aside, letting it cool and dry. After it has completely dried, grease the inside of the pot with a little bit of vegetable oil and let sit for a few days before wiping off. Just like with woks and other frying surfaces, never clean your stone pot with a scouring pad or other rough material.

Wooden Paddles (*Bap Jooguk*)   Rice is usually served with a wooden paddle. To keep the rice from sticking to the wood, dunk the paddle in cold water first. Wooden paddles can also be used for stir-frying and for toasting sesame seeds.

A Guide to Korean Language and Pronunciation

The Korean alphabet is made up of 24 letters—14 consonants and 10 vowels. The letters are combined to create syllables, so that at least one vowel and at least one consonant are combined to make a syllable. There are two problems with Romanizing Korean: (1) There is no standard and (2) some of the sounds in Korean don't exist in English.

Here is a simple guide to help with some pronunciation.

The Consonants

ㄱ — A cross between "g" and "k," as in such words as *kimchi* and *gochu*. Other than for *kimchi*, I spell it with the letter "g."

ㄲ — A double consonant with the sound of a hard "g" or "k," as in the Spanish *casa*. I spell it "gg."

ㄴ — Pronounced the same as "n."

ㄷ — A cross between "d" and "t," as in *daechu*.

ㄸ — A double consonant with the sound of a hard "d/t," as in the Spanish word *tio*. I spell it "dd."

ㄹ — A cross between "r" and "l," similar to the Spanish *gracias*.

ㅁ — Pronounced like the letter "m."

ㅂ — A cross between the letters "b" and "p" I spell it with the letter "b."

ㅃ — A double consonant with the sound of a hard "b" or "p," as in the Spanish *Pepe*. I spell it "bb."

ㅅ — Similar to the letter "s."

ㅆ — A double consonant with the sound of a hard "s," as in the word "sour." I spell it with "ss."

ㅇ — When used in the beginning of a syllable, it allows the vowel to be sounded without a hard consonant sound. At the end of a syllable, it sounds like "ng," as in the end of the word "song."

ㅈ Pronounced like the letter "j."

ㅉ A double consonant with the sound of a hard "j." I spell with "jj."

ㅊ Pronounced like "ch."

ㅋ Pronounced like "k."

ㅌ Pronounced like "t."

ㅍ Pronounced like "p."

ㅎ Pronounced like "h."

The Vowels

ㅏ Pronounced like "ah," as in "spa"

ㅑ Pronounced "ya."

ㅓ Pronounced "uh," as in "umbrella."

ㅕ Pronounced "yuh."

ㅗ Pronounced "oh," as in "rope."

ㅛ Pronounced "yo."

ㅜ Pronounced "ooh," as in "stew."

ㅠ Pronounced "yu," as in "you."

ㅡ Pronounced "eu," as in "good" or "hood."

ㅣ Pronounced "ee," as in "see."

ㅐ or ㅔ A combination vowel pronounced "eh."

ㅒ or ㅖ A combination vowel pronounced "ye," as in "yes."

ㅘ A combination vowel pronounced "wa."

ㅞ or ㅙ A combination vowel pronounced "whe," as in "sweat."

ㅝ A combination vowel pronounced "wuh," as in "was."

ㅟ or ㅚ A combination vowel pronounced "wee."

ㅢ A combination vowel pronounced "eui."

Resources

Web and Mail-Order Companies

CHONG'S GROCERY

A tiny little family-owned business in L.A. that makes the best sesame oil at a reasonable price from fresh toasted sesame seeds. They will ship via UPS to anywhere in the United States.

> 3560 W. 8th Street
> Los Angeles, CA 90005
> 213-387-0651

COSMOS FOODS

Korean company that makes *kimchi,* rice ovalettes, and toasted sesame seeds.

> 2405 Forney Street
> Los Angeles, CA 90031
> 323-221-9142
> 323-221-8173 fax
> http://www.cosmosfood.com

GARLIC FESTIVAL FOODS

What's Korean food without garlic? You can mail order whole garlic, minced bulbs, and a variety of garlic products.

> P.O. Box 1145
> Gilroy, CA 95021-1145
> 888-GARLICFEST or 408-842-7088
> 408-842-7087 fax
> http://www.garlicfestival.com

I-CLIPSE, INC. OR PACIFIC RIM GOURMET

Although they are not a good resource for specifically Korean ingredients, they have a decent collection of rice cookers, small clay pots, and other Asian cookware.

> 4905 Morena Boulevard, Suite 1313
> San Diego, CA 92117
> 800-910-WOKS or 858-274-9013
> 858-274-9018 fax
> http://www.pacificrimgourmet.com

KOREAN MARKETPLACE

If you click on the "Food" link, there are links to companies that make basic Korean food products. Unfortunately, you can't order from them directly.

> http://www.bestsme.com

KGROCER.COM

Although they specialize in "instant" food, they are still an excellent online source for such nonperishable items as Korean pastes, spices, dried fish, and implements.

> 923 E. 3rd Street, Suite 115
> Los Angeles, CA 90013
> http://www.kgrocer.com
> info@kgrocer.com

IKOREAPLAZA.COM

An excellent online source for nonperishable Korean food items. They even carry dried bellflower roots, fresh Korean peppers, and a variety of frozen seafood. Although their site is a little difficult to navigate, they also have a nice variety of Korean cookware.

> 2370 Telegraph Avenue
> Oakland, CA 94612
> 510-238-8940
> 510-238-8942 fax
> http://www.ikoreaplaza.com
> biz@ikoreaplaza.com

Where to Get Korean Groceries

This list was current when the book was published, but since stores come and go, please make sure the market is still in business before you make a special trip.

ALABAMA

SING SING INTERNATIONAL GROCERY
503 15th Street East #B
Tuscaloosa, AL 35401
205-752-4922

ARIZONA

KIMPO ORIENTAL MARKET
5595 East 5th Street
Tucson, AZ 85711
520-750-9009

KIM'S ORIENTAL MARKET
4002 N. 43rd Avenue
Phoenix, AZ 85031
602-278-0002

KIM'S ORIENTAL MARKET
2205 S. Craycroft Road
Tucson, AZ 85711
520-790-6945

KOREAN MARKET
1821 E. Southern Avenue
Tempe, AZ 85282
480-820-4097

OLYMPIC MARKET
1130 West Guadalupe Road #5
Mesa, AZ 85210
480-345-0002

CALIFORNIA

ARIRANG SUPER MARKET
8281 Garden Gove Boulevard
Garden Grove, CA 92844
714-539-2702

ASSI PLAZA
3525 West 8th Street
Los Angeles, CA 90005
213-388-0900

CALIFORNIA MARKET (GAJU MARKET)
450 S. Western Avenue
Los Angeles, CA 90020
213-382-9444

CALIFORNIA MARKET (GAJU MARKET)
15933 Pioneer Boulevard
Norwalk, CA 90650
562-924-2345

DO RE MI SUPERMARKET
9772 Garden Grove Boulevard
Garden Grove, CA 92844
714-537-1234

GALLERIA MARKET
3250 W. Olympic Boulevard #100
Los Angeles, CA 90006
323-733-3800

GRAND MARKET
1318 S. Garey Avenue
Pomona, CA 91766
909-622-6982

HAN KOOK MARKET
124 N. Western Avenue
Los Angeles, CA 90004
323-469-8934 or 323-469-0674

HAN KOOK MARKET
831 N. Pacific Avenue
Glendale, CA 91203
818-247-4949 or 818-547-5445

HAN KOOK MARKET
17643 Sherman Way
Van Nuys, CA 91406
818-708-7396

HAN KOOK MARKET
171 E. Live Oak Avenue
Arcadia, CA 91006
626-821-0171

HAN KOOK MARKET
15000 S. Crenshaw Boulevard #105
Gardena, CA 90240
310-324-2222 or 310-324-9710

HAN KOOK MARKET
18317 E. Colima Road
Rowland Heights, CA 91748
626-913-7796 or 626-912-0569

Han Kook Market
14551 Red Hill Avenue
Tustin, CA 92780
714-368-1527

Han Kook Supermarket
1092 East El Camino Real
Sunnyvale, CA 94087
408-244-0871

Hanmi Market
13321 Artesia Boulevard
Cerritos, CA 90703
562-926-7196

Han Nam Chain
2740 W. Olympic Boulevard
Los Angeles, CA 90006
213-382-2922 or 213-382-2913

Han Nam Chain
(Market World)
3030 W. Sepulveda Boulevard
Torrance, CA 90505
310-539-8899 or 310-539-9523

Han Nam Chain (Fullerton)
5301 Beach Boulevard
Buena Park, CA 90621
714-736-5800 or 714-736-5805

Han Nam Chain
2108 Golden Springs Drive
Diamond Bar, CA 91789
909-839-1121

Han Nam Supermarket
4941 La Palma Avenue
La Palma, CA 90623
562-865-4116

Kaju Market
2000 Judah Street
San Francisco, CA 94122
415-664-6677

Korean Farm Market
12500 E. Slauson Avenue, #B1-A
Sante Fe Springs, CA 90670
562-789-4989

Korean Food Market
332 14th Street
Oakland, CA 94612
510-835-8889

Kukjea Market
3130 Noriega Street
San Francisco, CA 94122
415-681-0333

Kyopo Market
3379 East El Camino Real
Santa Clara, CA 95051
408-244-1234

Lotte Market
2135 Foothill Boulevard
La Cañada, CA 91011
818-957-8184 or 818-957-8185

Lotte Market
1031 W. Orangethorpe Avenue
Fullerton, CA 92633
714-870-7566

Nam Soo Oriental Food
5817 Watt Avenue N.
Highland, CA 95660
916-338-0208

Oriental Food
9180 Kiefer Boulevard
Sacramento, CA 95826
916-561-7120

Pusan Market
2370 Telegraph Avenue
Oakland, CA 94642
510-986-1234

COLORADO

Oriental Circle Market
1443 Chester Street
Aurora, CO 80010
303-366-0454

Oriental Pantry
374 Whitney Avenue
New Haven, CO 06511
203-895-2849

FLORIDA

Seoul Market
200 N. State Road 7
Hollywood, FL 33021
954-987-7085

Woo Sung Market
5065 Edge Water Drive
Orlando, FL 32810
407-295-4077

GEORGIA

Han Kuk Shik Poom
3656 Buena Vista Road
Columbus, GA 31906
706-689-1398

Hangang Supermarket
3355 Steve Reynolds Boulevard
Atlanta, GA 30093
770-495-7005

Kim's Oriental Market
2324 Lumpkin Road
Augusta, GA 30906
706-790-3431

Kim Sun Market
5038 Buford Highway NE
Atlanta, GA 30341
770-457-2492

LOTTE ORIENTAL FOOD
5224 Bulford Highway
Doraville, GA 30340
770-458-5949

SEOUL ORIENTAL MARKET
118 Manor Court
Warner Robins, GA 31093
912-923-3179

HAWAII

DAE HAN KOREAN GENERAL
FOOD
1602 Kalakana Avenue
Honolulu, HI 96826
808-949-8653

SEOUL MARKET
2019 Waterhouse Street
Honolulu, HI 96819
808-841-0084

ILLINOIS

ARIRANG SUPERMARKET
4017 W. Lawrence Avenue
Chicago, IL 60630
773-777-2400

ASIA SUPERMARKET
9800 N. Milwaukee Avenue
Des Plaines, IL 60016
847-297-4949

CHICAGO FOOD CORPORATION
3333 N. Kimball Avenue
Chicago, IL 60618
773-478-5566

CHICAGO FOOD MARKET
5800 N. Pulaski Highway
Chicago, IL 60646
773-478-0007

CLARK MARKET
4853 N. Kedzie Avenue
Chicago, IL 60625
773-479-2262

GO HYANG FOOD MARKET
5731 N. Lincoln Avenue
Chicago, IL 60659
773-275-1397

HANA SUPERMARKET
8526 G-K Golf Road
Niles, IL 60714
847-470-4415

HYUNDAI SUPERMARKET
2837 Pfingsten Road
Glenview, IL 60025
847-480-8977

KANSAS

ARIRANG KOREAN STORE
626 Cherokee Street
Leavenworth, KS 66048
913-680-1381

KENTUCKY

CHOI'S ASIAN MARKET
607 Lyndon Lane
Louisville, KY 40222
502-426-4441

ORIENTAL SUPERMARKET
1211 Gillmore Drive
Louisville, KY 40213
502-966-0400

ORIENTAL SUPERMARKET
5083 Peston Highway
Louisville, KY 40213
502-966-0400

LOUISIANA

ORIENTAL MARKET
3324 Transcontinental Drive
Metairie, LA 70006
504-457-4567

MARYLAND

ASSI KOREAN GOURMET
Aspen Hill, MD
301-942-8989

BO YOUNG ORIENTAL GROCERY
409 East 32nd Street
Baltimore, MD 21218
410-467-6250

DAE JUN SUPER
1808 N. Patterson Park Avenue
Baltimore, MD 21213
410-732-5480

DAE SUNG ORIENTAL GROCERY
2213 Green Spring Drive
Timonium, MD 21093
410-561-4467

EASTERN FOOD MARKET
2030 Paul Street
Baltimore, MD 21218
410-752-6327

HAN AH REUM
12012 Georgia Avenue
Wheaton, MD 20902
301-942-1806

HAN AH REUM ASIAN MART
800 North Rolling Road
Catonsville, MD 21228

HAN-A RUM ORIENTAL MARKET
10539 Greenbelt Road
Lanham, MD 20706
301-805-0099

JIN MI ORIENTAL MART
10800 N. Rhode Island Avenue
Beltsville, MD 20705
301-937-7171

KOREAN KORNER
12207 Veirs Mill Road
Silver Springs, MD 20906
301-933-2000

LOTTE MART
8801 Baltimore National Pike
Ellicott City, MD 21043
410-750-9656

LOTTE ORIENTAL SUPERMARKET
11790 Parklawn Drive
Rockville, MD 20852
301-881-3355

LOTTE WORLD
13625-A Georgia Avenue
Silver Springs, MD 20906
301-962-3355

MI-JU TOWN SUPERMARKET
14222 Cherry Lane Court
Laurel, MD 20707
301-604-8585

NU-KOR ORIENTAL FOODS
714 M York Road
Towson, MD 21204
410-296-2834

MASSACHUSETTS

CHUNG GE KIM'S
210-D West Main Street
Ayer, MA 01432
978-772-5213

LOTTE MARKET
Massachusetts Avenue
Cambridge, MA 02139
617-661-1994

MIRIM ORIENTAL GROCERY
MARKET
152 Harvard Avenue
Brighton, MA 02135
617-783-2626

RELIABLE MARKET
45 Union Square
Sumerville, MA 02143
617-623-9620

MICHIGAN

KOREAN MARKET
412 West Avenue
Ypsilanti, MI 48192
313-487-9898

HAN MI ORIENTAL MARKET
5060 Rochester Road
Troy, MI 48098
248-528-0022

MAN NA ORIENTAL FOOD
1156 Broadway Street
Ann Arbor, MI 48105
734-663-6868

SEOUL ORIENTAL MARKET
25840 Beech Road
Southfield, MI 48034
810-357-2828

MINNESOTA

HANYANG'S GROCERY STORE
1095 Moore Lake Drive E.
Fridley, MN
612-572-0079

KIM'S ORIENTAL
689 Snelling Avenue N.
St Paul, MN
651-646-0428

MISSISSIPPI

SWEET & SOUR GROCERY
307C Clinton Boulevard
Clinton, MS 39056
601-924-1800

NEVADA

ASIAN MARKET
953 East Sahara Avenue #7-9
Las Vegas, NV 89104
702-734-7653

NEW JERSEY

HANAHREUM
518-14 Oldposted Road
Edison, NJ 08817
732-248-1504

HANAHREUM
25 Lafayette Avenue
Englewood, NJ 07631
201-871-8822

HANAHREUM
251 Board Avenue
Fairview, NJ 07022
201-941-7117

HANAHREUM
260 Bergen Turnpike
Little Ferry, NJ 07643
201-814-0400

HANAHREUM
321 Broad Avenue
Ridgefield, NJ 07657
201-943-9600

HANS FOOD
433 S. Washington Avenue
Bergenfield, NJ 07621
201-384-8288

NEW YORK

ASSI PLAZA
131-01 39th Avenue
Flushing, NY 11354
718-321-8000

HANAHRUM
29-02 Union Street
Flushing, NY 11354
714-381-5500

HANAHRUM
141-40 Northern Boulevard
Flushing, NY 11354
718-358-0700

HANAHRUM
25 West 32nd Street
New York, NY 10001
212-695-3283

HANAHRUM
59-18 Woodside Avenue
Woodside, NY 11377
718-446-5880

HAN GARAM
2737 Erie Boulevard
Syracuse, NY 13210
315-449-0600

NORTH CAROLINA

HAN MI ORIENTAL FOOD
MARKET
128 N. Main Street
Spring Lake, NC 28390
910-497-7676

LOTTE ORIENTAL FOOD
4211 South Boulevard
Charlotte, NC 28209
704-527-8949

LOTTE ORIENTAL FOOD
8311-C Glenwood Avenue
Raleigh, NC 27612
919-571-7777

OHIO

DONG WON ORIENTAL MARKET
4271 Mayfield Road
S. Euclid, OH 44121
216-291-1241

TOUL BO ORIENTAL MARKET
5046 N. High Street
Columbus, OH 43214
614-848-3224

OKLAHOMA

KOREAN ORIENTAL FOODS
4520 S. Bryant Road
Oklahoma City, OK 73135
405-670-5681

OREGON

GO BU GI MARKET
4520 SW 110th Avenue
Beaverton, OR 97005
503-464-4989

PENNSYLVANIA

HAMAHREUM
7320 Old York Road
Elkins Park, PA 19027
215-782-1801

NEW SAMBOK ORIENTAL
MARKET
1737 Penn Avenue
Pittsburgh, PA 15222
412-261-9377

YU'S ORIENTAL FOOD
1925 Cheltenham Avenue
Elkins Park, PA 19027
215-572-1616

SOUTH CAROLINA

HYUNDAI ORIENTAL MARKET
1807 Decker Boulevard #1
Columbia, SC 29206
803-738-0702

TENNESSEE

PARK & SHOP ORIENTAL MARKET
3664 Summer Avenue
Memphis, TN 38122
901-327-9756

TENNESSEE ORIENTAL MARKET
1102 Charlotte Avenue
Nashville, TN 37203
615-726-2626

TEXAS

ARIRANG ORIENTAL MARKET
2142 Austin Highway
San Antonio, TX 78218
210-653-8471

DONG YANG MARKET
8626 Long Point Road
Houston, TX 77055
713-465-1249

HAN YANG KOREAN GROCERY
6615 Airport Boulevard
Austin, TX 78752
512-371-3199

IRVING SEOUL FOOD
930 N. Beltline Road #132
Irving, TX 75061
972-579-8989

KOREAN & JAPANESE GROCERY
& GIFTS
1729 East Riverside Drive
Austin, TX 78741
512-445-7458

KOREAN MARKET
6210 Fairdale
San Antonio, TX 78218
210-662-0498

NEW ORIENTAL MARKET
6929 Airport Boulevard #121
Austin, TX 78752
512-467-9828

PACIFIC MARKET ORIENTAL FOOD
5070 Old Seguin Road
San Antonio, TX 78219
210-662-0498

POONG NYUN MARKET
839 N. Beltline Road
Irving, TX 75061
972-986-6939

SEOUL MARKET
5610 N. Lamar Blvd.
Austin, TX 78751

SEOUL ORIENTAL FOOD
MARKET
2415 Harry Wurzbach
San Antonio, TX 78209
210-822-1529

SHIN CHON ORIENTAL MARKET
11422 Harry Hines #210
Dallas, TX 75243
972-243-0733

YOUNG'S ORIENTAL FOOD MART
8141 Latigo Plaza Drive
San Antonio, TX 78227
210-645-0570

UTAH

ORIENTAL FOOD MARKET
667 South 700 East Street
Salt Lake City, UT 84102
801-363-2122

VIRGINIA

ANNANDALE KOREA HOUSE
4231 Markham Street
Annandale, VA 22003
703-354-1515

DONG-A ASIAN MARKET
9590 Lee Highway
Fairfax, VA 22031
703-385-0430

HANAHREUM
8103 Lee Highway
Falls Church, VA 21222
703-573-6300

LOTTE PLAZA
3250 Old Lee Highway
Fairfax, VA 22030
703-352-8989

LUCKY WORLD
3109 Graham Road
Falls Church, VA 22042
703-641-8585

ORIENTAL SEOUL MARKET
13662 Jefferson Davis Highway
Springfield, VA 22191
703-491-6967

RICHMOND ORIENTAL
431 E. Belt Boulevard
Richmond, VA 23224
804-231-7624

SAM MI ORIENTAL MARKET
6674 Arlington Boulevard
Falls Church, VA 22042
703-532-2066

WEST SPRINGFIELD ORIENTAL
MARKET
6343-A Rolling Road
Springfield, IL 22152
703-451-5929

WASHINGTON

ARIRANG ORIENTAL MARKET
7940 Martin Way
Olympia, WA 98506
360-456-1858

AURORA ORIENTAL FOOD & GIFT
15202 Aurora Avenue N.
Seattle, WA 98133
206-362-5575

BOOHAN MARKET
9122 South Tacoma Way
Tacoma, WA 98499
253-588-7300

HANMI MARKET
4006 East 13th Street
Vancouver, WA 98661
360-694-9626

HO DO RI MARKET
23830 Highway 99 #105
Edmonds, WA 98026
206-672-9611

HYUNDAI FOOD MARKET
30919 Pacific Highway
Federal Way, WA 98003
253-946-6900

KOREA ORIENTAL MARKET
3815 Lacey Boulevard #E-5
Lacey, WA 98503
360-491-3509

PAL DO MARKET
8730 South Tacoma Way
Lakewood, WA 98499
253-581-7800

PAL DO WORLD
1720 Highway 99
Lynnwood, WA 98037
425-742-2237

SAERONA MARKET
31260 Pacific Highway #12
Federal Way, WA 98003
253-839-6255

SOUTH GATE MARKET
3900 Fractoria Boulevard SE
Bellevue, WA 98006
425-643-4244

Recipe List by Korean Name

Jat Jook (Pine Nut Porridge), page 33
Jencha (Meat Fritters), page 85
Jjukkumi (Grilled Baby Octopus), page 156
Junbok Jook (Abalone Porridge), page 34

Kimchi Bokkum Bap (Kimchi Fried Rice), page 31
Kimchi Jjigae (Kimchi Hot Pot), page 112
Kimchi Mandu (Kimchi Dumplings), page 133
Kimchi Sujaebi (Spicy Dough Flake Soup),
    page 125
Kohng Gooksu (Cold Noodles in Soy Soup),
    page 119
Kohng Jang (Seasoned Black Beans), page 65
Kohng Namool (Seasoned Soybean Sprouts),
    pages 24, 70
Kohng Namool Bap (Soybean Sprout Rice), page 19
Kohng Namool Gook (Soybean Sprout Soup),
    page 105

Mae-un Dak (Chicken in Chili Sauce), page 177
Mak Kimchi (Quick Kimchi), page 42
Mandu Gook (Dumpling Soup), page 135
Mandu Pi (Fresh Dumpling Skins), page 129
Manul Jang-ajji (Pickled Garlic), page 66
Miyuk Gook (Seaweed Soup), page 103
Mu Sangchae (Spicy Radish Salad), page 75
Myulchi Bokkum (Sautéed Dried Anchovies),
    page 62
Myulchi Gookmul (Anchovy Stock), page 10

Naengmyun or *Mool Naengmyun* (Cold Noodle
    Soup), page 118
Nokdu Buchingae (Mung Bean Flatcakes), page 82

Ogok Bap (Five-Grain Rice), page 17
Ohjinguh Bokkum (Spicy Stir-Fried Squid),
    page 157
Oi Naengook (Chilled Cucumber Soup), page 76
Oi Sokbaegi (Cucumber Kimchi), page 57

Pa Jun (Green Onion Pancakes), page 90
Pa Kimchi (Green Onion Kimchi), page 55

Pa Muchim (Seasoned Green Onions), page 9
Pot (Red Bean Paste), page 187
Pot Bap (Red Bean Rice), page 16
Pot Bingsoo (Red Bean Ice Dessert), page 188
Pot Jook (Red Bean Porridge), page 35
Put Gochujang (Fresh Red Chili Sauce), page 5

Roseh Gui (Sliced Roast Beef), page 168

Saeng-gang Cha (Ginger Tea), page 188
Samgaetahng (Chicken Ginseng Soup),
    page 100
Sanjuk (Korean Shishkabob), pages 171, 172
Shigumchi Namool (Seasoned Spinach),
    pages 23, 71
Shikeh (Sweet Rice Drink), page 189
Shin Sul Lo or *Jungol* (Wizard's Stew or
    Wizard's Barbecue), page 115
Song Pyon (Half-Moon Rice Cakes), page 196
Soojong Gwa (Chilled Ginger Cinnamon Tea),
    page 183
Soon Dubu (Tofu Hot Pot), page 111
Soondae (Korean Stuffed Sausage), page 170
Sullong Tahng (Beef Noodle Soup), page 107

Torang Gook (Taro Soup), page 104
Twigim Mandu (Fried Meat Dumplings),
    page 130

Yachae Mandu (Vegetarian Dumplings),
    page 134
Yak Bap or *Yak Shik* (Sweet Spiced Rice or
    Medicinal Rice), page 200
Yangnyum Dak (Seasoned Fried Chicken),
    page 176
Yangnyum Dwenjang (Seasoned Fermented
    Soybean Paste), page 5
Yangnyum Ganjang (Seasoned Soy Sauce), page 4
Yangnyum Gochujang (Seasoned Chili Paste),
    page 8
Yookgaejang (Spicy Beef Soup), page 101
Yuja Cha (Citron Tea), page 184

Index

mustard green, 56

Napa cabbage, traditional, 41

potato pancakes, 92

quick, 42

regional variations, 45–48

white radish water, 51

wrapped, 43–44

Kitchen equipment, 238–240

Knife noodles with chicken, 122

Knives, 238

Korean chives, described, 230

Korean language, pronunciation guide to, 241–242

Korean meals, anatomy of, viii–ix

Korean names, "Americanization" of, 68–69

Korean watercress, described, 237

Korean zucchini

mixed rice bowl, 23–26

seasoned, 73

L

Laver, described, 231

Lunar holiday celebrations, 222–225

Lunchboxes. *See* Side dishes

M

Mackerel, grilled, 147

Malt powder, described, 231

Malt syrup, described, 231

Marinated perilla leaves, 66

Matchmaking, 211–212

Meats, 159–161, 165–172, 175. *See also* Chicken; Turkey

beef

dumplings, fried, 130–132

fire meat, 166

fritters, 85

mixed rice bowl, 23–26

shishkabob, 171–172

short ribs, 161

short ribs, stewed, 169

sliced roast, 168

soups

noodle, 107

oxtail, 106

spicy, 101

soy stewed, 175

pork

ribs, spicy, 165

sausage, stuffed, 170–171

spicy sliced, 167

Medicinal rice, 200

Mixed rice bowl

master recipe, 23–26

stone pot, 26

Mountain rice, described, 20–22

Mugwort, described, 231

Mung beans. *See also* Black beans; Red beans

described, 231

flatcakes, 82–83

Mushrooms

described, 231

mixed rice bowl, 23–26

seasoned, 72

Mustard, described, 231–232

Mustard green *kimchi,* 56

N

Napa cabbage

described, 232

Kimchi, traditional, 41

New Year celebrations, 201–203

Noodles, 116–126. *See also* Dumplings; Soups

cold noodles in soybean soup, 119

cold noodle soup, 118

described, x, 232

dough flake soup

with potatoes, 126

spicy, 125

knife noodles with chicken, 122

sweet potato, 123

North Korea

kimchi variations, 48

rice cake variations, 194–195

O

Octopus
  described, 232
  grilled baby, 156
Oxtail soup, 106
Oysters, fried, 95

P

Pancakes. *See also* Flatcakes
  green onion, 90
  kimchi potato, 92
  seafood, 91
Pans, 238
Pastes
  chili
    red, 6
    seasoned, 8
    vinegar, 9
  red bean, 187
  soybean (fermented)
    described, 228
    seasoned, 5
Pear, described, 226
Peppers, stuffed, 97. *See also* Chile peppers
Perilla leaves
  described, 233
  marinated, 66
  stuffed, 96
Perilla seeds, described, 233
Persimmons, described, 233
Pickled foods
  described, x
  garlic, 66
  green chile peppers, 67
Pine nut porridge, 33
Pollack, egg-battered, 84
Pork. *See also* Meats
  ribs, spicy, 165
  sausage, stuffed, 170–171
  spicy sliced, 167
Porridges, 32–36. *See also* Rice
  abalone, 34
  described, xi

pine nut, 33
pumpkin, sweet, 36
red bean, 35
Potatoes
  dough flake soup with, 126
  soy-seasoned, 64
Potato pancakes, *kimchi,* 92
Pots, 239
Pumpkin porridge, sweet, 36
Pyongyang Province
  kimchi variations, 48
  rice cake variations, 194

Q

Quail eggs, described, 233
Quick *kimchi,* 42

R

Radish
  described, 233–234
  kimchi
    Asian, 49
    white radish water, 51
  salad, spicy, 75
Radish greens, described, 234
Raw foods
  crabs, spicy, 152
  described, xi
  fish, 142
Red beans. *See also* Black beans; Mung beans
  described, 234
  ice, 188
  paste, 187
  porridge, 35
  rice, 16
Red chili paste, 6. *See also* Chili paste
Red chili sauce, fresh, 5. *See also* Chili sauce
Regional cuisines
  kimchi, 45–48
  rice cakes, 193–195
Ribs
  beef, 161
  beef, stewed, 169
  pork, spicy, 165

KOREA

PEOPLE'S REPUBLIC OF CHINA

RUSSIA

Chongjin

Hamyong
Book-Do

Hamyong
Nam-Do

Pyong An
Book-Do

Shinuiju

Hamhung

DEMOCRATIC PEOPLE'S REPUBLIC OF KOREA
(DPRK, NORTH KOREA)

Pyong An
Nam-Do

Pyongyang

Demilitarized Zone
(DMZ)

Hwanghae-Do

Haeju

Gangwon-Do

EAST SEA
(SEA OF JAPAN)

Seoul

Chunchon

Inchon

Ullung-Do

Gyonggi-Do

Suwon

Tok-Do

YELLOW
SEA

Choong Chong
Book-Do

Choong Chong
Nam-Do

Chongju

Daejon

Gyongsang
Book-Do

REPUBLIC OF KOREA
(ROK, SOUTH KOREA)

Jonju

Daegu

Julla
Book-Do

Gyongsang
Nam-Do

Ulsan

Gwangju

Changwon

Busan

Julla
Nam-Do

Korea Strait

JAPAN

Jeju-Do

Jeju